GW00671324

WHILE JUSTICE SLEPT

WHILE JUSTICE SLEPT

*The True Story of Nicky Kelly
and the Sallins Train Robbery*

Patsy McGarry

The Liffey Press

Published by
The Liffey Press
Ashbrook House, 10 Main Street
Raheny, Dublin 5, Ireland
www.theliffeypress.com

© 2006 Patsy McGarry

A catalogue record of this book is
available from the British Library.

ISBN 1-905785-04-6

All rights reserved. No part of this publication may be
reproduced or transmitted in any form or by any means,
including photocopying and recording, without written
permission of the publisher. Such written permission must also
be obtained before any part of this publication is stored in a
retrieval system of any nature. Requests for permission should
be directed to The Liffey Press, Ashbrook House,
10 Main Street, Raheny, Dublin 5, Ireland.

Printed in Ireland by Colour Books

CONTENTS

ABOUT THE AUTHOR

Patsy McGarry has been Religious Affairs Correspondent with *The Irish Times* since 1997. He has been working at the newspaper since 1994. A native of Ballaghaderreen, County Roscommon, he is a graduate of NUI Galway. He has worked for Independent Newspapers, the *Irish Press* group, *Magill* magazine, and freelanced briefly for RTÉ. In 1989 he set up the first independent radio newsroom in the Republic at Capital Radio (now FM104) in Dublin, having previously worked for four years on pirate station Sunshine Radio in the city. He was theatre critic at the *Irish Press* from 1990 until 1995. He received a national media award for comment and analysis in 1992 for *Sunday Independent* articles on the fall of Charles Haughey as Taoiseach and was awarded the 1998 Templeton European Religion Writer of the Year for articles in *The Irish Times* on Drumcree, the papal visit to Cuba that year, and articles criticising the Irish Churches for failing to practise what they preached on reconciliation. In 2001 he edited *Christianity*, a collection of essays published by Veritas. A collection of weekly columns he wrote for *The Irish Times* in 2000 was published by that newspaper in 2001 under the title *The Book of Jesus Report*, a contemporary account of the four gospels.

This book is dedicated to the memory of journalist Derek Dunne,
who died in 1991 after a brief illness. He was 35.
It is also dedicated to the Kelly family, particularly
their late parents Nicholas and Stella.

"What art mad? A man may see how this world goes with no eyes. Look with thine ears. See how yon justice rails upon yon simple thief. Hark in thine ear, change places, and handy-dandy, which is the justice, which is the thief? Thou hast seen a farmer's dog bark at a beggar?"

– *King Lear*, Act V, scene VI, 2

"Let no one pretend that our system of justice is a search for truth. It is nothing of the sort. It is a contest between two sides played according to certain rules, and if the truth happens to emerge as a result of the contest, then that is a pure windfall."

– Ludovic Kennedy, concluding
the book *Ten Rillington Place*
(published 1964)

THE PARDON

WHEREAS Edward Noel Kelly now residing at 14 Inisfallen Parade Dublin was convicted by a Special Criminal Court on the 15th day of December 1978 for the offence of stealing mailbags and the offence of stopping a train with intent to rob the mail and was sentenced to 12 years' penal servitude for each of these offences:

AND WHEREAS on the 2nd day of April 1982 the Court of Criminal Appeal dismissed an appeal by the said Edward Noel Kelly from such verdict and sentence as aforesaid which judgement was upheld by the Supreme Court on the 29th day of October, 1982:

AND WHEREAS upon consideration of a petition presented by the said Edward Noel Kelly on the 7th day of November, 1991 the Government, in the light of the Attorney General's advice following the receipt by him of the views of the Director of Public Prosecutions and relevant factual information, consider that it would be unsafe to continue to accept that the said Edward Noel Kelly's guilt is established beyond reasonable doubt:

AND WHEREAS the Government have therefore advised the President to grant to the said Edward Noel Kelly a pardon in respect of the said convictions and such full remission as is hereinafter set forth:

NOW I, MARY ROBINSON, President of Ireland, do hereby, on the advice of the Government, pardon the said Edward Noel Kelly in respect of the said convictions and wholly remit the said punishments of twelve years' penal servitude to which the said Edward Noel Kelly was sentenced as aforesaid to the intent that he shall henceforth stand released and discharged from all penalties, forfeitures and disqualifications incident to or consequent on the said convictions, as if he had not been charged or convicted.

GIVEN under my Official Seal
this 29th day of April 1992

Mary Robinson
Uachtarán na hÉireann

1

THE MAIL TRAIN ROBBERY

IT WAS ABOUT THREE O'CLOCK ON THE MORNING of Wednesday 31 March 1976 when the Cork to Dublin mail train emerged at last from the gloom. It was behind schedule.

"Frank" (as we shall call him) was positioned at a bridge over the railway track towards the Sallins side of Hazelhatch in north Kildare. He was carrying four flares, in case any might be defective. He fired one into the darkness above – a signal to other members of the 17-man gang further down the line to put detonators on the track. They did so, rapidly. The plan was that the train should stop beside fields where a Volkswagen van was parked to take away the haul.

Three detonators went off as the train passed over them. Immediately it began to stop; by regulation, the driver had to stop the train when he heard detonators. It was a signal of danger ahead.

When the train stopped it was boarded hastily by members of the gang. They were armed and wore balaclavas. They were "very aggressive," Frank recalled. It was planned that way in rehearsal, for quickest results. No one was hurt. No one was assaulted. The gang met "no real resistance".

Over the next minutes 12 bags containing registered letters and old bank notes, which he valued at "close to £1,000,000", were thrown from the train to the fields below, where they were lifted into the blue Volkswagen van. It had been commandeered by gang members about four hours earlier from greengrocer (and New Zealander) Ray Reynolds in Palmerstown, County Dublin.

The official estimate put on the haul by the authorities later was £221,000, an amount described then as the biggest ever taken in a robbery in the Republic. So large was the haul that the van had to be pushed out of the field by seven or eight of the gang members, he recalled. The entire operation took less than 25 minutes.

The only house near the scene had been commandeered by gang members about two hours earlier and its phone cut off. Living there were Conal and Marion O'Toole, their three children, and Marion's mother, none of whom was aware of what was happening or of what had been planned. There were three cars in the driveway of the O'Toole home. Two would be used by the gang.

When the Volkswagen van was pushed out of the field and drove off, other members of the gang followed. Frank took one of the O'Toole cars. He recalled that one car drove in front of the Volkswagen van and one behind. Two Garda patrol cars passed them, heading for the crime scene.

The van, unable to pull the weight, stalled at Captain's Hill, near Leixlip. Both cars emptied as gang members got out to push the van uphill. "It looked amateurish after such a professional operation," Frank commented. Then the van "disappeared into the night," he said.

He assumed its contents would be going to IRA prisoners' dependants, but he didn't know. "You did the job you were asked to do and then it was on to the next operation," he said. "I have no idea what happened to the money. It was handed over and that was not an issue with me. It could've been used to set up ten builders, when I look back. Anything could've happened [it]."

Frank drove on to Templeogue in south Dublin where he had parked his own car the previous evening. He put the keys of the O'Toole car under its back bumper and left it there, and drove in his own car to the house where he was then staying in north Kildare. He got word of their car's whereabouts to the O'Tooles "four or five days later", he said.

He was in bed "ten minutes" when two detectives from Dublin arrived at the house. It was about 6.45 am. "I was their main suspect and they gave me an alibi," he said. He would tell them so later. They had found him in bed. Had they touched the bonnet of his car they would have felt it was warm. They did not do so.

In a raid on the (now) TD Tony Gregory's house in Dublin that morning, also in connection with the mail train robbery, he was saved from arrest when detectives found the bonnet of his car was cold. Gregory was already by then a well-known political activist in Dublin's city centre, a member of the Irish Republican Socialist Party, as were most of the other suspects arrested.

Gardaí were correct in being suspicious of Frank's role in the robbery. For six weeks beforehand he had been involved in planning it. He had identified the train to be robbed and its schedules. He had bought a bike so he could do surveillance of the rail line in the north Kildare area to establish where the best place to mount the robbery would be, remoteness and accessibility being priorities. He chose the location.

It had been necessary to bring in "outsiders" to help the local IRA cell mount the operation. That cell, as with all such IRA cells, consisted of four. When an operation was to be mounted instructions would come from headquarters to just one member of the cell; that way the flow of information could be controlled.

The robbery had been well rehearsed beforehand in sheds around north Kildare. Every detail was anticipated and planned for, except the weight of the haul. To the best of Frank's knowledge not one of the other 16 gang members was ever held or questioned in connection with the mail train robbery. Nor was he again, after being pulled from his bed by two detectives that morning. Besides, most of the other 16 "didn't have permanent addresses", he recalled.

"Being a volunteer was a bitch of a job. You were lucky to have a house to go to. A lot of the time you go around in wet clothes, with no proper meals, going from shed to shed. How often did you have a warm bath? How often did anyone put an arm around you and said they gave a fuck? What kept you going was bravado or getting one over on the guards, whatever," he remembered. "One thing the IRA could never allow happen was for a ceasefire to go on over ten days. Volunteers might get used to a normal life, a warm bed, money for the pub."

Frank had been active in IRA operations for 12 years and was on the run for short intervals during that period. He had been arrested and remanded in custody many times, occasionally for things he didn't do, but was never charged or sentenced to a jail term. "Even in Green Street [Special Criminal Court] they had to have some sort of evidence," he said.

He remains totally convinced the authorities knew from very early on that neither Nicky Kelly nor any of the others charged in connection with the mail train robbery had anything to do with it. "I can guarantee you, the State, the Government, everyone with the slightest interest, knew Kelly didn't do it, and from the beginning knew it. Why were they at my house [where he stayed that night; it was not his home] if they didn't?" he asked. "They knew only the IRA could have pulled something like that off." He added: "Kelly and the rest couldn't have robbed a chip van."

Besides, Frank told the gardaí directly. About 15 months later he was arrested in connection with another IRA operation. He teased the detectives about not doing their job properly over the mail train robbery. He told them they had given him an alibi, where it was concerned, because they hadn't checked the bonnet of his car. He told them they should have done their police work better. They were "embarrassed", he said.

But he would never accuse the guards of being stupid. Some were "highly intelligent". "They are like any organisation. Like the IRA. You meet every kind, the good, the bad bastard and everything in between," he said.

In his sixties now, Frank is from rural Ireland. A fit man of medium build and stature, he drinks little and speaks in an intense, staccato style. He drinks alcohol on occasion but has no problem in dispatching coffee, cup after cup. "It never keeps me awake," he said. When we met in July 2006, he recalled the silence in his primary school classroom when his old IRA teacher spoke of his own activities during the War of Independence.

But Frank is insistent that no one but himself was responsible for his activities during the more recent Troubles, none of which, apart from the mail train robbery, he wished to discuss in any detail. He regretted it all. "I gave too many years of my youth to it," he said. All that came of it was that "it gave a lot of people reasons to visit graveyards." He now believes that, with the EU and normal population trends, the North "would have sorted itself out. The Troubles were a mistake".

He blamed "a lot of naïveté" for ever getting involved. "Reality comes with age," he commented. Looking back, he said, for instance at Padraig Pearse's speeches, "he was a raving lunatic, wasn't he!"

However, Frank's views on Gerry Adams and Martin McGuinness are very different. He has "the greatest of respect" for both. They were "two incredible soldiers and two incredibly able politicians" whose "greatest achievement was to be able to secure the peace process to where it is without allowing the IRA to split. It has never been done before."

As for himself, Frank ended his activities with the IRA before the peace process began and he has never been politically active. He doubted he would have been involved at all but for what he learned while in the US army during the 1960s. The Vietnam War was escalating and he was drafted. "We were all trained for field intelligence with long-range reconnaissance patrols." At the time the casualty rate for such patrols in Vietnam was as high as 90 per cent, he was told.

He and others questioned what it was all for. "Who gives a fuck for Vietnam?" they asked. He realised that he was "an Irish farmer going to kill Vietnamese farmers with whom I had far more in common." He refused to go to Vietnam and was honourably discharged. He believes that if he had not got that army training he "would never have got involved here [Ireland]." Not that he was blaming the US army either. The responsibility lay with himself alone, he insisted.

It was from his US army training that Frank taught IRA members how to handle interrogations, he said. "You take control of the situation. Refuse to answer questions. Concentrate on a white spot on the wall and remember the fear is based on what you know they can do to you, not what they are doing to you," he recalled.

He also said he introduced the cell system to the IRA, whereby no more than four in an area belonged to the organisation. "It worked very, very effectively," he said. "The four would know each other intimately. If something needed to be done in a particular area headquarters would contact one member of the cell. That way it was very easy to find out what happened if anything went wrong. Very few did [go wrong] because of that."

There was a downside, however. "It was why supergrasses lasted such a long time," he said. Because those involved knew each other so well there was no suspicion and there was an element of trust: "You didn't squeal on a buddy."

When an instruction came from headquarters "you didn't ask why," he said. "You just got on with the job, and when it was done you waited for the next instruction." Despite this, Frank insists he was never actually a member of the IRA. "I worked on my own. It's the reason I survived as long as I did. I was always independent," he said. However, he believes the IRA considered him a member.

He "disagreed entirely" with the IRA shooting RUC men in the North and indeed with the shooting of British soldiers there, believing instead the campaign should be targeted at those responsible in the UK. He blamed the British for starting it all in 1972, when internment was introduced in the North. So doing they "declared war", he said. He believed they did so deliberately, so their soldiers could have training in that type of warfare "and republicans fell into the trap". Otherwise he believes the Troubles would not have happened at all.

Internment led to the IRA having more recruits than it could accommodate. Such was the chaos, he said, the Provisional IRA was "a sad fucking bunch when we started". He dismissed outright suggestions that Fianna Fáil or Charles Haughey had any part in their creation. "Not at all. They were created by the British army," he said. He had high praise for Haughey. "He was one of the greatest Irishmen we ever had." He had been "directly responsible for the peace process being started. Himself and Fr [Alec] Reid. They had been dealing with the IRA behind the scenes from the early eighties," he said.

And Frank's praise was not party political. "The biggest [arms] dump in this country was on a Fine Gaeler's land," he remembered as an example. Such "everyday people took huge risks of their own free will," he said.

Today Frank owns and runs the small service business he set up when he "retired" from active service with the IRA. He reared his children to think for themselves, to be independent, and not to make his mistake, not to waste their youth as he believed he had his own. They are now young adults. His family is all to him, and particularly his wife, who stood by him through "the stupid years" when she suffered harassment because of his activities.

It is for the family's sake that he didn't want his name used in this interview. He didn't want them to be a focus of any attention it might provoke. The guards "know who I am", he said. He was not concerned that they would identify him.

Yet he retains many of his subversive views. He sees the Gardaí as "enemies of the State set up after the 1918 election". He believes refining diesel along the border and smuggling activities there to be "patriotism" – not that he is involved in either, has been, or benefited in any way financially from such, or from any IRA activities. He defines a patriot as "a man who fights his Government for his country".

As for Nicky Kelly and others charged in connection with the mail train robbery, he is dismissive. They were "pub talkers who talked too loud and too long".

He was direct and forthright, which is why he has been dubbed "Frank".

2

CONFESSION

DESCRIBING THE FINAL MOMENTS before he signed a confession to his part in the mail train robbery, Nicky Kelly told the Special Criminal Court, "Well, they just started to beat me again."

He was beaten with a blackjack, he testified, which he described as being about a foot long and seemed to be made of leather. He was beaten, he said, "on the upper arms and thighs, the back of the thighs, the insides of the legs, near the privates".

He recalled "the real stinging pain" of the blackjack. It was, he agreed with counsel, "a horrific and frightening experience" though "I was frightened the whole day". They were shouting and punching him at the same time, he said.

Then he said he made up a story about guns in Bray. "What I was personally thinking at the time was that again we would get out of there and discover there were no guns and they would search and it would save me three or four hours beating," he told the court. "Anytime that I was prepared to tell something they wanted to hear, they would stop beating me," he said.

He was still wearing the ski-jacket in which he had been arrested almost 40 hours previously. The beatings continued. "The second beating was [when] they wanted me to make a statement, which I eventually agreed to. I don't know whether it was on the third occasion or prior to me agreeing to make the statement or when I refused again to sign it that Sergeant Q and a number of other people came into the room. The worst stage was eventually when the statement was written out. I wasn't beaten when it was being written out but when I refused to sign the statement on the last occasion, there was a number of people in the room. I was just being thrown. I didn't know what was happening," he testified.

"The only two people who beat me with the blackjack were Det Sgt O and Guard B on three different occasions," he recalled. They were with him together during two of the blackjack beatings, he said. He was unsure whether Det Garda B was present for the third.

Over the three beatings he estimated he received between 30 and 40 blows from the blackjack. The first blackjack beating was administered by Det Sgt O, he said, the second by Det Garda B, and the third by Det Sgt O. At one stage, he said, Det Garda B threatened to break his nose with the blackjack. "Sergeant O held my head and he [Det Garda B] was coming down for my nose [with the blackjack] and he just pulled it back . . .," he said. They seemed to concentrate on the same areas, the upper arms, and inner thighs, "once or twice near the privates".

At one stage, he said, Det Garda P offered him a deal. He suggested "that I should set up Seamus Costello" (President of the Irish Republican Socialist Party, of which Kelly was a member). Det Garda P offered him a new identity, Kelly said. They would get him to the US and he would be given "a large sum of money".

He recalled Inspector A coming "in and out on a number of occasions and he only seemed to be interested had I owned up or made a statement". It was on the second occasion when they were beating him that he agreed to make a statement. "They asked me was I prepared to make a statement and I said I would." Det Sgt O wrote the statement out, he said. "I was never touched for about half an hour."

"They were telling me how the robbery was done and who took part in the robbery," he said. "There were putting a number of names and a number of people, different people doing things."

At one point, he remembered Det Garda B trying to get him to sign notes he was waving about. Kelly refused to do so. He didn't even know what was in them. Then they presented him with the statement to sign, he said. "I didn't want to sign it," he said.

There then followed his third beating with the blackjack, by Sergeant O, he testified, and "by far the worst" beating he had received. "It was very sore." There were a number of people in the room, "seven or eight overall," he recalled.

He was "being thrown all over the place in the room and they were shouting and roaring at me to sign the statement and I was being punched a number of times and at least on a couple of times I fell on the ground and on one occasion I remember being on the ground amid a lot of legs and they were shouting at me. They dragged me up off the floor. I was trying to get into a corner."

He could not identify all the gardaí who had been present but agreed Det Sgts O and Q, Det Gardaí B, P, and S were present, as was Det Sgt R, who was in his shirt sleeves and was sweating and whom Kelly recalled saying at one stage, "this is a hard way to earn a living". Eventually he agreed to sign the statement.

"I don't think I could have taken any more," he told the court.

"Any more what?" asked defence counsel Seamus Sorohan.

"The whole continuous beatings. I was left under no impression – the impression I was given that they were not going to stop until I signed the statement."

THAT WAS AT 5.15 AM ON WEDNESDAY, 7 April 1976, almost exactly a week since the mail train robbery took place.

Five men, all activists in the Irish Republican Socialist Party, were charged in connection with that robbery. Four were tried, three were convicted, two had their convictions overturned on appeal, which left one.

That man, Nicky Kelly, failed in every appeal he made to the courts in this country to have his conviction overturned despite "exhausting the appellate jurisdiction of this state", as then Chief Justice Tom O'Higgins put it in 1982.

He was eventually pardoned by then President Mary Robinson in 1992 and received £750,000, plus legal costs (estimated at another £250,000), in compensation from the State.

To this day it has never been established how or why this gross miscarriage of justice took place, nor has it ever been officially inquired into. During the 16 years which spanned the period between the robbery and his pardon in 1992, Nicky Kelly spent two and a half years awaiting trial, 18 months on the run, four years in jail, 38 days on hunger strike, and was failed at every turn by the Courts. In 1984, he was released from prison on "humanitarian grounds" by the then Labour/Fine Gael Coalition.

There was no forensic or circumstantial evidence linking Kelly to the robbery. There was only that confession he signed in the Bridewell Garda Station in Dublin, at 5.15 on the morning of Wednesday, 7 April 1976. By then he had been in custody for 43 hours, since 10 am on Monday 5 April and had faced interrogation by gardaí for a total of 27 hours. He claims that, altogether, he slept six hours during the entire period.

At his trial Kelly alleged that he had been severely and continuously beaten during his interrogation. According to medical evidence his injuries were "consistent with these allegations". All allegations were strenuously denied by the gardaí, many of whom were present in court.

Of the State witnesses for the prosecution, three were doctors from Mountjoy and Portlaoise prisons, who related their findings on examining Nicky Kelly when he was admitted to each. Another witness was an attendant to one of the doctors. The remaining 47 prosecution witnesses were gardaí.

Mr Justice Liam Hamilton (later Chief Justice) decided that Nicky Kelly's injuries had been "self-inflicted or inflicted by collaboration with persons other than members of the Garda Síochána", and the confession was allowed as evidence. That decision still stands in law, despite the presidential pardon.

The confession was investigated, separately, by two British scientists for the *Wednesday Report* RTÉ television programme in October 1991. Both concluded that it "could not be accepted as the utterance of Mr Kelly". Yet this discredited document retains a standing in Irish law because of its acceptance as valid by the Special Criminal Court.

3

A STORY FOR OUR TIMES

THE NICKY KELLY STORY is an example of how a democratic
state, and some of its most important institutions – its Government; its judiciary; its intelligence services/ police –, can react
in the face of a perceived threat, and in particular of how readily
those basic rights and principles which are the bedrock of democracy can come to be abandoned.

It is a story of how innocent people can be scapegoated,
whether because their political sympathies are deemed suspect or
they incur the displeasure of the police/intelligence community
for reasons unconnected with their supposed crime; and/or they
are simply useful in getting the authorities off the hook when under great pressure to deliver.

Though this book focuses on the Ireland of the 1970s to the
1990s, it is a story for our time.

In April 2006 two young Englishmen arrived in Dublin to pro-
mote *The Road to Guantánamo*, a film about their experiences while
detained by the US for two and a half years at the Guantanamo
Bay detention centre in Cuba, and how they came to be there.
Both were tortured and interrogated before being freed without
charge in March 2004.

Shariq Rasul (28) and Rhuhel Ahmed (24) were not even prac-
tising Muslims (they are now) when they set off with their friend
Asif Iqbal (24) from Tipton, near Birmingham in Britain, in September 2001 for Asif's wedding in Pakistan. The marriage had
been arranged by Asif's parents. Rhuhel was to be best man.

One evening in October 2001 they attended a meeting at a mosque in Karachi, where they heard appeals for humanitarian aid for the people of Afghanistan. "We were young. You do stupid things. I was 18," Rhuhel recalled in an interview with this reporter for *The Irish Times*, published on 6 April 2006. "And there was the adventure," said Shafiq. In Afghanistan what money they had was used to buy food and medical supplies for the people. However, they stood out as strangers and ended up as prisoners of Northern Alliance forces.

At the end of December 2001 they were handed over to US special forces, who beat them and tied them up before flying them to the US detention centre in Kandahar. "If your head wasn't touching the floor or you let it rise up a little they put their boots on the back of your neck," recalled Shafiq. They were kept like that for hours. They were also questioned on their knees while in chains and always at gunpoint.

In mid-January (Shafiq) and February (Rhuhel) 2002 they were flown to Guantánamo Bay. They were shaved, body searched, put into orange jump suits and dressed in a "three-piece suit" – a body belt with a metal chain connected to leg-irons with hand shackles attached. They would wear them until released in 2004.

They endured brutal interrogations and torture which extended from beatings, some especially severe; stress-inducing loud noise; being tied with their heads touching the ground "for six or seven hours", as Rhuhel recalled it; and solitary confinement which could extend for three or four months.

There were 48 men detained in each cell block, of 46 nationalities, both men said, not one of whom, they believed, had any involvement in terrorist activity. They remembered comments of Americans at the Guantánamo Bay detention centre: "You are in the US now. We can do what we want [to you]." It is understood there are currently as many as 500 men held in the Guantánamo centre, none of whom has faced charges.

When the family of Shafiq Rasul in Britain were told of his situation they contacted Gareth Pierce, the human rights lawyer who had exposed the miscarriages of justice in the Guildford Four and Birmingham Six cases, the most glaring examples of where a British Government allowed the abuse of basic rights and principles. By chance Shafiq's brother Habib had been studying Irish miscarriages of justice cases and knew Gareth Pierce was the right person to contact. It is believed her early and formidable intervention was what led to the young men being freed from Guantánamo Bay.

❧   ❧   ❧

LEST WE THINK SUCH EVENTS as occurred to Nicky Kelly belong to the past in this State we need only heed the reports to date which have emanated from the Barr Tribunal, the Morris Tribunal, and the Birmingham Commission in July, August and September 2006 respectively.

In July 2006 the damning conclusions of Mr Justice Barr were published following his investigation into the killing by gardaí of John Carthy at Abbeylara, County Longford in 2000. He found that the death of John Carthy at the hands of the Garda Emergency Response Unit was a "disaster" and "should not have happened". This finding contradicted an internal report by former Garda commissioner, Pat Byrne, which said that the killing "could not have been avoided". The Barr Tribunal also exposed the willingness of some gardaí to manipulate public opinion through the "leaking" of false information to the media.

Attempts by elements within the Garda to prevent an independent inquiry into the killing were initially successful. In 2001 an Oireachtas committee of inquiry was established, following intense public pressure. This was fiercely resisted by gardaí in the courts. In 2002 the Supreme Court, by a five to two decision, found that the committee had exceeded its powers. The Government then appointed the Barr Tribunal.

In an earlier life as a Senior Counsel, Mr Justice Barr was prosecuting counsel in the Nicky Kelly case.

In its latest, fifth report in August 2006, the Morris Tribunal, which is investigating the conduct of certain gardaí in Donegal during the mid-1990s, said it was "staggered by the amount of indiscipline and insubordination it has found in the Garda force. There is a small, but disproportionately influential, core of mischief-making members who will not obey orders, who will not follow procedures, who will not tell the truth and who have no respect for their officers". Justice Frederick Morris continued: "the Tribunal was used as a sounding board for deceit in the hope that it too could be inveigled into believing lies."

That Morris Tribunal is inquiring into the arrest and detention of 12 people in Letterkenny Garda station for suspected involvement in the death of cattle dealer Richie Barron in October 1996. It has already found that Mr Barron was the victim of a hit-and-run accident. One of those arrested in connection with his death, Frank McBrearty Jr, allegedly made a false confession but has denied signing the statement.

The experiences of the people detained at Letterkenny Garda station in connection with the death of Richie Barron in 1996, as told to the Morris Tribunal, bear a striking similarity to the experiences of those detained in connection with the Sallins mail train robbery in 1976, as told to the Special Criminal Court.

There is also a connection to major British miscarriage of justice cases. In April 2006 the Morris Tribunal heard evidence from Prof Gisli Gudjonsson, Professor of Forensic Psychology at King's College, London, an internationally renowned authority on interrogation and false confessions and whose reports were instrumental in reopening the Guildford Four and Birmingham Six cases, resulting in those convictions being overturned.

Then in September 2006 the results were published of an investigation by the sole member of the relevant commission, George Birmingham SC, into Garda handling of the Dean Lyons case. It found that the homeless drug abuser had falsely admitted to the 1997 murder of two women at Grangegorman in Dublin as a result of leading questions asked by gardaí and that Lyons acquired detailed information on the murders of Mary Callinan and Sylvia Sheils from those questions.

It also described as "extremely difficult to understand and even harder to justify" a decision by the Garda to press ahead with the murder charges against Dean Lyons even after another man had by then provided a detailed confession to having carried out the killings.

ᡐ   ᡐ   ᡐ

IT IS DIFFICULT NOT TO WONDER whether the Barr, Morris or Birmingham Tribunals/Commissions would ever have been necessary if what happened to Nicky Kelly, and others held in connection with the 1976 Sallins mail train robbery, had been properly investigated by the State.

In 1984, on publication of *Round Up the Usual Suspects*, a book about the Nicky Kelly case by journalists Gene Kerrigan and Derek Dunne, future President Mary McAleese wrote in an *Irish Times* review, "This book should be compulsory reading for everyone with a vote . . . its allegations need to be answered, not just for Nicky Kelly's sake but for all our sakes." Twenty-two years later, those allegations remain unanswered but, as the President indicated, the imperative that they should be has not gone away.

It has been said that those who ignore history are condemned to repeat it. The history of the Nicky Kelly case has been ignored by the Irish authorities to date and, as evidence to the Barr, Morris and Birmingham Tribunals/Commissions suggests, it may well have since been repeated.

A democracy is only as healthy and strong as the vigour with which the fundamental rights of its people are defended by its institutions. And whereas measures must be put in place to deal with real threats, these should not then be utilised for cynical purpose, with inevitable corrosive effects.

That, as he have seen here in Ireland where the Garda and particularly the judiciary are concerned, can lead to a dangerous erosion of confidence in institutions which are crucial to a healthy and strong democracy.

In the wider world we have seen how damaging such abuses have been to respect for the world's most powerful democracy, the US. Its moral standing internationally has rarely been as low.

We in these islands, who had been dealing with the tactics of terrorism for over 20 years before 9/11, should have been in a position to give authoritative advice to our friends in the US – were it sought – on how to deal with menace while simultaneously standing by basic democratic rights and principles.

But we couldn't, because we hadn't.

4

NICKY KELLY

IT WAS EVENING. "I went down to check out the local railway sta-tion. There was a freight train stalled there with no one about, its engine facing towards the US. Some of the carriages were open-top, with a tarpaulin cover. I climbed under one of the covers – bag in hand – like a hobo in one of those old films or a Woody Guthrie song. I lay there waiting in the dark for what seemed ages before the train began to move. 'Philadelphia, California, USA, here I come!' I thought. But it didn't turn out like that."

That is a memory Nicky Kelly retains from those days in early July 1979 when he was on the Canadian side of Niagara Falls, try-ing desperately to get into the US. He had been there nearly two weeks by then and had been seven months on the run from the Irish authorities. Niagara Falls was not a place he had ever planned to visit but then so little of what had happened over the previous three years in his life was planned either.

In December 1978 he had gone into hiding when, at his trial in Dublin on charges connected with the mail train robbery in 1976, the Special Criminal Court decided to admit his confession as evi-dence. He knew then his fate was sealed but was determined he would not do prison time for something he had no hand, act or part it.

ço   ço   ço

AT HIS INAUGURAL MASS in Rome's St Peter's Square on 24 April 2005, Pope Benedict XVI said of human existence, "We are not some casual and meaningless product of evolution. Each of us is the result of a thought of God. Each of us is willed, each of us is loved, each of us is necessary."

It may be so, but Nicky Kelly would be inclined to attribute his existence to something altogether more prosaic – a faulty bicycle chain. Stranded at Niagara Falls, he had plenty of time to reflect on that existence and his own past.

Stella Brophy was his mother. In the summer of 1948 she had been nursing an old woman in Arklow and, on a day off, she took out her bicycle and went for a spin through the countryside near the town.

She cycled along the beautiful valley beside the Avoca River where people were saving hay in the fields. The chain on her bicycle came loose. She laid the bicycle against a ditch and tried to get the chain back on when a young man emerged from one of the fields.

He fixed the chain. Then he asked her if she'd go with him to the pictures in Arklow. She agreed. Within six months they were married. The man was Nicholas Kelly, then farm manager on an estate near Arklow town.

Neither he nor Stella was from the area. Her people were from Graiguenamanagh in County Kilkenny. His came from Murrintown near Wexford. His father Edward had worked as a sawyer in the timber mill at Johnstown Castle there for 50 years. Nicholas's brother Tommy worked there for as long, as the gardener.

When Stella and Nicholas married they moved to Ferrymountgarret, near New Ross, in County Wexford. He was head steward there and they lived in the gate lodge. A house usually went with those jobs, for as long as they lasted. There was a lot of moving around at the time, with men being hired usually on a short-term basis.

And so, on 9 January 1951, Edward Noel Kelly (known as "Nicky") was born there, or, to be more accurate, in New Ross. It was a difficult birth, during which Stella was given the last rites. The baby was christened after his paternal grandfather. His family have always known him as "Eamonn" while everyone else calls him "Nicky".

When he was about two the young family moved to Danestown, near Tara in County Meath. When that job ended two years later they moved to Stella's hometown, Graiguenamanagh, where a baby girl, Breda, was born.

Nicholas got a job clearing forestry locally, but there wasn't enough work. He had to emigrate. Both he and Stella went to Birmingham. He worked on building sites and she nursed. The two children stayed with their grandparents in Graiguenamanagh. It was a not uncommon practice at the time.

Stella and Nicholas came home on visits three to four times a year. There'd be great excitement in the weeks leading up to their arrival, with a hackney car sent to collect them at Rosslare. Even still, Nicky Kelly can remember lying in bed at night waiting to hear the car engine as it turned into Cottage Row, where they lived, and the unbearable excitement of that sound.

In between those visits there were regular parcels of clothes and comics, with a money order inside. They brought him a Meccano set one Christmas, with a great big crane. He remembers being "a very content and fairly typical young fellow, quiet enough in my own way. Mad about hurling, fishing, and Brandon Hill beside us. I even liked school, which was almost unheard of in those days.

"Our house on Cottage Row was a traditional whitewashed cottage with a slate roof. It had a huge fireplace that you could almost sit into, and there was always a fire in the hearth. This was mainly to cook the feed for my grandmother's pigs. It used to be my job to keep the bellows going, making sure that whatever was in the big round skillet pot was getting plenty of heat. She always kept a few bonhams, and one of my earliest memories is of being with her down at the fair in 'Graig', as she bargained with a pig farmer for bonhams to replace the fattened pigs she had sold to the factory in Goresbridge or Bagenalstown. Another of my jobs was to collect two cans of milk from the creamery every day for the pigs."

He remembers his grandmother Margaret Brophy as a "strong sturdy little woman. She smoked a clay pipe – a *dúidín* as it was called – and wore a shawl for as long as I knew her. Jim Brophy, my grandfather, was a quiet, religious man. He had worked on farms around the town, but was best known for his work on holy wells in the area."

St Michael's holy well is near Graiguenamanagh, on the site of an old Celtic church. His grandfather always said he got his sight back there. Stella remembered him being blind and having to guide him across the bog to that well. He bathed his eyes in the water and suddenly announced he was cured. There was a story that a woman brought there in a wheelchair was cured too.

Also living in the house at Cottage Row was Nicky's Aunt Bridie and his cousin Seamus, who was a good bit older than him. "Bridie was the one who made myself and Breda do our lessons first thing after coming in from school every evening. She and my grandmother used to make beehives in the old style, which people came from far and wide to buy. The hives were cone-shaped and made from straw interlaced with dried briar bark. Beehive making was an old country skill which now seems to have died out."

It was a lively house, a rambling house with people always dropping in for a chat. His first memories of it include falling out of a tea chest, and the Blackstairs mountains. "They were the first thing you'd see from our front door, rising high across the river Barrow in County Carlow. We called them 'The Black Hills', after the song 'The Black Hills of Dakota'. Brandon Hill rose high to the side of our house, with Coppenagh Hill behind us. We were surrounded by hills and mountains, with the river Barrow flowing through the valley between and through Graig."

At the time Graiguenamanagh was a small hilly town, with a population well below a thousand. "The first school I went to there was the convent, where the nuns taught all boys and girls until they reached second class. A big grey old-fashioned building, staffed by a formidable set of women who you crossed at your own risk. It was there I made my First Communion. I always associate the smell of cocoa with that school. We used to drink it all the time, it seems."

Beside the school was a narrow trail between trees which led to the boys' senior school, or "the top school" as it was known. On the day before finishing second class, the boys were brought by the nuns along this path to the senior school where they would spend one school day before the summer holidays began. "Many times I remember looking at that path wondering whether the day would ever come when I too would walk along it and be 'big'," he recalled.

Mr O'Connor was principal of the boys' senior school. He was strict and had strong beliefs about things. There were never any discipline problems, as he held total respect and control. He was an excellent teacher and an understanding man. Kelly remembers him as being "good to me".

Mrs O'Connor was the other teacher there, and was not, as might be thought from their common surname, the principal's wife. He remembers her as a good-humoured woman with a deep love for history and the Irish language.

"I enjoyed myself at that school, and was a fairly good pupil. There was always great fun at breaktime, when we would play hurling. I was hurling mad. In the summertime we'd go to school in our bare feet, with the melting tar sticking to our toes. We'd get it off afterwards with butter."

In the wintertime one of the jobs the schoolchildren had every week was to collect sticks for the school fire, usually in the wood behind Dr Tierney's, the local GP. "On cold days that fire would blaze and we'd take it in turns to sit before it."

Across the road from the school was a steep bank leading down to the River Barrow. "We'd roll down there all the way. Down to the spot in the river, across from a hill called 'The Devil's Eyebrow', where we'd swim in the summertime. Or we'd walk to 'The Rock of Solaire' where it was said a nun had drowned. Drownings were always part of the folklore of our childhood," Kelly recalls. "It was probably a way of keeping us away from the river, which even still has its regular share of drownings at Graig."

He became an altar boy. "I started serving Mass fairly early, at about the age of seven. It was still said in Latin then, and I still remember those responses as clearly as if it were yesterday. As a boy I was very religious. Up to devilment one minute, a saint the next. Our church was Duiske Abbey right in the heart of Graig-namanagh. It gave the town its name – the 'village of the monks'."

Its churchyard is full of old, weather-beaten headstones. Some lie along the walls right up to the vestry door. "It was not a place to be on a dark winter's morning, or evening. But when I was serving early Mass, or devotions in the winter, there was no choice. It attracted tricksters. Hooded figures frequently lay in ambush behind those headstones. I did it myself. Worst though was to be tied to one of them and be left there in the dark imagining all sorts of things. There was plenty of talk about ghosts who were supposed to be there too.

"I think I saw one myself early one morning as I was going to serve Mass. There was this strange-looking dog, not one I recognised, and I knew every dog in the town. He just crossed between the headstones and walked right through the church wall. I ran like hell to the vestry. Nearly everyone had a similar tale to tell."

"Duiske" is derived from "Dubh Uisce" in Irish, meaning Black Water, which is the name of a river that runs from Brandon Hill to the Barrow. The Abbey was founded by Cistercian monks in 1204 and was their largest monastery in Ireland, with hundreds of monks and brothers there at one stage. It had a hospital, a hostel, a school, and a farm.

The monks reclaimed great tracts of land in the area. They started a wool trade, and built eel weirs on the Barrow, two of which still survive. Henry VIII closed down the Abbey. The monks were massacred and soon it was abandoned altogether. For centuries afterwards it was said the monks could be heard singing there at night. During penal times a thatched "Mass House" was built in the ruins, where people went to Mass in secret.

Over 250 years ago restoration work on the Abbey began. This went on right up to 1980, when the present building, with its white-washed walls, and narrow Gothic windows, was opened. "Gone is a lot of the darkness that was there when I was an altar boy. But the knight is still there. This is a stone effigy of a thirteenth-century Norman knight which we believed contained his corpse and which we were always afraid to go near, especially at night."

However, all was not fun and games. Times were tough. Clothes and school books had to be bought "and though I never remember being short of pocket money, we kids did our bit too". They picked *fraughans* – small, sweet berries – in late summer, and blackberries in October. The lanes up to Brandon were full of briars and they'd pick the blackberries there. Picking *fraughans* had to be more organised because more people would be involved, and a greater acreage had to be covered.

In both cases the picking was done for a neighbour of Kelly's, a man known as "The Bishop" Holden. Nearly everyone in Graiguenamanagh had a nickname. "I was called Nicky at school because someone had come across a character called Nick Kelly in either the *Topper* or the *Beezer* comics." There was a lad in the village called "The Lark". He was always early for school and one morning a nun said, "Ah, here he is as usual, up with the lark". "The Bishop" employed the children to pick berries for jam making. He paid by weight, packing the berries in barrels which he sold to a jam factory. Picking stones for local farmers was another thing the children would do, as well as snagging turnips. The pay was about five shillings for a 100-yard drill of turnips – "not a lot but we knew no better".

Another job they had was delivering the evening papers around the village and in Inistigoe, a few miles away. "The cans we used to carry the berries in, as well as the ones I used to bring milk from the creamery in for granny's pigs, were made by an old tinker man called Miley Doran. He was camped in a clearing off High Street, between Cottage Row and the rest of Graig. Miley was always a great one for stories, and we spent many hours sitting there at the camp fire listening to him. A settled travelling family, they were the first people in Graig to get a television. I remember watching a snowy BBC there. It was a great novelty in those days.

"Even radio was still new then. Most people had a wireless, of the wet battery variety. I remember how we'd all gather outside some neighbour's house on summer Sundays. The wireless set would be brought outside, with its earth wire stretching across the street, so we could all hear Micheál O'Hehir's commentary on some match or other. We'd cheer on our men like Seamus Cleere, Ollie Walsh, Martin Coogan, Phil Larkin, Billy Dwyer, Eddie Keher, and Johnny McGovern. That was really the beginning of my interest in GAA. Football and hurling have been great interests ever since."

Every summer Kelly would stay for a few weeks with his uncle Tommy at Sceachmolin, near Murrintown. "He and my father were the only two boys in that family. John, another brother, died at the age of nine, and I was the only Kelly boy of my generation. Tommy lived with Aunt Kitty in the family home, an old two-storey house whose windows had a lot of small panes. Besides my aunt Kitty, my father had two other sisters, May and Phyllis. A third sister, Peggy, died at the age of 14." He remembers that on summer visits there he'd help out with the haymaking and "pretend to be useful". In that house he was always called Nicky, after his father.

"My mother's people, the Brophys, had no interest in politics at all, but the Kellys were different. They had clear views on everything and were loyal followers of Fianna Fáil and de Valera." Towards the end of the nineteenth century Nicky Kelly's grandfather had returned from Widnes in England as a young fellow, to live with his grand-aunt Kate Dunne. "She was a hardy woman and an active Land Leaguer, who used to distribute leaflets and make rousing speeches against the landlords at the Bull Ring in Wexford town. She was arrested a couple of times and at one stage was threatened with eviction. But she fought off the bailiffs herself, with the help of a dog.

"My father went to school in Wexford town, where he maintained he even learned English through Irish. During the War of Independence it was said the function of the Kelly children was to lure the Black and Tans in their Crossley Tenders to a local swamp, where they'd get stuck in the muck. My aunt Kate's house was a stopping-off point for IRA despatch riders and a 'safe house' for men on the run. As my uncle Tommy described her, 'she was a true one'. And the husband of another grand-aunt of mine – my grandmother's sister – who lived near Enniscorthy, died of pneumonia while on the run during the War of Independence."

The area around the house in Sceachmolin was also replete with history. Stones under a bridge in the stream near the house were tinged red with what was said to be the blood of a priest killed there by the English during penal times. And the landlord of a local estate was beheaded by rebels there during the 1798 uprising. It was rebel country.

"Despite the Kelly's passionate loyalty to de Valera, generally speaking, politics did not touch their lives much while I was growing up. They'd be out at election times, but apart from that they were too busy making a living. As uncle Tommy would say, the times were 'too hardy' for anything else."

He recalls being "in Graig on two occasions when politics came our way. De Valera was in the town on a visit during an election campaign in the late fifties, probably the 1959 presidential election campaign. The Square was packed, with bands playing, and a lot of cheering and yahooing. I was on top of a building from where I could see everything, but all I remember is thinking that I had never seen so many hats in the one place before.

"The second time was when President Kennedy was assassinated in November 1963. It was dark and I was sitting in a cart, feeling sick, outside what was then O'Neill's pub opposite Duiske Abbey. I had been helping one of the lads in the pub, who was a friend of mine, to bottle stout. This involved pouring the stout from a barrel into a vessel which had six nozzles, with a bottle attached to each one. The nozzles often got air-locked and we would suck them clear each time. I had never taken drink before, so it wasn't long before I felt the effects. And that was the state I was in when someone came running out of the pub shouting, 'President Kennedy has been shot'. Just five months before I was one of hundreds of school children who had been brought to New

Ross to see him on his visit there and to wave our Stars and Stripes flags at him."

KELLY'S PARENTS RETURNED to Graiguenamanagh from Birmingham in 1959. They got a house a couple of doors up from Stella's parents. Breda and he went to live with them. His father got work in Carrick-on-Suir and would cycle the 40 miles there every Monday, returning by bicycle the following weekend.

Within a year, however, the family was on the move again. His father got a job with the Department of Forestry near Arklow, at Shelton Abbey. He would work in the grounds there for 28 years. When he got the job, both he and Stella moved to Arklow. It was decided that Nicky and Breda were so settled in Graiguenamanagh they should stay there until they finished national school. So they went back to live with their grandparents.

As he progressed at school Kelly was given responsibilities, which at times meant taking charge of the class whenever Mr O'Connor was away or sick. Fourth, fifth and sixth classes were in the one room and he did no more than supervise them in Mr O'Connor's absence.

He was also being pushed to go for secondary school scholarships. Missionary priests used call to the sixth class lads, to see whether anyone might have a vocation for the priesthood. Kelly won a scholarship, but he had no interest in boarding school. The idea did not appeal to him at all. Besides, it was more or less understood that when he finished primary school in Graiguenamanagh he would go to live with his father and mother in Arklow, which is what he did.

They lived at Tinnahask in the Fishery part of the town, down by the harbour. It is the core of old Arklow with a strong seafaring tradition. It could hardly have been in greater contrast to inland Graiguenamanagh. The only times Kelly had seen the sea before were on altar boy day trips to Tramore, and a few visits there with his father. This was a completely different world. Most of the people made their living from the sea, whether working on the harbour, fishing, or working on deep-sea tankers and cargo ships. Tourism was thriving and ship building continued there into the 1960s. "Gypsy Moth II", which Sir Francis Chichester sailed around the world, was built there. Afterwards, in the mid-sixties, he paid a visit to the town, to say thanks.

It was not unusual in the Fishery for men to be away at sea for six to eight months at a time. Some, on shorter-haul journeys with the P&O Line, Blue Line or Irish Shipping, would arrive home with loads of money after, say, six weeks at sea. There would be an almighty binge of tales and drink before they were off again. Arklow men had a reputation for letting their hair down when on shore leave, wherever they went, and it was said one city on the Great Lakes in Canada had a sign up which read 'No Arklow Men Allowed'.

Certainly the world-wide experience of many people in the Fishery gave the place an unusual flavour. Another thing that set it apart was the fish itself. Even in Famine times there was food in the Fishery, which helped keep surrounding areas going as well. This gave the area status locally, and a pride in itself which made many say that it was an 'independent republic' in its own right.

Like all seafaring communities, it has had its share of tragedy through drownings at sea. Hardly a year goes by without some-one from the locality being drowned. There is a certain acceptance of this, and whenever word comes through of another drowning the people gather in a line along the harbour waiting for news while the search goes on at sea. All of which means the Fishery is a close-knit community.

At the start of his time there, Kelly was homesick for Graig – for his grandparents, aunt, cousin and friends. But he settled in fairly quickly. He knew some lads of his own age from Arklow already. Members of the Arklow Boys' Club used to go to Graiguenamanagh in the summer every year and camp in the school playground.

Through those early teen years the Green in Arklow was where they all met. For the boys it was soon the most important place in town. It consisted of about six to seven acres of wide open space in the Fishery, which has now all but disappeared under development. It was there they played Gaelic football, soccer, rounders, golf and hurling – though this was not hurling country. There was great rivalry between the town gangs, each protecting its own territory using catapults. Sorties into enemy territory were regular.

The Fishery often came under attack. It had some of the most envied places in the town – the sea, the Brow, the golf club, the last a particular bone of contention with "enemies" as it was mainly Fishery lads who caddied there, often making a tidy sum of money.

They also played a lot on the boats in "The Dock". Crews on the trawlers sometimes gave them *scrann* – fish left over after a catch had been boxed for the market. The children would sell it house to house, or bring it home for the next day's dinner.

Another favourite pastime involved the beach, but not in the usual sense. There were cotton wool-type shapes of hardened gun powder in the sand, which went back to the days when there used to be a munitions factory in Arklow. It had been there up until the First World War and was run by the Chamberlains, one of whom, Neville, later became Prime Minister of Britain. The factory had been built during the Boer War but was destroyed in a massive explosion early in the First World War. Local people have always believed it was hit by a missile from a German U-boat. Over 100 people were killed and a monument in the local graveyard commemorates them. In the explosion so much of the gunpowder was dispersed that it was never possible to clear it completely from the sand. So Kelly and his friends would go in search of it; pack it into Brasso tins; tie on made-up fuses; light them; and run like hell.

South towards Clogga, where they used go on long treks, is the Deer Leap. According to local stories Fr Murphy, the 1798 rebel leader, was surrounded there on all sides by the English. It looked like he couldn't escape. A deer was passing and he got on its back. It jumped over the soldiers to a spot beyond their range below where, they say, its imprint can be seen to this day.

Dancing days began with the pioneer hop, which was run by local priests and took place at the Ormond Hall on Sundays during the summer. There would be a lot of girls from out of town at these hops too; tourists from as far away as Dublin even. Arklow had a thriving tourist trade then. Kelly and friends would meet beforehand in a pub where the older boys would be drinking to steel their nerves. From the hops it was a short step to dances. The Entertainment Centre locally was where they really wanted to go. It was there big bands such as the Freshmen, the Miami and the Royal Showband came when they visited Arklow.

But the youngsters had no money. So they would go around the back where there was a swimming pool. When the Centre was crowded, the management would open exit doors leading to the pool. One of the greatest dares was to get over the wall and into the hall without the bouncers seeing. Climbing over that wall one night, Kelly landed right on top of one of the bouncers, and that was that.

They also started going to dances in Courtown, County Wexford, about 12 miles away. Friday and Sunday nights were the best there with the Entertainment Centre in Arklow tops on Saturdays. Getting lifts to Courtown was never a problem. But if you met a girl there then it was likely you'd have to walk home, as everyone would be gone when the courting was over.

Another lively spot in those days was Gardiner's pub in Coolgrainey, County Wexford, particularly on Monday nights. It was a great place for folk and rock groups, and it was there Kelly first heard Donal Lunny play. He was with a group called Emmet Spiceland.

Kelly started attending the Tech in Arklow and hated it. For someone who was so happy at national school this was a surprise and something he never really understood. He began to mitch and would spend days walking along by the seashore or up at the golf course caddying for a few bob.

Eventually he talked it out with his father and mother. "They realised I had gone beyond the point of no return," he said. He got a job with the White Swan Laundry, where under the guidance of a man called Tom Ryder he made deliveries all over the county. He worked there for a year and remembers it as one of the happiest and most carefree times of his life. "Tom Ryder felt I could do better for myself and it was he who encouraged me to go for a job with Nitrigin Éireann Teoranta (NET) at their new fertiliser factory in the Avoca valley."

It was a huge plant, employing over 1,200 people, and growing all the time. NET had a huge impact on Arklow. For the best part of 20 years it changed what was a fishing port with a steady tourist trade into an industrial town. These days, it is extremely unlikely that NET would have been allowed build a big fertiliser plant in the very centre of one of the most beautiful, unspoilt valleys in the country. But back in the early sixties, jobs were all that mattered and there was little environmental awareness. The plant was built in stages, beginning in 1963.

Between construction jobs and those in the plant itself – all of which paid very well – Arklow was a boom town for many years and with that went a hectic social life locally. "In the late sixties it was a good place to be young and to have money. I got a job in the canteen at NET, working at everything from stock control to cooking to serving food to running the factory shops. I stayed there for three years," Kelly recalls.

He was living at home then. There had been two further additions to the family – Margaret, born in 1961, and Stella, born four years later. The two girls were more like a second family in the house, such was the age gap between them and Nicky and Breda. Breda was so homesick for Graiguenamanagh she returned there after a short time in Arklow.

"In 1968, when I was 17, I made my first foray abroad, though it is probably something of an exaggeration to describe the Isle of Man as 'abroad'. I was on holidays in Port Erin there for two weeks that summer." When he came home he decided to go to Dublin. He got a job in an off-licence/delicatessen in Ranelagh and lived in a bed-sit close by. "The place was full of young people, most of them students with a taste for parties and politics. I began to regret not having furthered my education and seriously considered ways I might rectify this so I could go to university and study subjects like politics and history."

Many of the students were like himself. They came from families with no history of higher education and were among the first to benefit from the new free education scheme introduced by Minister for Education Donough O'Malley in 1967.

"There were political meetings of all sorts taking place and at one of these in the Mansion House I met a girl who was studying medicine at UCD. We started to go out together, which consisted mainly of hanging around with her and her gang of eight to ten fellow students. Their confidence and articulation impressed me very much and I was often intimidated into silence.

"I had never been a great reader but if I was to have any pride left in that company at all it was essential I read some of the books they kept referring to. And I did. Books by Connolly, Marx, Engels and Mao, mainly.

"I also envied them all the time they had to learn and talk. It seemed a great way to live, and there was so much to talk about as 1968 went on. I clearly remember, in March that year, watching on TV the scenes from that hotel balcony in Memphis where Martin Luther King died.

"I remember the news broadcasts from Los Angeles that June of Bobby Kennedy's assassination. Then there was the ending of the student revolt in Paris; the Soviet invasion of Czechoslovakia in August; and the RUC attack on a civil rights march in Derry that October. That year, which began with so much promise, went from bad to worse, ending with the election of Richard Nixon as President of the US."

He went home to Arklow after being away eight months. It was there his political education was about to begin in earnest.

5

POLITICS

N O SINGLE INDIVIDUAL has had more influence on Nicky Kelly than Seamus Costello.

"I had heard his name mentioned often around Arklow during the mid- to late sixties, in association with fish-ins, the Bray Housing Action Group, and the beaches campaigns. It was on a protest during the beaches campaign I first saw him," Kelly recalls. That was in 1968 at Brittas Bay, a fine sandy beach near Arklow which stretches for miles. Some local landowners began to charge people who wanted access to the sea across their lands, which lay between the beach and the public road. There was a lot of anger at this and around the issue generally – that people should have to pay for access to beaches in their own country, access they had had down the years without question.

With hundreds of others Nicky Kelly went to the meeting at Brittas, which was to be addressed by Seamus Costello, who was then leading opposition to the charges. He had the support of trade unionists, various action groups, and the more radical elements in the Labour and Fianna Fáil parties. There were a lot of gardaí present to prevent people from crossing the private lands to the beach below. That was an eye opener for Kelly.

Costello rose to speak and did so with great passion and clarity. Kelly recalls, "I was very impressed. I had never heard a politician – he was a county councillor – speak so honestly before. Nor had I ever agreed with a politician so much before. So I began to take part in the beach protests, and travelled to fish-ins around the country, which were about the same issue – the right of the

Irish people to avail freely of the natural facilities in their own country."

Kelly remembers travelling to a fish-in on the Blackwater River, near Lismore in County Waterford. Fishing rights on the river were reserved for the private use of a landlord. "A group of us from County Wicklow went there by private bus. When we arrived at the river we unloaded our fishing rods and tackle and stayed fishing for the day. That evening we went home." Indeed the protests were as much social occasions as political ones.

Costello had been a Sinn Féin councillor on Wicklow County Council and Bray Urban District Council since 1967. He won both seats as a result of his work on the Bray Housing Action Committee and the Bray Tenants Association, which he set up a few years earlier to tackle the housing crisis in the town. He also exposed corruption in the planning process in the county, and the abuse of planning procedures by some councillors. But his main concern was with the building of new houses, and he organised communities towards that aim, with great success.

"Among the other councillors he stood out like a new pin, or maybe 'a sore thumb' would be more like it. He always stood by his convictions. His people were well-off cattle dealers from the county, with strong republican leanings," Kelly recalls.

Costello had been involved in the IRA Border campaign which ended in 1962. He was interned and released in the early sixties, after which he went to work as a salesman for Walden's in Dublin, then one of the biggest car dealers in the country. He won a "salesman of the year" award with them one year.

He lived in Bray and became involved with the trade union movement and in community development groups there. This led him to the County Council in 1967. During the summer of 1968 he stood for Sinn Féin in a by-election which followed the death of Labour's James Everett. He polled a healthy 2,009 first preferences.

That experience led him to question seriously for the first time Sinn Féin's abstentionist policy, whereby elected Sinn Féin TDs refused to take their seats in the Dáil. Costello was convinced that if the people believed he would have taken his seat in the Dáil on winning it, he would have been elected, Kelly said.

"I was not around for that election [1969], and would have only been vaguely interested then anyhow. Some have described Costello as arrogant, but I never saw that. Certainly he did not tolerate fools gladly, and he didn't beat about the bush. He was direct and forceful in his opinions.

"He was a very determined, forthright man with natural authority – a born leader of people. At the time I thought there was no one else like him. To a young man beginning to be interested in politics, he was a beacon which cast bright light and no shadows," Kelly remembers.

On his return to Arklow from Dublin in 1968, Nicky Kelly got a job in a plastics factory near the harbour, making drainage hoses. He lived at home, now at Tyndall's Lane in the Fishery area, to where the family had by then moved. "Soon I was back into the swing of things again, but this time there was more politics involved. I was beginning to become keenly aware of the injustices around me and, driven by idealism, set about building up the confidence to do my own bit about improving things. But I was by no means politically committed. I was uncertain about too much."

He packed in the factory job after about six to eight months, and set off for the Isle of Man again in the summer of 1969. "I got a job at the Port Erin Hotel where I had stayed the previous year. There were two Gallagher brothers working there. I had met them the previous year. They were from Glasgow, but originally came from Donegal. It was a wild time. I worked in the bar and nearly every drink served was accompanied by 'one for yourself', as a tip. By the end of the night there'd be a stack waiting to be drunk."

It was not unknown for bar staff to fall asleep in the lift on the way to bed. They lived in at the hotel. "The boys and myself toured all over the island, climbing Snaefell, visiting Ramsey, and travelling on the miniature train system that crossed along the coast. We spent a lot of time in Douglas, which was a mad place then. There was a lot of tension and fights were regular, mainly between Scots and gangs from Northern Ireland." These fights

were one reason why the three decided to base themselves in Port
Erin.

"I remember watching the moon landing that July morning in
a pub in Douglas. Everyone was in great form as Neil Armstrong
bobbed along the lunar surface. Then in August there were the
attacks on the Bogside in Derry, as well as Bombay Street and the
Falls in Belfast. I remember the then Taoiseach Jack Lynch going
on TV and announcing the South would not stand by and watch
the attacks continue, and the Minister for External Affairs, Dr
Paddy Hillery, going to the UN to demand intervention, and the
UN refusing him."

In the middle of all that, Kelly fell in love with a girl working
on the Fleetwood to Douglas ferry. "She was a good bit older than
me. I followed her to England, but she was having none of it, and
I went back to the Isle of Man. After that I returned to Arklow."

There was lots of work in the town at the time. He got a job at
NET, where the second stage of building the plant was underway.
He worked for a contractor installing pipes and water tanks,
something he would do a lot of in the years ahead, with different
contractors around the country. There was plenty of construction
going on at the time. Jobs were plentiful and the money was good.

Hi political activity also resumed: "I began to take part in various local protests and was gradually drawing closer to Sinn Féin."
In time the beaches campaign was successful; the county council
bought a large site near Brittas Bay and turned it into a car park
which allowed direct access by the public to the beach.

He began to visit Dublin again, calling to see some of his student friends. He also visited the North for the first time when he
took a trip to Derry. "That was the thing to do – spend a weekend
in Free Derry. It was just after the arrival of the British army and
the place was full of sightseers like ourselves. Smoke seemed to
always hang over the tiny houses in the Bogside and further up in
the Creggan, where the housing was more modern but people
were very poor too.

"The most amazing thing was the generosity of the people to
all of us sightseers who had come to gawk and gawp, because

they didn't seem to have much to spare. But, whether looking for a place to lie down or for a bite to eat, they were kind to a fault.

"There was a great atmosphere, a bit like a *fleadh ceoil*, with euphoria in the air. We felt we were watching history in the making. The local people were running the Bogside themselves, with a great spirit of excitement and dynamism. Everyone seemed to be helping everyone and nearly all seemed to be on the streets debating and discussing things, as decisions were made on the hoof.

"It seemed so democratic with no major personalities to the fore, deciding or leading – though I did see John Hume, Bernadette Devlin, Paddy Doherty and Ivan Cooper, at various stages. But none of them tried to dominate things. The people themselves were deciding their own destiny. For someone whose idealism was prone to suffer easily this was inspiring, and I bonded with these people and their spirit."

He would pay many similar visits to both Derry and Belfast in the coming years, mostly for similar weekends, just to see what was happening at first hand. And he would get annoyed at the presence of tanks and guns, barricades and blockades. "The North would play an ever-increasing role in shaping my political thinking."

In 1970 he joined the local branch of Official Sinn Féin in Arklow. "For two reasons: they were the only people who seemed to genuinely care about local issues and to be effective in getting things done about them; and because of Seamus Costello."

He became more involved in protests as well, such as those organised by the Irish Anti-Apartheid Movement against the all-white South African Springbok rugby tour in 1970. "I felt they should be banned from playing in Ireland. I was on the anti-Springbok marches in Dublin and in a picket outside the Bray hotel where they stayed. But it was in July of that year that I first became really involved in a political campaign."

There was a referendum on whether Ireland should join the Common Market, now the European Union. He was opposed and did the usual things – postering, distributing leaflets, painting slogans on roads and walls. "I was totally opposed to the notion of joining the Common Market, just as much as while still in

Graiguenamanagh I remember being opposed to the Anglo-Irish Free Trade Agreement signed by Sean Lemass in 1965. That was probably the first time ever I had strong political feelings. They were the same feelings. Both meant, as far as I was concerned, that we were surrendering our economic independence and that would soon be followed by our sovereign independence.

"We were lowering our barriers to multinationals who had no loyalty to us, nor would have. All they were interested in was making money out of us – money which, apart from wages, they would take away again. I saw no virtue in that, and seeing Irish politicians push both as a gravy train to ever-increasing employment and prosperity diminished further what little respect I had left for them."

Meanwhile, despite his increasing involvement politically, Kelly worked and played hard. "I had plenty of money and I was 19 and living in a lively spot. A new acquaintance I made that summer was Pat McCartan. He was from Gorey, County Wexford. I met him through his sister Claire, whom I got to know going to dances. He was then a law student at UCD and very interested in politics, particularly left-wing politics. So we had that in common to begin with. We also attended dances and went on sessions together. As often as not when I'd visit Dublin I'd stay at his flat."

There he met other students, most of whom were also interested in politics. Through debate with them he became more knowledgeable on various political theories. He began to read new writers who had immediate appeal for him, people like the German radical Rosa Luxembourg as well as Patrick McGill, Liam O'Flaherty and Peadar O'Donnell.

"I met O'Donnell on a number of occasions and was present at the Burlington Hotel in 1986 to see him presented with the Order of Vietnam by the Vietnamese Government. I also read some of the work of Sean O'Faolain, who had preceded O'Donnell as editor of *The Bell*, a magazine which was probably the only socially critical organ of its day in this country, during the 1940s and early 1950s."

One man whose historical writing appealed to Kelly particularly was Ernie O'Malley. "I liked his two books, *On Another Man's*

Wound and *The Singing Flame*. Both are very fair, honest, unglamorous accounts of the War of Independence and the Civil War. But only the foreword in *Raids and Rallies*, appealed to me, in which he described someone and concluded that 'it is worth travelling through life when you meet a human being of such sincerity'.

"Another writer, a greatly underestimated one, and whom I feel might have fitted that very description, was Breandán Ó hEithir. He had a great love for Ireland and I was fortunate enough to be able to sit down and talk about that powerful gut feeling with him before he died. He is a man whose talent and contribution I believe has never been appreciated enough. This was definitely the case throughout most of his life.

"It was around then too I began to read Dónal MacAmhlaidh. Years later he would write to me when I was a prisoner in Portlaoise, and we corresponded regularly. What all these people had in common was that they wrote out of direct experience of life. That was what interested me, and what I respected."

By the early seventies he felt more confidence around the students, more sure of his ground. He was travelling a lot in the job and had discovered that the building site was every bit as good a way of learning about people and life as a university campus.

IN DERRY, ON SUNDAY 30 JANUARY 1972, 13 people who had been taking part in a march against internment, which had been introduced in the North the previous August, were shot dead by British paratroopers. Yet another person died later in hospital. The country went hysterical.

The day of the funerals in Derry was declared a day of national mourning in Ireland. A huge march took place to the British Embassy, then on Merrion Square in Dublin. Everyone was expecting something to happen. A small detachment of gardaí outside the Embassy was no match for the thousands of demonstrators. Soon windows in the Embassy building were broken and petrol bombs were being thrown in. It was burned to the ground.

"I missed the burning," Nicky Kelly recalled. "I was working and couldn't get to Dublin until the following evening. A few of us came up from Arklow. The ruins of the Embassy were smouldering and about 30 young seminarians from somewhere in Meath were holding a vigil. Hundreds were coming and going all night and the following day. Many, like ourselves, were just there as a gesture of solidarity with the dead in Derry. We must have stayed about 36 hours."

The following Sunday there was to be another march in Newry. "We went to that. Thousands from the South came along to support it. It was amazing. We got off the trains at Dundalk and walked behind a group of women singing 'Faith of our Fathers'. Behind us there were convoys of cars as far back as the eye could see. When we got to Newry the town had been blocked off and the march had been declared illegal."

British army helicopters circled above, with barricades covered in razor wire across the roads, and behind those were armed British soldiers. "Anything could have happened; everyone was tense. I saw Neil Blaney for the first time then. He strode forward to one of the barricades and tore at it with his hands. A soldier stepped forward. Blaney roared at him, 'Go back to your own country'. But there was no getting through." Blaney, the Donegal TD and former Fianna Fáil Minister, had been sacked from Government by then Taoiseach Jack Lynch in 1970 for allegedly conspiring to import arms for use in Northern Ireland.

During the 1973 general election campaign Nicky Kelly canvassed for Seamus Costello in Wicklow. "I had never been involved in a general election campaign before. It was a great experience, whether handing out leaflets, erecting posters, organising strategy, manning polling booths, canvassing itself, or whatever." Costello did not win a seat but that election saw into office what was optimistically described as "the Government of all the talents" – a coalition of Fine Gael and Labour. Sixteen years of uninterrupted Fianna Fáil rule had come to an end.

ဆ   ဆ   ဆ

MEANWHILE, WORK WAS GOING WELL. Nicky Kelly's job now involved the installation of pipes and steel chimneys, some of which came in 22-metre lengths. These would be bonded and then welded. Kelly discovered that he could earn a lot of extra money by working at the heights required to install these chimneys. He became involved in installation work around the country, at Tarbert, Shannonbridge, and Turlough Hill, the Pigeon House, as well as at NET. There was a lot of construction going on and plenty of work available in that line.

Kelly then went to work for the William Press Engineering company in Arklow, where he ran the site office at the Gypsum Plant being built there. His job included time-keeping, the collation of wages and the general administration of the site. "It was there one day I had my first encounter with death. A subcontractor in his twenties fell through the asbestos roof onto the concrete floor below. He never regained consciousness but died as I held his oozing head in my arms. It was a shocking experience and I was deeply shaken by it."

Around this time, Kelly started up the Hospital Action Committee in Arklow. There was a lot of talk, and had been for some time, about the necessity for a hospital in Arklow. It was one of the largest industrial towns in the country with no accident or emergency service. A cottage hospital there had been closed down years before, and now when an accident happened the victim had to travel over 30 miles to the nearest hospital in Dublin.

"I convened a meeting at the Royal Hotel in Arklow. It was packed, with hundreds in attendance, people from all walks of life, employers, trade unionists, community groups, the politically active, the politically uninvolved. The issue was one a lot of people felt very strongly about in Arklow."

It was decided to elect a committee and he was elected chairman. "I threw myself heart and soul into the campaign. We had some officials down from the Department of Health to investigate the situation, and a delegation met the then Minister for Health, Brendan Corish. He was friendly, but seemed more interested in talking about relatives of ours he knew than about the issue."

His reason soon became clear. The Fitzgerald report, published not too long after the Arklow delegation met him, recommended a general centralisation of hospitals in Ireland, the closure of smaller hospitals, and the building of larger ones. "It was not very encouraging for our campaign. But we kept going and I continued to be very actively involved, returning from Dublin, or wherever, in order not to miss any meetings, until 1976. Then, when I was charged in connection with the train robbery, I thought it was in the best interest of the hospital campaign if I resigned." This was resisted by the committee, but that is what he did.

When their contract at the Gypsum Plant finished, his employers left Arklow and he was out of a job. He got another with a local firm, Edward Dornan Engineering, which employed about 50 to 60 of the most skilled installers in the country. The company had the name of being a good employer who paid well.

"I got on very well with Eddie Dornan, who became a friend. The company had a major job going at the Clondalkin Paper Mills in Dublin, installing a plant to refine timber from logs, through chips, to the fine pulp that becomes paper. We were working alongside the Swedish manufacturers of the plant, in its installation. This was in 1974, and as the job looked like going on for a long time – it lasted until 1976 – I moved to Dublin."

Pat McCartan was living in a flat on Goldsmith Street in Phibsboro and Kelly moved in with him for a while. Shortly after that Kelly and his girlfriend Nuala Dillon moved into a smaller flat in the same house. "I met Nuala, who was from Celbridge in Kildare, when she was working in Arklow. We had been going out since 1972. She also was working at the Clondalkin Paper Mills. She had no interest in politics, so putting up with someone like me and my absences at meetings and protests cannot have been very easy for her. We were together until 1976, when the trauma of my arrest and its aftermath was too much."

Politically, affairs were very turbulent within Official Sinn Féin during 1973. Seamus Costello was never happy with the ceasefire declared by the Official IRA (the military wing of Official Sinn Féin) in the North in 1972, and Costello was soon at odds with the party leadership. He became frustrated with attempts by the leadership to end further discussion on the matter.

Early in 1974 he was suspended from Official Sinn Féin for six months. He was also instructed by the party not to stand in the upcoming local elections. But that June he stood as an Independent Sinn Féin candidate in Bray and held his seat. Kelly canvassed for him again. "Then he was expelled from Official Sinn Féin for being 'generally unsuitable', basically because he continued to defy directives from the party leadership. I was very angry about this and stood by Costello. I knew no one in public life who could match his integrity and abilities, and besides, I had misgivings of my own about the way the Officials were developing.

"The party was attracting a particularly high-powered, manipulative breed of ambitious people who seemed obsessed with carving niches for themselves in urban working class areas as a base on which to build political careers. They had an air about them which was more pragmatic than idealistic, and they seemed to be just in it for themselves," Kelly remembered.

He also agreed with Costello's line on the North which he had come to see as an artificial state that could not be democratised and was beyond reform. "I did not see it as the prerogative of any political party, particularly a 32-county socialist party, to abandon the aspiration to a 32-county socialist republic for what I saw as political expediency. Nor did I like the way rural Ireland was being ignored by the party in favour of the urban working class. Few in Official Sinn Féin seemed to have any feel for the people and country of Ireland. What they had a feel for was ideas. So when Seamus Costello split, I was ready to jump too."

But first there was the Official Sinn Féin Ard Fheis of November 1974. Costello had hoped to be readmitted to membership and spent the months previous to the Ard Fheis travelling around the country trying to win support among delegates. He was not allowed attend the Ard Fheis himself, and some of his more prominent supporters were stopped from going in. "I, however, got in without any bother and tried to bring up the issue of Costello's expulsion, but was stopped. That was the end of my association with Official Sinn Féin."

As Official Sinn Féin was tearing itself apart in Ireland even more dramatic things were happening in Britain. In October 1974 five people were killed when a pub was bombed in Guildford, and in November, 21 people were killed in an explosion in Birmingham.

In the aftermath of both bombings there was tremendous pressure on the police in Britain to deliver. Both events also led to the introduction of tougher security legislation there and to pressure being put on the Irish authorities to step up security measures in the Republic. "Resulting from all of this, the Birmingham Six and Guildford Four were jailed in Britain, and I was here."

જી   જી   જી

THE RESPONSE OF THOSE who supported Seamus Costello after the November 1974 Official Sinn Féin Ard Fheis was to set about the formation of a new political party. Soundings around the country showed there was a lot of support for the creation of a party with the aim of establishing a 32-county socialist republic. There was substantial support in Derry and Belfast from among groups who were never happy with the Official's ceasefire.

In the south, particularly in Dublin, Cork, Limerick and Waterford, support came from those who were not happy with what they saw as the anti-democratic and conspiratorial approach of the Official's leadership, and who believed that the party's pragmatism would tempt it to further dilute its original socialist and republican principles.

The great draw to the new party was what many saw as the rock solid integrity of Seamus Costello. No one doubted either his republicanism or his socialism.

A series of meetings took place, at Costello's instigation, with various groups including Provisional Sinn Féin, Labour, trade unionists, and the Communist Party of Ireland, with a view to creating a co-ordinated group on the left which could act as one force with one voice. In general a lot of socialists joined who felt the new party could wed both republicanism and socialism without damaging either. Among those was Bernadette (Devlin) McAliskey. Her decision to join the party was a major boost.

The Irish Republican Socialist Party was formally launched at a meeting in the Spa Hotel in Lucan, County Dublin, that December. Seamus Costello was elected chairman. The party's first public meeting took place in February 1975, with Costello and Bernadette McAliskey on the platform.

There was a large attendance. Costello pointed out that the fight for freedom and the emancipation of the working class was the same one, but that the immediate aim must be the unity of Ireland. The response of the Officials to all of this was first sullen, then anxious. Some of their members, particularly in the North, defected to the IRSP. The Officials were afraid this trend might continue and that the growth of the IRSP would be at their expense. There had been a lot of bitterness in Belfast in particular over the split, which led to shootings and killings.

In May 1975 Seamus Costello was driving back to Dublin after a party meeting in Waterford when a motorcyclist sprayed his car with sub-machine gun fire. Costello's windscreen was shattered but he escaped assassination by veering and weaving the car away at high speed.

If the Officials responded to the emergence of the IRSP by hoping to crush it at one end, the authorities were just as determined to crush it too. The harassment of party members rose to remarkable levels during 1975. "I was used to petty harassment by the gardaí, as a member of Official Sinn Féin – being stopped on the street by plainclothes Special Branch men, being verbally abused by them, that sort of thing – but this was of a new order," Kelly recalls.

It was after the IRSP was formed that Nicky Kelly was first "lifted" on a Dublin street by the Special Branch and brought up to the Phoenix Park, where he was then let out to walk all the way back into town again. On another occasion he was taken off a bus near the North Circular Road by the Special Branch, lectured to "in a language once unknown to the clergy", then told to "ske-daddle". And he was held in detention under Section 30 of the Offences Against the State Act a number of times.

Other party members came in for worse treatment. Some were arrested under Section 30 of the Offences Against the State Act on Friday evenings and held in custody for the 48 hours allowed, which meant the weekend. This happened regularly. The numbers of people arrested under Section 30 rose from 607 in 1975 – the year the IRSP was founded – to 1,015 for 1976, an increase of 408 in just one year.

IRSP offices were regularly raided, as well as members' flats and houses. "Seamus Costello's offices in Bray were raided so of-ten – and so many important papers relevant only to his work as a county/urban district councillor taken – it almost made it impos-sible for him to do his job as a public representative. All this har-assment led us to believe the authorities had set out to destroy the party before it could get off the ground. Allied to this, the media were being fed regularly with well-publicised misinformation and downright lies which were rarely checked out before being printed. As a result some members lost their jobs," Kelly says.

IT WAS IN THIS CLIMATE that "The Heavy Gang" came into being in the Garda. Their activities were much talked among the chattering classes throughout 1975 and in early 1976. "There were all sorts of stories circulating, of people being beaten in custody, being made to stand for hours in the one position; being kept without sleep, belted in the groin, pushed, dragged, and pulled from one detec-tive to another, etc."

Cases being talked about included one on in Cahir, County Tipperary, where a man jumped out the second storey window of a local Garda station because he said he was being beaten by de-tectives from Dublin. This was denied by the gardaí. After the jump it was discovered the man's pelvis and nose were broken, and that there were lacerations on his face, arms and legs. He was released without charge.

Another man claimed he too was badly beaten while in custody. The guards said he fell down the stairs. A doctor who examined the man was not so sure. Similar stories came from all over the country, some involving republicans and some involving people with neither affiliation nor politics," Kelly remembered. What the stories of brutality had in common were the names of certain detectives.

Between 1970 and 1974 two people died in the Republic's prisons or in Garda custody. Between 1975 and 1979 that figure rose to 20. All were described as "suicides".

ONE SUNDAY MORNING IN JUNE 1975 part of a railway line was blown away near Sallins, County Kildare, coincidentally not far from the scene of the later mail train robbery. Shortly beforehand a train had passed that way carrying 300 Official Sinn Féin members and supporters to Bodenstown, for their annual commemoration of Wolfe Tone. Christopher Phelan, a local man who had apparently happened upon the bomber, was killed. His body was found in bushes near the rail line. The gardaí concluded that the IRSP was responsible for both the killing and bombing.

A fingerprint discovered at the scene was later found to belong to a loyalist paramilitary who subsequently took part in the Miami Showband massacre in July 1975, when the band was ambushed by the Ulster Volunteer Force near the border on their way back to the Republic from a dance in the North. Three of them were killed.

After the Sallins railway bomb, Garda sources leaked "information" to security correspondents in the media and some newspapers carried banner headlines announcing that the IRSP was to blame for the Sallins incident. When it turned out otherwise, none bothered with a correction.

"I was sitting in a pub in Arklow that Sunday night when the Nine O'Clock News came on the TV. An RTÉ report on the incident carried a description of some of those the gardaí wished to interview in connection with it. I recognised myself from one of the descriptions, as did most in the pub. It was a strange feeling to be among people in such circumstances. I left," Kelly recalls.

Six IRSP members were later arrested under Section 30 and questioned in connection with the Sallins incident, reinforcing the story. The six included Seamus Costello, Nicky Kelly and some members of the party Ard Comhairle. "We were asked to account for our movements prior to, at the time of, and after the explosion and murder. We did. We were released. But the finger had been pointed, and that would make it easier for the authorities the next time out."

This was the context in which a gang of armed men stopped the Cork to Dublin train at Hazelhatch, near Sallins, shortly after 3.00 am on the morning of 31 March 1976. According to the authorities they robbed it of approximately £221,000, though the figure was always believed to be much higher. The amount was never officially established. Regardless, at £221,000, it was still the biggest and most audacious train robbery in the Republic's history.

"At the time I was fast asleep, but my life would be changed irrevocably by that train robbery," observes Nicky Kelly.

6

IN CUSTODY

BRIAN MCNALLY LIVED IN SWORDS with his wife Kathleen and their four children. He was from Derry and had moved to Dublin with his family two years before. In the early days he had been involved with the IRSP but wasn't any longer. He played drums with a country and western band and that interested him more than politics now. He and Nicky Kelly got on well as they also shared a strong interest in GAA. So they kept in contact.

That Tuesday evening, 30 March 1976, Kelly decided to drop out to see McNally. "I got the bus to Swords, walked to his house, and knocked on his door, which was answered by Kathleen. Brian wasn't there. I went in, had a cup of tea, chatted to Kathleen, played with the children, and watched TV for a while."

It was getting late. "I left to catch the last bus home, with Kathleen telling me I could stay in their box room if I missed it. There was a woman at the bus stop as well as myself. Someone she knew was passing by in a car and stopped to give her a lift. After a while I decided it was pointless waiting there as the last bus must have gone. I would take up Kathleen's offer, but first I had to find a phone."

He rang Nuala Dillon at the flat to let her know what had happened. Shortly after he returned to McNally's, Brian arrived home. "He had been in town, met a few people and gave them lifts home. We had more tea, talked about football and politics, and eventually went to bed." It was well into the early hours of the morning by then.

"The next thing I remember was being woken up by a stranger. It was about 6.00, 6.30 am. He asked me my name, and I gave it. That seemed to satisfy him and he left the room. There was great commotion in the house, so I put on my clothes and went out onto the landing. It was crowded, with two plainclothes Special Branch detectives, the four children, Brian and Kathleen. 'What's up?' Brian asked." The Branch men were leaving by then.

"We asked them what all this was about and one turned and said, 'Listen to the radio'." Radio Éireann, the only radio station in the State, was not on the air for another half to three quarters of an hour.

"We all went into the kitchen, where the kettle was boiled as we speculated what this raid was about. The 'O'Donnell Abu' signature tune began to play on RTÉ eventually, and we got the 7.30 headlines. That was the first we heard of the robbery at Hazelhatch, County Kildare. And, apart from general curiosity, we took no more heed. Then it was down to the business of the day at the McNally household. Kathleen organised the children for school, while breakfast was prepared."

Later that morning Brian McNally gave Nicky Kelly a lift into Dublin. "I called to the IRSP offices on Gardiner Street, where stories were coming through of similar visits by gardaí to other party members that morning. I was not working that day. The job at Clondalkin Paper Mills had ended a few months earlier and I was now employed by another company, Saggart Engineering. But the work was not as steady."

He went to Bewleys Café on Westmoreland Street and rang Nuala Dillon at work, something he did every day. She told him gardaí had been to their flat in Goldsmith Street that morning, looking for him. "I told her what had happened in McNally's and assured her there was nothing to worry about."

That afternoon, after he left the IRSP offices, another party member, Osgur Breathnach, was arrested under Section 30, on suspicion of having robbed the train. Osgur was editor of the IRSP paper *The Starry Plough*. He was taken from the IRSP offices by a Special Branchman, brought to the Bridewell Garda station, and put in a cell. Breathnach, who would only speak in Irish, repeatedly asked for a solicitor, naming Pat McCartan. But throughout his time in custody no solicitor ever came. The gardaí insisted later that everything was done to get a solicitor for him.

That evening, up to four Special Branchmen questioned Breathnach at various times, and each gave up when he refused to answer questions until a solicitor was present. He was held until the following Friday afternoon, when he was released without charge. He had spent almost 48 hours in custody, without getting access to a solicitor, and without being questioned by anyone for 42 of those 48 hours.

"Annoying as all this was, none of us was surprised that such a thing could happen," remembered Kelly. "Too many members had similar experiences already. Indeed, instead of intimidating us, this harassment increased our determination to go on as a party."

By the weekend Kelly had forgotten the Special Branch visit to McNally's and the flat on Goldsmith Street. "It was life as normal. The Friday after the train robbery, 2 April 1976, the same day Osgur was released, Nuala and myself went to Arklow for a funeral. We stayed at home, in Tyndall's Lane, with my family."

On Sunday evening Nuala Dillon returned to Dublin. "We had been invited for a night out that Sunday with my former boss Eddie Dornan and a few friends, but Nuala was working in Clondalkin the following morning." He saw her to the train at Arklow station.

The get-together at Dornan's continued into the night with, eventually, just a few left playing cards. It was a late session and ended nearer dawn than midnight. "I slept on a couch for about three hours and woke up parched and hung-over. I went to make a cup of tea."

At about 10.00 am there was a knock on the door. There were three gardaí there looking for Nicky Kelly – a local detective, a Special Branch man, and a uniformed garda. They asked him to accompany them to Arklow Garda station. "I got my ski jacket and went with them."

What happened from then until the following Friday, when he was released on bail from Portlaoise Prison, would remain a matter of deeply divided opinion, with Nicky Kelly saying one thing and the gardaí saying another.

What follows is an account of those events based entirely on the transcripts of what was heard at the Special Criminal Court.

7

INTERROGATION

THERE WOULD BE TWO TRIALS in the case, with the first one aborted in circumstances related later in this book. Nicky Kelly began his evidence to the Special Criminal Court on the afternoon of 20 November 1978, the twenty-eighth day of the second mail train robbery trial.

He began his evidence by relating the details of his personal circumstances, and his movements in the days and hours leading up to the time of his arrest, as they have been described in the previous chapter.

He had spent the weekend prior to his arrest on Monday, 5 April 1976, in his hometown, Arklow, County Wicklow for a funeral on the previous Saturday morning. The following, Sunday, night about eight to ten people attended a party at his friend and former employer Eddie Dornan's house in Arklow and were playing cards, chatting, and drinking. It was very late when it ended. At about five o'clock in the morning, he fell asleep on an armchair and remained there "until seven".

He woke up parched with thirst, and made tea. At about 10.00 am there was a knock on the door. Three gardaí were looking for him. They asked him to accompany them to Arklow Garda station. He was arrested under Section 30 of the Offences Against the State Act.

He told the court he had been arrested under this Act "at least three times – three, four or five" times before. The longest he had been held was "maybe 24 hours" and his experience was that whenever he accounted for his movements and they (the gardaí) had held him for a day, he was freed again. "That, or if you were persistent enough looking for a solicitor [you would be released], rather than [they] getting a solicitor for you". He said that on every occasion he was held under Section 30 he had asked for a solicitor, and that one had never been made available to him.

At Arklow Garda station he was given Section 52 of the Offences Against the State Act to read. He was asked to account for his movements at the time of the mail train robbery, which he did. When he realised they planned to take him to Dublin he asked for Pat McCartan, by then a qualified solicitor (now a judge of the Circuit Court).

The gardaí said that as McCartan was in Dublin it would make more sense to contact him when they got there. This was denied by the gardaí in their evidence. They said that at no time during the period Nicky Kelly was in their custody had he asked for a solicitor.

He was taken to Dublin with a garda sitting each side of him in the back seat of the car, another in the front passenger seat, and a garda driving. One of his main recollections of that journey were comments made by the gardaí insinuating he had been on his way to Rosslare and they had caught him just in time. This too would be denied by the gardaí in their evidence to the court.

He had no idea where he was being taken to in Dublin but assumed it was to the Bridewell, where he had been detained under Section 30 a number of times before. However, when they turned to the right at Ballsbridge he knew he was being taken somewhere else. They arrived at Fitzgibbon Street Garda station at around midday. He had never been there before.

HE WAS TAKEN ALONG A CORRIDOR to a small room at its end. It had one window, a number of lockers against one wall, a table, chairs and a light which was switched on from the outside.

There was a bathroom opposite and he was allowed go to the toilet. He heard one garda comment to another that he did not look particularly worried, to which the reply was that he would be when they were finished with him. In court the gardaí denied such an exchange ever took place.

He made another request for a solicitor but said he was again ignored. This also was denied by the gardaí. He was placed in the small room. Two gardaí entered the room shortly afterwards. They did not identify themselves. He was asked to account for his movements on the night of the robbery. He did so. One garda began to shout at him and said that he was not telling the truth. gardaí told the court consistently that they had never shouted during the interrogations.

He was left alone with one of the gardaí, who "was shouting . . . and he seemed to be hovering over me that he didn't believe me". Detective Garda A (as we will refer to him) denied this in court and all allegations made against him by Nicky Kelly.

Kelly, who was 25 at the time of his arrest, explained to the court he was 5' 7" or 8" in height and weighed about 11 st 8/9 lbs at the time. Det Garda A was 38 at the time and told the court he was 6' 1" or 2" and weighed over 15 stone.

Kelly said that at one stage Det Garda A told him Nuala Dillon would be arrested for conspiracy and, at another stage, that his (Kelly's) mother, on hearing of his arrest, had had a heart attack and was in St Vincent's Hospital. Kelly also said he had been slapped on the face and ears. All this was denied in court by Det Garda A.

Kelly recalled that later that day Det Garda A said he had been speaking to Kelly's school teacher, who said he was "an odd ball", and that then Det Garda A began calling him "a psychopath and an atheist". The detective sprinkled water on him which Det Garda A described as "holy water", from "a cup or something", while shouting "fucking atheist and communist". He (Det Garda A) was "cursing the whole time". Everything with the detective was "fucking . . .", Kelly told the court.

In his evidence, Det Garda A described Nicky Kelly as "a nice fellow", "not the normal villain". He agreed he had taken part in the investigations of major crimes in the State over the previous five years, since he had joined the Technical Bureau of the Garda. He was "not an expert" in any particular field, such as ballistics, fingerprints, or cartography.

He agreed he had extensive experience of interviewing people. He agreed he didn't believe Kelly's protestations of innocence. He agreed it would be "very improper" to sprinkle somebody in the manner Kelly suggested.

It was put to him that he had admitted producing "a crucifix to a prisoner or prisoners in the past". He agreed that "one case, in the trial of the [Senator] Billy Fox murder case, I admitted having my rosary beads and producing it to a prisoner." (On 11 March 1974 Fine Gael Senator Billy Fox was murdered at Tircooney near Clones, County Monaghan, while visiting his girlfriend. In May 1974 five men were jailed for the murder and also for membership of the IRA.)

Det Garda A denied saying to Kelly that by the time he had dealt with him, he would "be like the fellows down in Cavan, . . . barking like dogs". He agreed the name of solicitor Pat McCartan "came up in conversation . . . in relation to the flat in Goldsmith Street [where McCartan once resided also] and other matters", but that at no time did Kelly request a solicitor. He felt "it would not be fair for me to relate the conversation about – that took place [about McCartan]".

He denied accusing Kelly of taking part in a bank robbery at Cloghran, near Dublin airport (which occurred at around the same time as the mail train robbery) and "several other robberies". He had no conversation about any bank robbery with Nicky Kelly.

Nor had he brought Kelly out into the corridor where a man and woman were standing, or that he and Kelly had stood in "front of this man and woman for a good few seconds" before Kelly was returned to the room.

This had not happened, said Det Garda A, nor had he returned to the room some time later and said the couple had identified Kelly as one of the men "concerned in this bank robbery". It "never happened", he said. (Neither Nicky Kelly nor any of the other accused in the mail train robbery case were charged in connection with any other robbery.)

ACCORDING TO THE GARDA TIMETABLE Det Garda A was relieved from the interrogation of Nicky Kelly by Det Garda B at 1.00 pm that Monday afternoon. Det Garda B was with Kelly until 2.20 pm approximately on that occasion. Det Garda B was based at Store Street Garda station in Dublin but had been asked to go to the Central Detective Unit (CDU) in Dublin Castle at noon that day.

In his evidence he said that he had spoken there to a number of people and was told to go to Fitzgibbon Street station. He had not been involved in the mail train robbery investigation up to that point. He was the only member of the Garda at Store Street asked to assist in the investigation but "was unable" to throw any light on why he was "so signally singled out," as Seamus Sorohan, senior counsel for Kelly, put it in court.

Det Garda B agreed he believed Kelly "may have been involved in the robbery, to what extent I don't know". He had "learned in Dublin Castle, in relation to information received, [which] indicated that the IRSP organisation were responsible for the robbery".

Kelly testified that when Det Garda B entered the interview room he "made some remark to Det Garda A had I made any admissions or owned up yet and Garda A said to me you'd better do something better for this man".

Kelly told the court that when Det Garda A had left Det Garda B asked him to turn out his pockets, which he did. Keys were all he remembered handing over.

Det Garda B then began questioning him, "asking me was I prepared to make a statement, was I ready to own up . . . near enough the same line as Garda A had been on previously". He was slapped in the face "a couple of times", he said.

This was denied by Det Garda B, who also denied making Kelly sit/stand up on a chair. "When I was sitting on the chair he would tell me to stand up, sit, stand up, and then on one occasion he pulled the chair from under me and I fell on the ground," Kelly told the court. He also said he asked Det Garda B for a solicitor: "I asked everyone for a solicitor." This too was denied by Det Garda B. "I seemed to get worse treatment when I asked for a solicitor," said Kelly. Asked by counsel whether he kept asking for a solicitor "to the last minute" or whether he eventually desisted from doing so, Kelly recalled "the worst banging I ever got" on the Tuesday afternoon (6 April). "I doubt if I asked after that," he said.

He said Det Garda A and Det Garda C, a member of the Special Branch, had been responsible for that. Both gardaí denied the allegations in court, with Special Branch Det Garda C insisting he had not been involved in interrogating Kelly at that time.

Kelly said he knew Special Branch Det Garda C "pretty well". He elaborated by saying "on a couple of occasions I had difficulty keeping him out of my flat". Prior to the train robbery, "I would have had a lot of contact with him", he said. Det Garda C was "on duty in the area," Kelly testified, "we didn't like each other for a start".

On that Tuesday on which Kelly alleged the "worst banging" incident took place when he asked for a solicitor, he recalled Special Branch Det Garda C saying something like, "I suppose you want your friend McCartan". Then, Kelly told the court, "they started to punch and slap me". Both gardaí (Det Garda B and Special Branch Det Garda C) "passed adverse and crude remarks about Mr McCartan", Kelly said.

"In actual fact they beat me I think for the sole reason – they beat me a bit heavier because I asked for McCartan. I didn't ask for McCartan specifically afterwards," he said. All of this was denied in court by both gardaí.

In his evidence Det Garda B said that as far as he could recall Kelly denied involvement in the robbery and then they had a general conversation. "I do believe the general conversation I had with him would have covered his background, his association with the IRSP and any other information which I believed would have assisted me if it was my duty afterwards to interview him", Det Garda B testified.

The source of information that the IRSP was responsible for the robbery, he said, was Det Inspector A of the CDU, who had received it from "a reliable source". (Det Inspector A, who by the time the case came to trial had been promoted to the rank of Superintendent, was never asked by the court to substantiate this information, which formed the basis for all arrests in connection with the mail train robbery. In court proceedings he continued to be referred to as "Inspector" or "Det Inspector").

According to the Garda timetable Det Garda A relieved Det Garda B at 2.20 that afternoon (5 April 1976). He was with Kelly until 6.15 that evening.

Kelly testified that a number of other gardaí were also with him during this period, one of whom he claimed was Special Branch Det Garda C, referred to already. Kelly said he was photographed that afternoon. He was not subsequently able to identify the photographer.

"I was placed near a wall when I was being photographed", he explained, and Special Branch Det Garda C said to him "'Get up, you fucking cunt' or 'Get up against the fucking wall', something to that effect. He was effin' and blinding and the like, while he was shouting at me to turn left and turn right I was photographed three or four times . . . I don't know exactly."

This episode was denied by both gardaí with Special Branch Det Garda C telling the court he did not see Kelly that day in Fitzgibbon Street station at all.

One garda who Kelly testified had questioned him that afternoon in Fitzgibbon Street for a short time was Special Branch Det Garda D. Kelly told the court that this detective worked in the part of Dublin which included his flat. He knew him "previous to the time". Asked what Special Branch Det Garda D's manner was like, Kelly replied, "It was pretty aggressive. Well, his parting note was that if I ever got out of this I would get a hole in the head."

In his evidence Special Branch Det Garda D said "I don't recollect, in my memory, being in Fitzgibbon Street [that afternoon]." He replied to each of the allegations – that he had been aggressive to-wards Kelly; that he had questioned him; or that he would like to see he get a bullet in the head – "That is not correct, my lords." "I didn't see, nor did I question Mr Kelly at Fitzgibbon Street station."

Asked whether he knew Kelly, he said "No, not at that time (of the robbery/interrogations), but I know him by sight". He also denied that "a giant of a fellow . . . over six feet" entered the inter-rogation room as he left.

According to Kelly's evidence this "giant" was "six foot two/ six foot three", well built, with a country accent, whose "fists seemed – in proportion to my head they would be near enough the same size". He "took him to be a detective". This man, he said, grabbed him and said "something to the effect that he would be back this evening". Then he left.

COMING UP TO 6.00 PM, Kelly said Special Branch Det Garda C left, explaining that he was on his way to arrest Nuala Dillon. "He made some reference to a bus, because he would have known she was coming from work," Kelly said. The bus, from Clondalkin, would have stopped on Dublin's Aston Quay near O'Connell Bridge.

He believed the garda was in earnest as "a number of gardaí over the day in Fitzgibbon Street had stated that she would be charged with conspiracy". Special Branch Det Garda C, he said, "kept looking at his watch and saying to me I had so much time to do something for her". All of which was denied by the gardaí in court with Special Branch Det Garda C repeating that he wasn't there at all.

Throughout that afternoon Kelly said he was "being slapped on the face or punched on the . . . all the time they seemed to con-centrate along here", he pointed to his upper arms. Of Det Garda A, he said, "the majority of his occupied time was spent on these two arms rather than . . . he didn't hit me anywhere else".

Asked whether these alleged punchings were accompanied by the Garda saying anything, Kelly replied, "Well, if he wasn't shouting for me to own up he was shouting insults at me, just general insults, reference to family, friends, different things." This too was denied in court by Det Garda A.

According to the Garda timetable, Garda E was with Kelly in the interrogation room from 6.15 pm until about 8.10 pm that evening (Monday, 5 April 1976). Garda C brought in "chips and fish or chips and chicken or something," the first food Kelly had had since the cup of tea at Dornan's in Arklow that morning. He recalled that his stomach was upset.

Asked by counsel whether "interrogation or was it interviewing or was it general conversation or what?" took place with Garda E. Kelly replied "there was absolutely no, what they classify as general conversation. What I have heard the gardaí give in evidence as general conversation never happened. You know it [interrogation] was the whole time. If it wasn't people beating me to get me to make a statement or to own up, it was people questioning me, counter questioning me and continuously . . . everybody, as far as I can recollect, got an account of my movements."

Garda E, he said, questioned him but never shouted at him and never laid a hand on him.

At about 8.10 pm Det Garda B arrived accompanied by Det Garda F, who had been among the arresting gardaí in Arklow that morning. Garda E left.

In his evidence Det Garda B agreed that he and Det Garda F had worked on a number of cases together. He told the court that at about 3.30 pm that day he had received "confidential information", by phone, at Fitzgibbon Street to the effect that in a phone call to Nuala Dillon on the day of the robbery Kelly had said "the job went alright". Kelly agreed that he had called Nuala Dillon at work that day – he called her at work "every day" – but both he and his girlfriend denied Det Garda B's account of what Kelly said to her.

The information came from someone in the Special Detective Unit (Special Branch) who had called to Fitzgibbon Street, Det Garda B testified, but he could not remember who this man was or his rank. "As a result of receiving this information", Det Garda B explained," I left Fitzgibbon St and travelled a number of miles, with a view to gaining any further information." He returned to the Garda station at "6.00 approximately, or 6.15 pm."

Kelly explained that on being arrested he was wearing a ski jacket over a jumper and a shirt, and on numerous occasions during the interrogations he had been refused permission to remove any of his clothing, despite the heat in the room which, he said, was small and where the radiators were on.

৩০   ৩০   ৩০

NICKY KELLY WAS ABOUT TO ENTER a period he described to the court as "the greatest torture of the whole lot" and which he said lasted from 8 pm to 9.45/10 pm that evening. There were four or five lockers in the room, which was also used as a sergeants' mess. He said Det Garda B grabbed him by the ski-jacket and the back of his trousers and began banging his head off these lockers "about five, six" times.

He pleaded with Det Garda F and shouted at Det Garda B to stop. "I was pleading with him [Det Garda F] to get him [Det Garda B] to stop . . . or take him off."

Next, Kelly testified, Det Garda B spread-eagled him against a wall. He was made spread his legs as wide as possible "to where I had reached the extremity". Then they would jab him in the sides and kick the feet from under him. When he fell to the ground they accused him of falling.

This happened "five or six times", he said. On one of those occasions "when I was knocked to the ground and accused of falling, I refused to get up, and Det Garda B hit me with a chair," he said. He was hit "on the back", he said.

Asked whether he had felt pain as a result, he replied, "I would have been in pain already so I don't know whether I felt pain. It was just to me another one of those things that happened to me in the presence of Garda (B)." Both Det Garda B and Det Garda F told the court that none of this took place.

"On one or two occasions – I can't say exactly – they went out and switched off the light," Kelly continued. He had his back to them, so didn't know whether both had gone out or not. He was facing the wall throughout these episodes, so couldn't see them. The door would then open suddenly. He had been placed standing near it, and he would be knocked to the ground by it. This too was denied as ever having taken place by both gardaí.

Eventually Kelly said he just lay on the ground and refused to get up, as "the best refuge for me was to be on the ground or the corner, cuddling, it was the only chance I had". Then, he said, both gardaí pulled his hands above his head, palms upwards, and Det Garda B placed the two front legs of a chair on his palms while Det Garda F held his hands in place. Det Garda B sat on the chair, Kelly testified, and leant forward briefly looking into his (Kelly's) face and leered at him. He hurled insults at him, "general insults", "about my mother and Nuala Dillon", and began to spit in his face. Kelly said he moved his head from side to side to avoid the spittle.

The episode lasted "seconds", Kelly said, and he described it as "more weird and frightening than painful". He "probably did scream. Yes, I was crying. I was degraded. It was totally degrading," he told the court.

"The whole interview with those two individuals seemed to come to an end then, immediately," he said. They suddenly left him, to be replaced by Det Garda G, a man whom, he said, he found sympathetic. Both Det Garda B and Det Garda F denied to the court that the chair episode ever took place. Counsel for the prosecution, Robert Barr BC, described it as "a further lurid refinement to add to your [Kelly's] story about lies of ill-treatment by the Garda Síochána". To which Kelly replied "I am suggesting the lurid refinements were developed by Garda [B]."

According to the Garda timetable, both Det Garda B and Det Garda F were replaced at 9.45 pm by Det Garda G and Det Garda A. Kelly recalled being alone with Det Garda G for "maybe 20 minutes, a half hour".

"I can recollect someone brought me over and sat me down at the table," he told the court, remembering what had happened when Det Garda B and Det Garda F had left, "and I was sitting very close to him and it was then this conversation took place".

The "conversation" involved a distressed Kelly. "I was crying", telling Det Garda G what had happened, he told the court. "I showed him everything," he said, of what he alleged had been done to him. Det Garda G, he said, told him he didn't agree with what was happening, but urged him to make a statement or it would get worse.

"He was suggesting to me to own up to my part and it was during this stage I said to him that if ever I made a statement it would be for something I didn't do," Kelly told the court. According to Det Garda G, however, when he entered the room with Det Garda A, Kelly was "just sitting there at the table relaxed. He was after having a meal, he had some chips".

"Had you enough to eat?" Det Garda G asked, and Kelly said he had. "Did he look distressed?" asked Seamus Sorohan, senior counsel for Kelly. "Not in the least," replied Det Garda G. "Anything different to how he looked at 12 noon [when Det Garda G last saw Kelly]?" asked Sorohan. "Not a bit", replied Det Garda G.

"He didn't look like a man that had been shoved around, assaulted, punched?" continued Sorohan. "No way," replied Det Garda G. ". . . Badgered, shouted at, nothing like that in his appearance, as far as you could see?" asked Sorohan. "No, my Lord," replied Det Garda G, "he never mentioned that to me either."

According to the Garda timetable Det Garda A was with Kelly from 9.45 pm on Monday 5 April 1976, to 12.55 am on Tuesday 6 April. Apart from the recorded presence of Det Garda G until 10.15 pm, Kelly said that other gardaí were coming and going while Det Garda G was there with him, something he claimed was going on throughout that day.

Det Garda A interrogated him during this session once more. "He was punching me in the arms, slapping me and shouting. At one stage he had papers in his hands and he was saying I was implicated in statements by other people," Kelly testified. The language Det Garda A used was "pretty violent", according to Kelly and curses "were pretty prominent in his speech".

Sometime during this period he said he asked Det Garda A for both a doctor and a priest. "I was so desperate that I was asking for anything," he recalled. "I had been asking for a solicitor all day, I got no response." He felt "very sick. I felt nauseated that evening," he said. He asked for a priest because he thought this might make some impact.

He referred to the holy water episode, allegedly involving Det Garda A, that afternoon, and that he was getting nowhere asking for a solicitor. "In actual fact I was just being beaten when I asked for one," he testified. Det Garda A, in response to his request for a priest, "started shouting, calling me an atheist". Det Garda A denied all of the above allegations in the course of his testimony.

IT WAS DURING THIS SESSION TOO, Kelly said, that Det Garda A told him Nuala Dillon was in a cell in Fitzgibbon Street "and that she was crying and that she wanted to see me" and that he (Kelly) was the only one who could help her.

"He was shouting and roaring, making reference to her father [Michael Dillon, then a prominent personality on TV and radio farming programmes] about the headlines in the papers, his daughter charged with conspiracy," said Kelly, who "may have said to him [Det Garda A] I did not believe she was arrested ".

Det Garda A was then absent for "a very short time". He came back and soon afterwards dragged him to the room door, Kelly said, and pointing up the corridor said, "Look you fucking cunt, you thought we were joking."

Kelly saw Nuala Dillon at the other end of the corridor, "either her back or her side" in his direction. "I seen her face but she wasn't full front to me," Kelly testified. There was a man along with her whom he did not know. As soon as he had seen her he was pulled back into the room, he said.

"Up to that stage," Kelly told the court, "I would not have really believed him about Nuala Dillon or about my mother [being in St Vincent's Hospital with a heart attack] but then . . ."

Det Garda A denied the above, telling the court he was not aware Nuala Dillon was in Fitzgibbon Street station that night. "I didn't become aware at any stage [of her presence] my lords", he said.

Nuala Dillon was in Fitzgibbon Street Garda station that night.

Det Garda B testified that after his 8.10 pm to 9.45 pm session with Kelly he had phoned Nuala Dillon and made an arrangement to meet her at Mountjoy Garda station, to clear up matters about the phone call Kelly had made on the day of the robbery. As Mountjoy Garda station was under reconstruction – "the place was covered in dust" – he decided to take Ms Dillon to Fitzgibbon Street, "which was a few minutes' drive down the road". Det Garda B agreed that normal Garda business was being carried on at Mountjoy station despite the reconstruction, but he felt it more appropriate to take Ms Dillon to Fitzgibbon Street "because of the condition in which I saw the station".

Accompanied by Det Garda F he took her to Fitzgibbon Street by car. He agreed that the interview with Nuala Dillon took place at Fitzgibbon Street in a room at the far end of the corridor "off which corridor the room that Mr Nicky Kelly was being questioned by Garda [A] was situated", as it was put by Seamus Sorohan.

Det Garda B agreed "it was quite possible" Nuala Dillon may have been there (in the corridor) "for some seconds before we checked the room to establish if there was anybody in it". He agreed with Seamus Sorohan there was "no stratagem, no plan for Mr Kelly to see Nuala Dillon" that he (Det Garda B) was aware of or took part in.

For her part, Nuala Dillon testified she received a phone call that Monday night "at about 11 o'clock". Somebody said to her, she told the court, "Nick wants to see you", and she went to Mountjoy Station.

Two plainclothes gardaí were there to meet her and they drove her to the station she now knew to be Fitzgibbon Street.

There she was brought to a room "and Garda [A] came into the room". She pointed out Det Garda A in court.

He told her, she said, "Nick has confessed he made a phone call to you on the day of the robbery, and that he had said 'the job went alright'." She denied he had said that and accused Det Garda A "of putting words in my mouth".

Det Garda A then said to her that her story did not agree with Kelly's. After this she was moved to another room, then to a smaller one again. About 15 minutes later she was "brought out to some corridor", she recalled. "I thought I was waiting to see Nick Kelly, and then after – I don't know – I was talking to whoever was with me for about five minutes – it could have been longer or shorter, I was told I could not see him. I was brought back to my flat."

DET GARDA B TOLD THE COURT that at 12.45 am (on Tuesday 6 April 1976) he received a call from Dublin Castle instructing him "to the effect that both prisoners [Kelly and co-accused Bernard McNally] be brought to the Bridewell" at which time he believed both accused "had been put down for the night".

In his evidence, Kelly testified that he recollected Det Garda B coming into the room at this time. "He had the smell of drink of off him," he told the court, and that Det Garda B said "I think it was to Guard A . . . something to the effect had I owned up, had I admitted my part?"

Kelly said he was then taken out of the room by Det Garda B, "Upstairs, up a flight of stairs, concrete, as far as I remember." They got to a landing where there was a young fellow he assumed was a prisoner. He got the impression this "young fellow" was being taken by a uniformed guard out of a cell, "which it transpired was the cell I was brought into".

He said he was brought to the cell by Det Garda B, who "pulled the door behind him. He pushed me up to the corner of the cell", by which time Kelly described himself as "the very same – to use a country euphemism – as a sack of spuds".

Questioned by Robert Barr, Kelly said that by then he "was physically and mentally tired".

"And of all those that you encountered the one that terrified you the most was B, is that correct?" asked Barr.

"B and A," replied Kelly.

"B most of all?" continued Barr.

"Well, B because he always seemed to leer and grin at me, and A because he seemed to hover – this thing – he seemed to be above me and shouting and roaring the whole time, but the two still left the most psychological mark on me."

In the cell, he said, Det Garda B "grabbed me by the hair and he was pushing my head up and down towards the toilet bowl. Maybe five or six times." He elaborated: "My head never actually hit the water." At the same time, "he was passing remarks to me that tomorrow would be another long day".

Kelly then said Det Garda B took him out of the cell and put him up against a wall, where he told him "he was adopting me", and "something to the effect that when he was finished with me I would sign any statement".

Kelly then said that Det Garda B "spit in my face". He also said he "got a knee in the thigh", after which he was taken back to the cell where, he agreed, Det Garda G found them: "You sitting on the bed, Guard B at one end with his foot up," as Robert Barr put it.

Barr wondered, "And he really, in effect, could have done what he liked with you at this stage?"

"Well, if I had been like I am at the present time. . ." responded Kelly.

"Of course, but as you were then, he had got you so beaten, so distressed, so cowed down, that he could have done what he liked with you at that stage?" queried Barr.

"Well I wasn't in a position and I didn't make any effort to hit him," responded Kelly.

After further clarification of the alleged incidents in the cell, Barr went on to suggest that "if there was any reality in this you would have complained in vehement terms to Det Garda G and you didn't".

Kelly replied, "It seemed pointless. I did not differentiate between one [Garda} and the other . . . to my effect I might even have it in my mind that he [Det Garda G] was a senior officer."

Det Garda B testified that none of this had taken place. He did not know why Kelly had been brought up to the cell in Fitzgibbon Street when he was about to be transferred to the Bridewell, but said, "I didn't bring him up".

"Bernard McNally had been put down for the night and I believed Nicholas Kelly had also been put down for the night," he testified. He had received the phone call directing that both prisoners were to be transferred to the Bridewell.

He agreed that he was "in a cell alone with Mr Kelly, when Det Garda [G] arrived. "It was a matter of seconds, my lords," he said. He agreed with the evidence of Det Garda G, who had testified that Kelly had been sitting at one end of a bed in the cell, when he arrived on the scene, and Det Garda (B) was standing at the other "just inside the door, his foot on the bed".

Det Garda G also testified that Det Garda B "went back [to the cell] just before me to get Nicky Kelly [to take him to the Bridewell]". He had noticed little change in Kelly's appearance from that morning. "He may have looked a bit tired, that's all," Det Garda G said, but everything was "just the way it would normally be".

Both he and Det Garda B brought Kelly to the Bridewell, by car. He drove, and recalled that Det Garda B sat in the back with the accused.

This was disputed by Kelly, who said Det Garda B sat in the front passenger seat, and "at one stage Guard [B] turned around and said, if I had a gun would I shoot him? He asked me what did I think of him," to which question Kelly said he did not reply.

Det Garda G told the court: "I can't remember any conversation. If they were speaking, I didn't hear." When he was asked specifically whether he had heard Det Garda B "saying to him

[Kelly] 'if you had a gun now, would you shoot me?',", Det Garda G replied, "No, that never happened."

Det Garda B, who testified he sat in the back of the car with Kelly, agreed he had some conversation with him on the way to the Bridewell. "The conversation was in relation to cigarettes," he said. "I asked him had he enough cigarettes and, as far as I recollect, he took a packet, a 20 packet from his pocket and I think it was full or almost full."

"There may have been some other general conversation," he said, "there was very little spoken on the way to the Bridewell."

"You are sure this conversation took place about the 20 Major; my client will deny it absolutely?" said Seamus Sorohan.

"I made a note of it," replied Det Garda B.

KELLY TESTIFIED THAT WHEN HE ARRIVED at the Bridewell that morning of 6 April 1976 he was escorted to a cell in the women's section. "My recollection is that either Guard B said it to me or to the jailer to put me in a quiet place," he said. Det Garda B told the Court, "I don't believe I spoke to the jailer" and agreed with the suggestion that he "didn't give any directions or make any suggestions [to the jailer]".

Kelly described the bed in his cell as "a heavy timber plank, bracketed on to the wall, with a circular shape log for the pillow". There was no mattress, but there were blankets. He used a jacket as his pillow.

Det Garda G agreed in his evidence that there was a mattress in the Fitzgibbon Street cell from which Kelly was taken to the Bridewell, but responded "no" when Seamus Sorohan put it to him that "so far as you are concerned, no suggestion that Mr Kelly was taken from Fitzgibbon Street station to the Bridewell to sleep on a wood plank bed so that he would have less chance of getting a night's rest, nothing like that entered your mind?"

It was 1.30 on the morning of Tuesday 6 April, when Kelly was placed in the cell, on his own, at the Bridewell. It was not a restful night. "My legs and arms were pretty stiff and sore. I felt pretty sick as well, even from earlier on that evening I had a very bad headache", he said. He told Robert Barr "I slept very little that night. I didn't even lie down. I sat on the wooden boards . . . I was sitting up against the wall and the jacket was against my head."

When asked why he had not requested a mattress, he replied "I was terrified another bunch of detectives might come in . . . I was afraid for when they came to look into the spy hole . . . I was going half crazy just listening to their footsteps on the tiles [outside] because every time they came near my door I thought it was me they were taking out."

"The greatest thing that was on my mind", he said, "was that I was going to get beaten again."

Later that morning a Garda Sergeant came to the cell and read over an extension order to him, "sometime between 6.30 am and 9.00 am," as the Garda Sergeant told the court. Breakfast of "tea and toast" was served. Kelly recalled being "very thirsty".

At about 10.30 am he was taken to "a fairly large room" in the police station section of the Bridewell. Det Garda A and Det Sergeant H were with him there, from 10.30 am to 10.45 am, according to the Garda timetable. "Well, I remember immediately I met Guard A again he asked me was I ready to own up now and I told him I was telling the truth," Kelly testified. "He said he didn't believe me. He started to shake me and said I had better do better than that, something like that."

At one point he said Det Garda A caught him by the shoulders, turned him around to face him and said, "Are you afraid or are you ashamed to look me in the eye?" Both Det Garda A and Det Sgt H denied this incident took place.

Det Sgt H "seemed pretty annoyed," recalled Kelly. "Well, he came in and he started shouting at me. He accused me of wasting police time. He said I didn't stay in McNally's house that night [the night of the robbery], that Fitzpatrick and Barrett [two others of the accused] had stayed there".

Kelly said he told him he was the only one to stay with the McNallys that night, and advised Det Sgt H to check this out with

Mrs McNally. He told the court that he understood that when the two gardaí left then it was "to check with Mrs McNally".

According to Det Sgt H's evidence Kelly was treated throughout this brief session in an acceptable fashion only, by both himself and Det Garda A, with no shouting or hectoring, and nothing physical.

Det Garda A and Det Sgt H were replaced at 10.45 am by Det Garda F and Det Sgt I. Det Sgt I asked Kelly whether Michael Barrett and John Fitzpatrick had stayed in McNally's house the night of the robbery. Kelly replied, "No, definitely not", after which they had "general conversation".

Det Sgt I explained to the court that he had been interviewing another of the accused, John Fitzpatrick, at the Bridewell earlier that morning, and decided to check details with Kelly. He was asked whether he had accepted Kelly's word on the matter. "Yes," he replied, "and we discovered afterwards it was a genuine mistake on Mr Fitzpatrick's part in relation to the date, so there was no need to check it any further."

According to Nicky Kelly, as well as the above having occurred, "Guard F was asking me was I ready to own up to my part in the robbery . . . he pushed me about. There was nothing really severe."

Both gardaí denied in court that Kelly had been pushed about, or abused in any way during this encounter.

Det Garda F and Det Sgt I were replaced by two other gardaí – Special Branch Det Garda C and Det Sgt J. Kelly testified that both gardaí "were shouting at me to own up. They started throwing me from one to the other". Det Garda C, he said, was "consistently passing insults about my mother and Nuala Dillon".

Then "at one stage I fell on the floor and Guard J picked up a chair and hit me with it. That was the second period I was hit with a chair . . . it was worse than the last time. I think it was to get me off the ground". He was hit "on the back or the side. I don't know exactly [he indicated an area above the left buttock]. They were shouting at me to get up off the ground. I was refusing to get up off the ground." He continued, "I remember afterwards having a very bad pain here [indicated spot above left buttock] for a number of weeks," he said. Det Garda C and Det Sgt J denied in court that any such incident took place.

At some stage during that session Kelly told the court Detective Inspector A arrived into the room. "He seemed to usher them out as he entered the room but my recollection is that Guard C stayed on for 10 or 15 minutes, or that he came in and was there when Inspector A was there."

Inspector A, he said, told him to sit down at the table and asked him to recount his movements on the night of the robbery. The Inspector wrote "on half sheets of paper". Read to the Court by Inspector A, these notes amounted to a detailed alleged confession by Kelly of participation in the mail train robbery. In the cell, when Kelly refused to sign the notes, he told the Court, Inspector A "just rose abruptly and he says if I wasn't prepared to help myself that he could do nothing for me. He would have to send in these men again."

He (Kelly) said he could see the two guards (Det Garda C and Det Sgt J) looking in through a glass panel in the door. "I was watching them more than I was watching Inspector A," Kelly told the court. He recalled the Inspector saying "that Nuala Dillon was a nice girl. It was a pity she had to be kept in a cell and he stated that when I was prepared to tell the truth that she would be released."

As Inspector A left Kelly said Det Garda C and Det Sgt J came in and accused him "of telling the Inspector lies". That was when he "discovered he was an Inspector", Kelly told the court. "They beat me, punched me," he said, "they were punching me on the arms and slapping me. Most of the beatings I got were on the upper body."

Det Sgt J testified that he wasn't in the Bridewell at all that day. Det Garda C, who denied any abuse of Kelly had taken place, testified he was in the Bridewell that morning but said he had "no recollection of seeing Det Sgt J [there] at any stage."

He accompanied Inspector A to an interview with Kelly in the Bridewell at 11.30 am. He remained in the room for some time, and then "just left it". Inspector A remained behind. He was not, as Seamus Sorohan suggested, "nodded [to] to go out, or whispered at to go out or told to go out by Inspector A"; nor was there "any urgent duty" he had to attend to; nor did he return to the room again.

Inspector A told the Court that at 11.30 that morning he interviewed Mr Kelly in an "office situated outside the prison section in the Bridewell". "My recollection, my lords, is that he was brought from the prison section to this interview room or, again, he could have been there – but he was on his own and C [Det Garda C] joined me a short time after that," he said. He had "no recollection of J [Det Sgt J] being around".

He introduced himself to Kelly and they "had a general conversation". He explained to him that he was investigating the mail train robbery and felt the accused might be able to help with enquiries, to which Mr Kelly replied, "I told you I was not involved in any robbery." After cautioning Mr Kelly he asked him to explain his movements on the night, which he did, and this was written down.

Kelly told the court he did not recall being cautioned by Inspector A that morning. (In fact he testified during the trial, "I was never cautioned". Garda witnesses testified at all relevant times during the trial that he was so cautioned.)

For his part Inspector A said no reference was made to Nuala Dillon during this interview, nor were there two gardaí outside the door, nor did he say there was "nothing I can do" or anything about "sending these men in again".

The interview ended at 1.00 pm, he said, and Mr Kelly was taken back to the prison section for his dinner.

ACCORDING TO THE GARDA TIMETABLE, and his own evidence, Det Garda A was with Nicky Kelly from 3.30 pm until 6.30 pm that day. Kelly testified, "Well, Guard A was with me for a long period but a number of other detectives, who I cannot name, were there as well. There was at least a few while I was being questioned."

He went on to recall, "Well, this was the first stage. They actually told me the part I played in the robbery. . . . Guard A was doing most of the talking, if not all of the talking. He was literally shouting the whole time. At one stage he was shouting that I was in the house, holding the people in the house. . . . O'Toole's house. [The O'Toole family home at Kearneystown, where the mail train robbery took place, was taken over by armed and masked men for a period before the train arrived.] At another stage he told me I had hi-jacked the van [used to take away the stolen mail bags]. He mentioned numerous names to me of people who had been in the robbery." To all of which Kelly answered: "I just kept telling them I knew nothing about it."

Describing what he alleged Det Garda A did to him during this interview period, Kelly told Robert Barr that, "He was hitting me, slapping me. The size of him, when he hit the table it jumped." Det Garda A was also, he said, "shouting" at him and hitting him "hard heavy punches" on the upper arms, which were then "tender from the prolonged beating of the previous day" as Robert Barr put it to him. Kelly agreed with this description.

Sometime during this interview Kelly recollected being taken out of the prison section to a small room by a number of gardaí. Det Garda A was among them, he said. He was told he was being taken to an ID parade. He said he asked for a solicitor once more, and "they said that made no difference, they would take me either ways".

He remembered, "This door was open into a room. There was a man there with a patch over his eye, and someone said, 'Is that one of them?' . . . I don't know how far I was inside the door. I confronted this man. He was sitting on a chair. He was asking, 'Is that one of them?'"

At this point in the evidence Seamus Sorohan said, "Someone addressed the words to this man, 'Did you see this man?', meaning you, before you. Did the man, in fact make any reply?"

Kelly responded, "I can recollect him saying, 'That's not one of them' or 'No'. The one thing that struck me, he had a peculiar accent." This man, it transpired, was Ray Reynolds, a 37-year-old

New Zealander whose van was taken from him by three armed men in Palmerstown, County Dublin, the night before the robbery. In a tussle with one of the hijackers he received a blow just above the left eye, causing a wound which required ten stitches.

Eventually Kelly was taken back to the interview room in the prison section at the Bridewell again. "From then on, it was Guard A impressing on me, Guard A saying I was one of the people in the house and this other thing was brought up again, about me hijacking the van," he said. But "nothing of significance" took place between then and when he was taken to his cell for tea, he said. That was at 6.30 pm, according to the Garda timetable.

Det Garda A's account, in court, of that Tuesday afternoon's interview was brief. "At 3.30 pm on the same day I saw Nicky Kelly at the Bridewell and Detective Gardaí F and B were with him at the time. I again asked him about the train robbery and had a general conversation with him, and at 6.30 pm I left him and he was given his tea and he was put in a cell."

Kelly drank his tea but "didn't eat anything". He told the court that "at this stage I was shattered". He was "sore all over. I was pretty sick. My stomach was pretty sick as well and my headaches were incredible. My head was just spinning the whole time."

At one stage he was taken out of the cell by a garda who he was unable to identify. "I didn't know what was happening. I was placed against a wall and it transpired I was measured."

The next thing he remembers is being put in "a small room" in the prison section. Det Garda A was already in the room, he said. "Nearly immediately he started shouting at me to put up my hands. He said, 'Put up your arms you fucking yellow bastard and fight'. I tried to get out in a corridor. He started calling me a coward and he was punching me in the arms. I was moving away from him. He was just punching me."

"He was asking me was I ready to own up. What sort of a man was I, allowing a girl to be kept in a cell," Kelly recalled for the court, agreeing that the girl referred to was Nuala Dillon. Det Garda A, he felt, was with him "for less than half an hour" on this occasion.

His next recollection of that particular period was the arrival of Inspector A. Det Garda A testified that after leaving Mr Kelly at 6.30 pm, he did not see him again until 11.50 pm that night.

Kelly was asked at this point in his testimony, by Seamus Sorohan, "Up to that stage have you a reasonably clear memory of the events in the Bridewell on this Tuesday?"

Kelly replied, "I suppose up to this stage, even further on." Asked to put "an approximate juncture" on when his memory begins to disimprove, Kelly said, "I don't know. The people, the gardaí who I would have known previous would be the ones I would have recognised who would be in that room over that period. Whether I have them in right sequence, from 12 [midnight] onwards, I do not know." He "couldn't be definite" as to whether all were in the right sequence up to 6 pm.

INSPECTOR A REMEMBERED ENTERING the room at about 9 pm. "I have no recollection of anybody being with Kelly in the room [as he entered]," he told the court. Questioned as to the possibility of "a doubt whether somebody may have just come out as you went in, is that the position?", Inspector A responded, "It could be, but I have no recollection."

He went in and "had a general conversation with him [Kelly] and I offered him tea, which he accepted, and biscuits." He left him then, after 15 minutes, and Det Garda N brought in the tea to Mr Kelly, he told the court.

In his testimony, Kelly agreed Inspector A arranged for him to have tea. The interview, he recalled, "was quite friendly but I knew where I stood with him". He explained to the court he did not trust Inspector A. "Well, it was obvious he had control over Guard J and Guard C on the previous morning because he had threatened me," Kelly said. "The actual words he used was, if I wasn't prepared to help myself he could do nothing for me. He would have to send these men in. That signified to me that he was in charge."

The Inspector, during this interview, Kelly said, "talked to me again about Nuala Dillon and he said the best thing I could do was to own up, save myself a lot of bother. And at one stage he said to me – the one thing that stood out in my mind – that if he wasn't with the guards himself he would be with the Provos." Inspector A denied in court that this ever took place.

Asked by Seamus Sorohan what was his objective in going in to see Kelly at that time, Inspector A replied, "Well, if he was on his own, like, and we were, sort of, on that friendly terms when I had parted with him that day, I'd have went back to see him."

"For what reason or reasons – not just to talk to him. Isn't that right?" continued Seamus Sorohan.

"I don't know, my Lords," replied Inspector A, "but that is what happened, like. Those things – you'll do those things. You'll just go in and have your confab and two years afterwards you are asked why, like. But there was nothing sinister, like."

"To use you own picturesque phrase, a confab, you went in for a chat?" suggested Sorohan. "Well that's what it turned out to be anyway," replied Inspector A.

BETWEEN 9 AND 10 PM that night Det Garda N of the Special Detective Unit visited Nicky Kelly in the interview room. It was the first time they had met. Kelly testified that he believed this was the last time he requested a solicitor. He did so as Det Garda N was new to him, and thereafter abandoned the idea as he felt it was useless and in instances only made matters worse.

He recalled that his interview with Det Garda N was taken up primarily with the phone call he had made to Nuala Dillon on the day of the robbery. "He was saying to me I had rang Nuala Dillon at lunch time on the day of the robbery and told her that everything was OK, the job went alright, something to that effect," he said.

This was being suggested to him "continuously", he said. At times Det Garda N would leave the room, he said, when there would be an "incursion of detectives" who would come in "shouting". They pushed him about and beat him for a short period before leaving and Det Garda N returned. This happened "on three occasions", Kelly said. One of those detectives he identified to the court as Det Garda A. Det Garda A denied in court he had been in the room at all at that time, nor is he recorded as being such in the Garda timetable.

At Det Garda N's return to the room on each occasion, Kelly told the court, he would ask him whether he wanted this to continue. He started to get Kelly to shout out his answers aloud. He demanded Kelly repeat after him aloud "one, two, three". Kelly said he refused initially but then gave in and started to shout "one, two, three" at the top of his voice.

Eventually he began to agree with Det Garda N that he had said during the phone call, "Everything is alright, the job went OK." "Whatever he wanted me to say, I said it," Kelly told the court, because, above all else, he wanted "to stop the beatings".

Either Det Garda N or Det Garda A began to mention some of Dublin's pubs, Kelly told the court. Grogan's on South William Street was named, and the County Bar on Parliament Street, as well as the Ormond Hotel. It was put to him he had been in the County Bar planning the robbery. That himself and Michael Barrett had discussed the robbery there, with Nuala Dillon in their company. This was put to him "a number of times" and he denied it each time. It was put to him that everyone who had been involved with the robbery had met at the Ormond Hotel before it happened. They continuously mentioned Nuala Dillon. They said that if he agreed to repeat some things in her presence she would be released.

He was asked to say (in front of her) that they (she and he) had been in Grogan's Bar with Michael Barrett and to repeat their interpretation of the phone call. If he agreed to do this he could see her and she would be released, they said. Eventually, he agreed. They (gardaí) then got a towel and washed his face, he told the court. "Guard A wiped my face and I either combed my hair or I was told to comb it," he recalled.

Then Inspector A arrived into the room with Nuala Dillon. Kelly still had his jacket on. They did not allow him to remove it at any time, he said. Det Garda A remained in the room with him, Inspector A and Nuala Dillon. He did not recollect Det Garda N being there for this confrontation.

Det Garda A said something like, "Say now to Nuala what you have said to us", and Kelly said to her, "Remember, Nuala, we were in Grogan's with Michael Barrett when the robbery was planned" and that during the phone call he had said, "Everything went OK, the job went alright."

Nuala Dillon "said absolutely nothing, as far as I can recollect now," Kelly told the court.

As regards his own state of mind at the time, he said, "I don't think I was even really conscious of the situation. I knew she was there". He was feeling "very bad" both "mentally and physically," he said. He remembered that as Inspector A led Nuala Dillon from the room he (Nicky Kelly) said something like, "Can she go now?" He didn't know what the reply was but he was left with the impression she was being released.

Then, shortly afterwards, when he assumed Nuala Dillon had been released, he denied to the gardaí the truth of what he had said to her – as regards the phone call and the meeting in Grogan's pub. That was "the first time the blackjack was produced", he told the court.

In his evidence Det Garda N said that when he entered the interview room Inspector A was still with Mr Kelly, but left then. Earlier Inspector A had told him he had received confidential information from a reliable source that in a phone call to Nuala Dillon at noon the day of the robbery, Mr Kelly had said to her, "The job went alright."

He (Det Garda N) cautioned the accused (which Kelly denied). Mr Kelly, he said, appeared a "calm, collected, normal person in every sense of the word". His demeanour was "pleasant". Twice during the session he had made him tea. (Kelly denied this and said that after the cup of tea he had received from Inspector A, and despite his requests for water, he received nothing to drink again until the confession was signed).

Det Garda N agreed Kelly denied any part in the robbery a number of times. There was "general conversation". Eventually, he told the court, Mr Kelly said he had been in the County Bar with Michael Barrett and John Fitzpatrick, about two weeks before the robbery. There was a third man there he didn't know. They discussed plans for the train robbery. That night he told Ms Dillon what they had been talking about.

Det Garda N then said he asked him (Kelly) about the phone call on the day of the robbery and Mr Kelly had told him he made it at 12 noon and that he had said to Ms Dillon, "The job went off alright." Det Garda N had notes of what Mr Kelly had said, some of which he told the court were contemporaneous. After these admissions from Mr Kelly he went out to talk to Inspector A and Inspector B, Det Garda N said.

He testified that Inspector A then went in to see Mr Kelly and said, "I believe you have told Det N certain things," to which Mr Kelly replied, "Yes."

Inspector A, Det Garda N recalled, then cautioned Mr Kelly and (he) Det Garda N read back his notes to him, which Mr Kelly agreed were correct but refused to sign. At no time had (he) Det Garda N shouted at Mr Kelly or slapped him or banged a table in front of him, he told the court. Mr Kelly had himself brought up the subject of Ms Dillon about this time, with Inspector A, he said. He mentioned she would be concerned about him, and he was about her, and he asked Inspector A if it was possible to see her.

Inspector A said he believed Ms Dillon was in the Bridewell and he asked Det Garda N to bring her in to see Mr Kelly, which he did. He left her there with Mr Kelly and Det Garda A for about ten minutes.

Inspector A was not present during the visit. Then he returned and took Ms Dillon out to the gardaí who had been accompanying her when he had brought her in to see Mr Kelly.

A short time later he realised Mr Kelly was on his own. He went in to him again and asked whether he might not like some fish or chips. While he was doing so, Det Sgt O and Det Garda P came in. He left. That was "the sum total" of his dealings with Mr Kelly, he told the court.

❧   ❧   ❧

NUALA DILLON TESTIFIED that at about 9.30 that night two detectives had come to her flat and said Nicky Kelly wanted to see her. She reminded them she had been told the same thing the previous night but was not allowed see him then. They guaranteed she would see him this time. They said he wanted clothes. She put some in a bag and was driven to the Bridewell. It was about 10 pm.

She was brought to a room which had a teleprinter in another larger room off it. Inspector A came in "quite often". He was "very friendly". She was asked about the phone call Kelly made to her on the day of the robbery. She knew he had phoned her.

"He phones me every day," she told the court, but could not remember what exactly he had said. But what they (gardaí) were saying "definitely was not said", she insisted.

At one stage Inspector A came in and said Kelly was now saying he and she had been drinking in Grogan's and that they had planned the robbery, and she had been drinking pints of Harp. She said this could not be true, "and it was not true", and he said "well come on and Nick will tell you". He then took her to the room where Mr Kelly was being questioned. She had no doubt that it was Inspector A. He accompanied her into the room where Kelly and Det Garda A were already.

"The room was hot – the first thing that struck me; the room was warm and he was wearing a ski jacket," she recalled. Nicky Kelly she remembered as looking "upset". He was running his hands through his hair and he was "sort of sweating slightly – his face . . . his hand was shaking at some stage". She asked him was he alright and he said yes.

Then Det Garda A said something like, "Tell us what you have been saying about drinking in Grogan's" and Kelly turned round and said, "Do you remember, Nuala, and we planned the robbery?" Then, she remembered, he turned to Inspector A and Det Garda A and said "... but she was not in [on] the final details."

He said something then like, "I phoned you the next day and said the job went all right." She said nothing. "I knew he was lying and I didn't know why. I had no idea," she told the Court. He then said, "Can she go now?" Then Inspector A took her out, to the same room she had been in previously.

She said to Inspector A she didn't know what he (Kelly) was talking about, "It wasn't true." She said she thought she needed a solicitor, to which Inspector A retorted, she told the court, that "If I [Nuala Dillon] continued in that vein I was lucky that I wasn't locked up already– that I wasn't in a cell – and I would be locked up." Plainclothes gardaí came and went, questioning her. She asked could she go, but was told to wait until Inspector A came to see her. He came at one stage and said Kelly was bringing them to the money, and asked her to wait until they came back.

The place got "very quiet" and she tried to sleep on a wooden bench but couldn't. Then she began to hear screaming. She heard someone shouting "please, not there" or something like that. She went out of the room and there were a lot of gardaí outside the door.

"Please let me out," she said, "I can hear someone screaming." A short time afterwards two plainclothes gardaí came and took her to Mountjoy Garda station. She asked to be allowed go home. They said no; they were waiting for Inspector A to give them the word.

At 8.00 the following morning they said she could go. As she was leaving she was re-arrested outside the Garda station under Section 30 of the Offences Against the State Act. She was brought back to the Bridewell and placed in a cell. She was held there until "about seven o'clock that evening". She was not interviewed "at all". She was taken out and photographed at one point. She was not told why she was being held, at any point. Then "they just came and let me go. Nobody said anything to me." She went home.

‰   ‰   ‰

NICKY KELLY TESTIFIED that when Nuala Dillon left the room after her visit along with Inspector A, he was left alone with Det Garda A. He "was always, as far as I can recollect, accompanied from then onwards by three or four detectives".

Kelly went back on what he had said to Nuala Dillon. "I was refusing to make the statement [of guilt] and I had gone back on what I had originally said to Nuala Dillon." He could not recall for certain who was there then but thought Det Garda A was present at that stage.

It was at this time, Kelly testified, that the beatings with the blackjack began, as reported in Chapter 2. "Well, they just started to beat me again," he began.

Dealing with this final phase of the interrogation, Robert Barr, senior counsel for the prosecution, said to Nicky Kelly, "Now we come to the blackjack. There were three episodes in this regard. It was always wielded by Det Sgt O?"

At which point Mr Justice Clarke intervened to remind him, "Once by Garda B, the second by B, and the final by Sgt O."

Robert Barr then asked Kelly, "Did Garda B have his own blackjack or was it the same one?"

"The same," replied Kelly.

"You were beaten again about the upper arms and on the thighs?" asked Barr

"The back of the thighs, the insides of the legs."

"A couple of times?"

"Near the privates."

"As far as the beatings on your legs, did they cause pain?" asked Barr.

"Yes."

Kelly went on to explain that the "real stinging pain" was felt as the instrument was pulled away, rather than on impact. "Perhaps a whiplash effect," was his description.

". . . It was a painful, horrific experience?" asked Barr.

"It was."

"Horrific and frightening?"

"I was frightened the whole day."

"This was behind it all. The blackjack was getting to be severe terror?"

"To somebody in that position, another variation"

"Here is an added instrument. Up to now there was only the chairs. This was the first instrument used, apart from the chairs?" asked Barr.

"Correct."

"Did you get more [blows] on the last occasion than on the other two?"

"On the last occasion, besides the blackjack being used, a number of people were moving through the room. I don't know, I thought it was immediately I said, immediately after that I said I would not sign the statement."

"When you were knocked to the ground – the third attack with the blackjack, had you been knocked on the other two occasions?"

"I was literally in between legs. They were grabbing me and shouting at me to get up."

"How did you fall? Was it a blow of the blackjack?"

"I did not fall. I was pushed to the ground in the same period when the blackjack was used. I got a beating from a greater number of men than had been in the room previously," said Kelly, adding, "They over-concentrated on my arms, my forehead. Kneed in different positions, the whole place was a frenzy."

"You are saying the whole object of the exercise was to get you to sign the statement?" questioned Barr.

"Correct."

"And once that happened . . . ?"

". . . Orange and tea. Orange and tea. The whole thing finished," answered Kelly.

"So that at the time you got to the end of the third blackjack and allied beatings your will was at that stage completely broken?"

"I could not take any more."

Mr Barr then went on to discuss Kelly's mental and physical condition at the time, and continued, "If what you allege did in fact happen to you, one would expect you must have been at that stage . . . your spirit must have been broken, cowed down, and you were utterly distressed?"

"Correct, yes," said Kelly.

"When did you get your wits together again?"

"When in Portlaoise prison [the following Friday]."

"Not until then?"

"To be frank, when I got bail."

"Not until you got bail?"

"It never sank down into me until weeks afterwards."

NICKY KELLY SIGNED THE CONFESSION, implicating him in the Sallins train robbery, at 5.15 am on Wednesday 7 April 1976.

ONE OF THE MORE BIZARRE EPISODES to happen following Kelly's signing of the confession that morning was a trip he was taken on by gardaí to the scene of the mail train robbery and then to Bray.

During his alleged final beating before signing the confession, Kelly mentioned about guns in Bray. It was "about 1.00 am", he told the Court. "What I was personally thinking at the time was that again we would get out of there and discover there were no guns and they would search and it would save me three or four hours beating," he told the Court. "Anytime that I was prepared to tell something they wanted to hear, they would stop beating me," he said.

In his evidence Inspector A told the Court they (gardaí) decided to take a trip to Ballymore Eustace, to where he said Kelly had told them the mail train robbery money would be found. Kelly, in his evidence, said that he "was told" he was going on a trip. The round-trip, taking in Ballymore Eustace and Bray uncovered nothing – neither money nor guns. Kelly was accompanied on the journey by Inspector A, as well as Detective Sgts O and R.

On return to the Bridewell later that morning, Kelly was soon joined by three of the other accused, John Fitzpatrick, Brian McNally and Michael Plunkett.

"We showed each other the bruises that were there and we discussed what happened. We had a discussion about a solicitor. We knew we were going to appear before a court," Kelly testified. It was agreed that if there was any press in court or anyone they knew, "Michael Plunkett would state what had happened to us."

He recollected telling Inspector A he wanted a solicitor and being told "we would be coming back there [to the Bridewell] and we could contact a solicitor when we came back." Inspector A, in his evidence, said he saw all four accused prior to the District Court hearing. They "had a chat". None of them requested a solicitor, he said.

The four accused were taken through a tunnel, escorted by detectives and gardaí "in front of us and behind and when we got there, there was a fair number in the court itself as well".

Kelly had difficulty going up stairs into the dock. He was stiff and sore. "There was no one in the court except gardaí, quite a number in plain clothes. In actual fact, they would have outnumbered the uniformed," he recalled.

Inspector A agreed at the Special Criminal Court that he had requested that the accused be remanded in custody. He could have said "to the following morning", but he was not definite about that.

Defence counsel Seamus Sorohan wondered at this. "Was it for any ulterior motive, so that it might eventuate in these persons being kept in the Bridewell and not being transported off to Mountjoy where they would be examined by a doctor on reception?" he asked. Inspector A denied any such motive. It was near midnight when the accused were brought back to the Bridewell, Inspector A told the Court.

He agreed that at the time he was aware of a *habeas corpus* application being made by another accused in the mail train robbery investigation, Osgur Breathnach, who was then in the Richmond Hospital. He was also aware that there were allegations that

Breathnach had been beaten by members of the gardaí. His own state of mind at the time was that "no person in Garda custody had been assaulted. The subsequent investigations by me showed otherwise," he told the Court.

Back at the Bridewell the accused were allowed two phone calls. Kelly called a friend of his parents in Arklow, and Nuala Dillon. He asked her to contact a solicitor.

Nicky Kelly and Michael Plunkett were placed in one cell while John Fitzpatrick and Brian McNally were placed in another. This placing of the accused in cells together would prove crucial in the admissions of their confessions as evidence by the Special Criminal Court.

Asked by Seamus Sorohan about the rules for the Bridewell, Inspector A said he had "never read them". Asked whether he was "aware there was a rule that persons charged with the same offence should be kept segregated from each other, or something to that effect, while in the Bridewell?", Inspector A replied, "I am not aware of it. I think if that is there it is a new one."

The following morning the accused were brought to the District Court again. There were "quite a number of friends there. Michael Plunkett spoke out in court about what had happened to them, and showed his bruises," Kelly testified. Bail was fixed and they were remanded to Mountjoy.

THE FIRST DOCTOR TO SEE NICKY KELLY on his admission to Mountjoy on Thursday 8 April 1976 was Dr Paul McVey, deputy medical officer at the prison. He confirmed to the court that Kelly had extensive bruises on both arms and the right shoulder. There was also bruising of both buttocks. He wouldn't rule out the possibility that there may have been a number of things he had left out.

Mr Kelly, he said, was also complaining of a headache, and he agreed the injuries were consistent with being hit or having fallen.

One of the judges (not identified in the transcripts) asked "Could they [the injuries] be consistent with being hit with a cosh or a blackjack?"

"Possibly," replied Dr McVey.

His superior, Dr Samuel Davis, examined Kelly the following day (Friday). His report read as follows: "Edward Kelly, 25 years. Eating. Bowels not open since Sunday. Left shoulder and scapula area has extensive bruising, going from the tip of the acronium towards the scapula. Linear bruising measuring 5" x 2" and 3" x 1", extensive bruising on left upper arm, completely bruised on outer and medical side, one third approximately on inner side, not bruised but sore and tender to touch. On lateral surface of forearm circular bruising approximately 2" on middle of forearm, above wrist 2" approximately. Circular bruise. Over pectoral area two superficial injuries approximately 1". Has appendix scar. Complains of tenderness over bladder area. Large superficial bruising of outer anterior surface of right arm, 7" x 7" continues into back of right shoulder. Complains of bad headaches. Bruising of right and left cheek of sacral region (buttocks). Bruising behind left ear. Bruising on front and back of left thigh."

Dr Davis had dictated his report to an assistant Mr Joseph Deignan, while examining Mr Kelly. Dr Davis explained in court that this was not his usual procedure, but he had arranged it in this instance as "we don't have a lot of cases with so many remarks to be made and to be done in case I missed out anything. Sometimes when you examine, you have to write down, you might miss something. I thought this [case] was important enough to have somebody receive my dictation".

He adopted the same modus operandi with all five accused in the mail train robbery case: Kelly, Plunkett, McNally, Fitzpatrick, Breathnach.

"Because of the number of injuries and the number of things you had to call out?" queried Seamus Sorohan.

"Yes," answered Dr Davis. The prisoners had, he said, complained that "they were beaten by the police".

"The injuries", Dr Davis testified, "were consistent with a person having come into contact with some object."

"A fist?" asked Sorohan.

"It could be," answered Dr Davis.

"Maybe a kick?" asked Sorohan.

"It could be," answered Dr Davis. The doctor agreed that wearing a shirt, a pullover and possibly outside that again a ski-jacket would tend to lessen the imposition of linear marks on the skin, from a cosh or suchlike.

Dr Richard Burke examined Kelly on his arrival at Portlaoise prison later that day, Friday 9 April 1976. His evidence to court was broadly in agreement with the findings of his two doctor colleagues.

Following Dr Burke's examination, Kelly was released on bail.

THERE WERE 51 WITNESSES for the prosecution against Nicky Kelly in the trial.

Four of those were Dr McVey, Dr Davis, and Mr Deignan, who confirmed Dr Davis's report, and Dr Burke. All the remaining 47 prosecution witnesses were members of the Garda Síochána. Apart from Kelly himself, there were three defence witnesses: Nuala Dillon, Dr Sean O'Cleirigh and Dr David Magee, who both examined Kelly at Mountjoy prison on Thursday 8 April 1976. Their medical evidence underlined that of the other three doctors involved with his case.

UNDER CROSS-EXAMINATION BY ROBERT BARR, Kelly was asked; "Are you saying to this court that there is a conspiracy of naked perjury involving a very large group of the Garda Síochána from the rank of Superintendent, if not even Chief Superintendent, downwards?"

"I am saying to the court what happened me in the custody of the gardaí," responded Kelly.

"You have heard the Garda evidence. They are lying, is it as simple as that?" asked Barr.

"Well, anyone who I have stated assaulted me and sat here and said that they didn't, to me they are not telling the truth."

"And anyone who said you looked perfectly alright and made no complaints when, on the contrary, you say you did make complaints, he is lying too . . .?"

"Correct."

According to the official Garda timetable, Nicky Kelly was interrogated by 14 gardaí over a period of 27 hours before he signed the confession. He insisted at the trial that many more were involved. Those listed on the official Garda timetable were as follows, with the length of time each spent with Kelly:

	Hrs/mins
Det Garda A (Technical Bureau)	11.45
Det Garda B (Store St)	6.15
Det Sgt O (Central Detective Unit)	4.30
Det Garda F (CDU)	2.50
Det Garda P (Special Detective Unit/Special Branch)	2.35
Det Sgt R (Finglas)	2.10
Det Inspector Edward Ryan (CDU)	2.10
Det Garda N (Special Branch)	1.50
Det Garda E (Ballyfermot)	1.45
Det Garda C (Special Branch)	1.30
Det Sgt I (Ballymun)	0.45
Det Sgt H (Pearse St)	0.45
Det/Garda G (Special Branch)	0.30
Det/Garda U (Special Branch)	0.05

Under cross-examination by Robert Barr, Kelly made it clear that he was not alleging all the gardaí involved in his interrogation had abused him. The majority had not, he said.

ON FRIDAY 9 APRIL 1976 another man, Michael Barrett, was also arrested in connection with the mail train robbery. He too was charged and released on bail.

On 9 December 1976, following repeated delays by the State in its preparation of the case against the six mail train robbery accused, and indications privately to District Justice Ó hUadaigh by the DPP Eamonn Barnes that he was undecided about pressing charges at all, Justice Ó hUadaigh discharged all the accused.

The DPP called a conference of 12 of the most senior gardaí involved in the mail train robbery investigation, where the guilt of the suspects was impressed on Barnes, who was also assured there had been no ill-treatment meted out during the interrogations. The DPP instructed that five of the accused be charged. He felt there was not enough evidence against the sixth man, Michael Barrett.

On 17 December 1976, four of the six were rearrested and charged – Kelly, Breathnach, Plunkett and McNally. The gardaí were unable to find Fitzpatrick.

His appearance at a press conference in Dublin seven years later would set the cat among the pigeons.

8

JUSTICE, AS SEEN TO BE DONE

THERE IS NO DOUBT the Government was very happy with the Garda's handling of the train robbery investigation. Minister for Justice Patrick Cooney told the Dáil on 5 May 1976, during a debate on the crime rate, that "there was an unfortunate rash of robberies some weeks ago but I am precluded, happily, from commenting on them because the vast majority are sub-judice". He continued, "They are sub-judice because we have an active, intelligent, dedicated, loyal police force whose morale is at its highest."

Indications that, among the gardaí themselves, this morale was not at all as Minister Cooney saw it, was available in the then current issue of the *Garda Review* magazine, published by the Garda Representative Association, wherein an editorial criticised Government policy towards the gardaí, which it said was based on misleading information provided by the Garda Commissioner, Edmund Garvey.

There was at the time general dissatisfaction within the force at Commissioner Garvey's style of leadership and growing concern over stories of "Heavy Gang" activities. It was even said that some Garda Superintendents would not allow known "Gang" members to be involved in investigations in their own areas.

Commissioner Garvey was furious at the *Garda Review* editorial, which he saw as rebellion. He sent senior gardaí to the Director of Public Prosecutions (DPP) with a copy of the editorial, parts of which he had underlined and numbered with references to accompanying notes.

He wanted the DPP to consider charging the editorial board of the magazine with subversion. He made suggestions for other likely charges, such as incitement to violence, for instance – any of which would have meant the gardaí responsible could be brought before the Special Criminal Court. No charges were brought by the DPP.

The result of this increasing concern among the gardaí themselves was that a number of their representatives went to see Minister for Justice Patrick Cooney himself. He was not encouraging. Dissatisfied with his response, they then went to see Minister for Foreign Affairs Garret FitzGerald, early in 1977, and told him of their worries. He was sympathetic but nothing happened.

When Garret FitzGerald brought the gardaí's complaints to the attention of the Taoiseach, Liam Cosgrave, they were waved aside. It is said that FitzGerald considered resigning then, but he didn't.

A member of that Garda delegation which attempted to have the alleged activities of the "Heavy Gang" curbed, and which protested at the severity of the Garvey regime generally within the force, was P.J. Culligan, later Garda Commissioner himself.

In February 1977, the alleged activities of the "Heavy Gang" were discussed in the public domain for the first time. *The Irish Times* published a series of articles by journalists Renagh Holohan, Don Buckley and Joe Joyce which alleged the existence of such a group and carried statements from people who said they had been beaten by the "Heavy Gang".

The revelations in the articles were backed up by lawyers, doctors, guards, as well as victims. The "Heavy Gang", it was disclosed, was employing similar methods to those used in Northern Ireland during the early 1970s, and which the European Court of Human Rights had described as torture. This followed a case taken by Ireland against Britain to that body, following allegations of ill-treatment of suspects in the North.

Two of those involved in presenting Ireland's case in that action were barrister Aidan Browne, who would later give evidence on Osgur Breathnach's behalf at the mail train robbery trial, and psychiatrist Dr Robert Daly of UCC, who testified on Nicky Kelly's behalf.

As well as beatings, the techniques allegedly employed in the North and condemned by the European Court of Human Rights included depriving people of sleep and disorienting them, sometimes by the use of hoods or high-pitched "white noise". Other techniques allegedly involved forcing people to stand spread-eagled against a wall for long periods and, in interrogation, the alteration of questioners between "nice" guys and "bad" guys.

The European Court later ruled these techniques as "ill-treatment" rather than "torture", as the perpetrators did not "take pleasure" in applying them!

Responding to the *Irish Times* articles, and subsequent opposition questions in the Dáil, Minister Cooney denied that the "Heavy Gang" existed or that there was any substance to the allegations being made about the treatment of people in Garda custody. He refused to set up an inquiry into the matter.

On 18 February 1977, Gerry Collins, then Fianna Fáil spokesman on Justice, said that the Minister had "a very grave responsibility to immediately set up a judicial inquiry into the allegations made and have the machinery there in operation ready at the push of a button to deal with allegations as they arise . . .". He continued, "If there is any truth whatsoever in these allegations . . . those who might be responsible for ill-treatment of persons in custody [then the Minister should ensure they] would be disciplined as they should be."

By the end of June 1977, Gerry Collins was himself Minister for Justice. In office he too refused to set up an inquiry into the *Irish Times* allegations, whether of the type he himself had demanded four months previously, or otherwise.

It was also in June of that year that Amnesty International sent a team to Ireland to investigate allegations of Garda ill-treatment of suspects. The team consisted of two people, Angela Wright from Amnesty's international secretariat, and Douwe Korff, a Dutch lawyer. They inquired into a total of 28 cases, seven of which involved people held in connection with the mail train

robbery, including Nicky Kelly. While their investigation was underway in Ireland the Amnesty team was shadowed continuously
by Special Branch gardaí. At the end of their investigation the
team sought a meeting with Minister Cooney, then still in office.
He refused to meet them. Generally, members of the Coalition
Government rubbished the Amnesty investigation and refused
point-blank to co-operate with it.

In August 1977, Amnesty sent its report to the Irish Government, now led by Taoiseach Jack Lynch. The report found that
people were being systematically brutalised while in Garda custody by detectives who specialised in extracting statements by
force. The report also found: "Allegations common to every case
examined are that the victims were at various times beaten and
punched, the most common targets being the ears, stomach and
groin; knocked or thrown against walls or furniture; thrown from
one officer to another; kneed in the stomach and kicked. It was
also commonly alleged that victims were pulled or swung by the
hair; arms twisted behind their backs while they were punched;
were spread-eagled against a wall and had their legs kicked apart
so that they fell to the ground."

It continued: "In five cases detained persons alleged they were
beaten with objects . . ." The report concluded that "The consis-
tency in the nature of allegations from persons arrested at different times and in different parts of the country lend weight to their
validity, as must the fact that during the past 18 months and
longer the same officers have been mentioned as being involved
in maltreatment of suspects in reports made at different times in
different parts of the country." It called for an independent inquiry into all the allegations.

But that Amnesty report went much further than just endors-
ing reports of the existence of the "Heavy Gang" and its activities.
It made observations about the Special Criminal Court. That
Court, it said, had refused or failed to examine allegations of brutality by the gardaí and that, in its conduct, the onus of proof had
shifted, effectively requiring the defence to prove beyond all reasonable doubt that brutality had occurred. The prosecution did

not appear to have to prove that it did not occur, as the law required the prosecution to do, it said.

This was the same court which would hear Nicky Kelly's case within five months, in January 1978. But, still, he was optimistic. So were his legal team. The reason was as simple as it was naïve – they did not expect his confession to be admitted as evidence or that he would be found guilty of something he didn't do.

In publishing that Amnesty report, the new Lynch Government deleted the section referring to the Special Criminal Court. It also refused the request for an independent inquiry into Garda conduct. Instead it set up a three-man committee, headed by Judge Barra O'Briain, with a brief to make recommendations for safeguarding people in custody and for safeguarding the Garda from untrue allegations. This committee was not allowed investigate any existing allegations of the ill-treatment of suspects while in Garda custody. When the O'Briain committee made its recommendations a year later, practically all of them were rejected by the Lynch Government.

THROUGH 1977 NICKY KELLY'S OPTIMISM about his case increased. The revelations about the "Heavy Gang" and its activities; the interest of Amnesty and other international human rights groups in the case, and that of the others, boosted his confidence that all would be well.

This was bolstered by the change of Government in June 1977, especially after Gerry Collins's call for a judicial inquiry into the allegations of ill-treatment of suspects while in Garda custody.

During the general election campaign that summer, Kelly canvassed again for Seamus Costello in Wicklow while doing the other usual political chores as well – postering, leafleting, etc. He always enjoyed elections and it was an opportunity to escape from a preoccupation with his own troubles. No one ever referred to the mail train robbery or the pending trial during any of his canvasses throughout the constituency. Nobody showed him any hostility.

It would be Seamus Costello's last election. Kelly was at a consultation in the Law Library in Dublin with counsel Tony Sammon and Seamus Sorohan on 5 October 1977 when the word came through. There had been a newsflash on the radio that Seamus Costello had been shot dead. Earlier that afternoon Costello had been sitting alone in his car on Northbrook Avenue in Dublin's North Strand, when a lone gunman stuck a gun in the window and shot him. He was 37. It was shocking news and Kelly was shattered by it.

"I left the Four Courts and went to be with his widow Melissa and their four young children. His funeral in Bray was attended by representatives of all the political parties, and thousands of the ordinary people he had fought for all his political life. Some of them wept in the streets as the hearse passed. In death he was praised as he never was in life. Costello's death cast a gloom over the remainder of '77 for me."

But early in the New Year of 1978 there was good news. Edmund Garvey, the Garda Commissioner, was sacked by the new Government.

THE MAIL TRAIN ROBBERY TRIAL began on 19 January 1978, before Justice James McMahon of the High Court, Justice John O'Connor of the Circuit Court, and Justice John Garavan of the District Court. Soon a routine had established itself.

"It was like going to work. We had to be there at 10.00 am, or risk contempt of court. At 10.30 we entered the dock and sat there until about 1.00 pm. There'd be a break for lunch, before resumption at 2.00 pm. Proceedings finished at 4.00 pm. This went on five days a week, for five months during the first trial."

At the beginning there was great public interest, with detailed reports in the papers. Then, as the case wore on, interest waned. Solicitors for the accused were Pat McCartan and Michael White (now also a judge, of the Circuit Criminal Court), who were partners in a practice at the time.

Seamus Sorohan was senior counsel for Nicky Kelly and Brian McNally. Paddy McEntee was senior counsel for Osgur Breatnach and Mick Plunkett. The prosecuting counsel were Noel McDonald and Robert Barr.

Relations between the defendants and their lawyers were not always easy. "We, and the IRSP, were anxious to launch a campaign on the case, with public meetings, marches, and other forms of protest, to highlight what we saw as an attempt by the gardaí to destroy the party by setting us up for a crime we did not commit. Our lawyers simply wanted to fight the case through the legal system. This was a great point of contention," Kelly remembered.

The IRSP campaign was to all intents put aside while the case slowly wound its way through the legal system. Its tardy progress was a constant irritation where the defendants were concerned. "Not only did this snail's pace prolong the agony, it made it impossible for us to think of a future beyond the case. The result was that we were often critical of what seemed like the laid-back style of our lawyers in court. Their lack of urgency and calmness before what was going on and what seemed like their acquiescence in the slowness of it all used to drive us crazy," he recalled.

Arguments between the defendants and their lawyers were frequent, and during the hearings they frequently sent messages to their lawyers pointing out details they thought had been forgotten or which they felt had not been made proper use of.

The trial trundled along. Defence counsel scored two major points early on, which livened things up for a while. Paddy McEntee succeeded in getting one prosecution witness to admit that a statement she signed in relation to the case had been prepared by a garda and sent to her for signature 18 months after the event.

Seamus Sorohan, cross-examining Special Branch Det Garda C, made another discovery. Det Garda C was one of the gardaí who questioned Nicky Kelly when he was in custody. Det Garda C told Seamus Sorohan he had not read the statement he made about the Kelly case since it was prepared almost two years earlier. He had not needed to, he said. Sorohan noticed that as Det

Garda C spoke he kept tapping one of his pockets. He asked Det Garda C if he'd mind emptying his pockets. Among the contents was a copy of the statement Det Garda C had made about the Kelly case almost two years previously. He said he had not looked at it before giving evidence.

But those were just two bright spots in what seemed endless boredom. Then the most bizarre of things began to happen. It was noticed that one of the judges seemed to be sleeping through the hearings. This soon became the main talking point, obscuring almost everything else where the trial case was concerned. As early as 1 February 1978 – the tenth day of the trial – people began to remark that Justice John O'Connor seemed to be sleeping.

This was reported by journalist Niall Kiely in *Hibernia* magazine on 3 February, but nothing happened. Lawyers for the defence were reluctant to do anything that would embarrass the judge, and this caused further strain in their relationship with the defendants. The lawyers hoped the presiding judge, Judge McMahon, might do something after the *Hibernia* report.

On Monday 6 February Martin Reynolds, a Fine Gael party activist, wandered in to see what was happening in the case. Annoyed at what he saw, he wrote to Garret FitzGerald, by then leader of Fine Gael, and asked him to take a personal interest in the proceedings. He also queried whether Judge O'Connor's condition might not be a reason to have the trial stopped. But nothing happened.

By then everyone was talking about "the sleeping judge". Everywhere, but in the Special Criminal Court, where matters continued as before. Then farce took over. Great big law books began to be dropped from a height as Judge O'Connor's head dipped nearer the bench. There would be sudden fits of loud coughing; a door near Judge O'Connor would be banged when necessary; some court officers would attempt to accidentally nudge him; and counsel's kidneys became over-active as frequent adjournments were sought so lawyers could go to the toilet.

All of this succeeded in bringing Judge O'Connor back to awareness in the Special Criminal Court, but usually only for a while before he fell into a slumber once more. Word spread that he was taking tablets for a heart condition and that a side-effect was drowsiness. People began to wonder whether the man was fit enough to work at all. But nothing happened about that either. There were reports that at a legal dinner his head dipped right down on to the plate of food before him. The man was obviously unwell.

The defence lawyers did not want to do anything in open court. They were afraid of the consequences for the case if they did. But the defendants were adamant something had to be done. So, on their instruction, defence counsel asked to see the three judges privately, in their chambers. There they outlined their concerns, but nothing happened. Judge O'Connor continued to sleep on.

It was time for firmer action. The defendants felt that if they were being denied such a basic right as trial before a jury then, at the very least, they were going to have the full attention of all three judges. On 26 April Seamus Sorohan made an application to the court to discharge itself and called for a new trial to be held. The application, which he said caused him deep personal and professional embarrassment, was being made as "from time to time it has appeared that one member of the court was apparently asleep in the sense that his eyes were closed and his head down".

Paddy McEntee added that Judge O'Connor appeared to be asleep on a large number of occasions during the course of the trial. "Not alone must justice be done but it must be seen to be done," he said. Prosecuting counsel Noel McDonald opposed the application, pointing out that the trial was 50 days old and that, had the problem been noted as far back as February, such an application should have been made then.

Judge McMahon announced that the Court itself would pronounce on the matter. All three judges – including Judge O'Connor – retired to decide whether Judge O'Connor had been sleeping. They returned and told the Court they had found that Judge O'Connor had not been sleeping. He was satisfactorily fulfilling his duties in accordance with "the solemn declaration he made on his appointment". Seamus Sorohan responded that the matter would be taken further.

Eight affidavits were sworn, one from each of the defendants; one each from solicitors Pat McCartan and Michael White; one from Fine Gael activist Martin Reynolds; and one from the *Hibernia* journalist Niall Kiely, who had written the 3 February story. Pat McCartan quoted from notes he had taken at the trial in January: "Judge O'Connor fast asleep – head on bench."

The affidavits were presented to the High Court on 28 April. Seamus Sorohan and Paddy McEntee asked for a conditional order prohibiting the Special Criminal Court from proceeding with the trial.

It was refused by the President of the High Court, Justice Thomas Finlay, for three reasons. He said the issue had already been ruled on by the judges of the Special Criminal Court; that they had established as "a finding of fact" that Judge O'Connor was not sleeping; that if he (Judge Finlay) agreed with the defence lawyers it would mean the end of the trial; and finally there was the matter of what he described as "the wholly unexplained delay" between when Judge O'Connor's alleged sleeping was first noticed and when action was eventually taken.

The defence counsel immediately lodged an appeal with the Supreme Court. It was heard the following week before Chief Justice Tom O'Higgins and his four colleagues, Justices Seamus Henchy, Frank Griffin, John Kenny and Weldon Parke.

They did not appear at all pleased with the application, least of all the Chief Justice. He was particularly hostile to Paddy McEntee, who went back to sixteenth-century English law to establish precedent. Exchanges between Justice O'Higgins and McEntee were sharp.

Paddy McEntee began, "Your lordship submits . . ." He was immediately interrupted by Chief Justice O'Higgins, who brusquely corrected him. "No, Mr MacEntee, I do not submit. You submit, and I decide."

The Supreme Court rejected the appeal, unanimously. By then nine of the country's most senior judges had heard the application and had ruled against it. The trial continued and Judge O'Connor slept on. It was back to dropping books, banging doors and seeking leave to go to the toilet once more.

On 4 May it became too much for Mick Plunkett. When Paddy McEntee returned from one of his toilet breaks, Plunkett rose to his feet and demanded it be put on the record that the real reason McEntee had sought the adjournment was so Judge O'Connor might be woken up. Judge McMahon ruled him out of order. He said Plunkett had no right to speak as he was represented by counsel.

On 11 May, *Hibernia* reported this incident, adding that before the McEntee adjournment Judge McMahon "seemed to make an unsuccessful effort to rouse O'Connor". It was a brave piece of journalism, which seriously risked contempt, as it was suggesting that despite rulings to the contrary at the Special Criminal Court itself, the High Court, and the Supreme Court, all was not in order with the trial's conduct.

It also implied that there were efforts by Judge McMahon and, elsewhere in the same article, by Judge Garavan, to continue what was basically a charade, to ensure the trial went on. It was expected action would be initiated by the Courts against the magazine. But nothing happened.

On the trial's sixty-fifth day, 6 June 1978, there was a delay in beginning as Judge O'Connor had not arrived. Word spread that he had had a heart attack and died that morning. The trial was abandoned. By then it had become the longest and most expensive court case ever held in the history of the State.

Feelings in legal circles about the Judge O'Connor affair, not least among the judiciary, were to stay strong. An indication of how strong can be gained from a remark made by Circuit Court Judge Diarmuid Sheridan, at a sitting in Thurles on 7 June, the day after Judge O'Connor's death.

"The events of more recent times may well have taken their toll on him and it might be prudent to observe that he deserved a little better than he got," he said.

9

TRIAL TWO

NICKY KELLY WAS BUSY THAT SUMMER while awaiting the new trial. Encouraged by growing public support, he spoke at a meeting of International Jurists held in Liberty Hall to discuss the cases and others affected by the alleged activities of the "Heavy Gang".

Nobel Peace Prize winner Sean McBride set up an unofficial inquiry into what had happened to the mail train robbery defendants, and groups such as the Association for Legal Justice and the Irish Council for Civil Liberties – notably through Kadar Asmal, a law lecturer at Trinity College Dublin and later a minister in South Africa's post-apartheid Government – continued to highlight the case as well.

More generally, there was a growing awareness that all was not well with the mail train robbery saga, an awareness heightened by the "sleeping judge" affair, but also by the remarkable similarity in statements made by the different gardaí involved in the interrogations to the Special Criminal Court already, and by the August 1977 Amnesty report.

Everything though was qualified by the impending trial. It began on Monday 10 October 1978. The defendants were optimistic once more. That optimism increased when they heard that Justice Liam Hamilton was presiding. His conduct of the trial was expected to be brusque and to the point, with none of the meanderings that bogged down the previous one. His colleagues would be Justices Gerard Clarke of the Circuit Court and Cathal Ó Floinn, President of the District Court.

The defendants were formally charged once again, after a long technical argument as to whether the first trial had or had not happened in law! When charged this time Nicky Kelly replied, "Framed by the Heavy Gang. Not guilty." The other defendants did the same. "[Inspector A's] Heavy Gang are guilty. I'm not guilty," said Mick Plunkett.

By then the defence lawyers were convinced of two things: that many prosecution witnesses were fudging the truth and that there appeared to be every semblance of a conspiracy at work among the gardaí, such was the extraordinary similarity in detail between separate garda statements.

But once again the central issue was whether or not the defendants' confessions would be admitted as evidence. Everything hung on that and it would take up the most part of this second trial, as it did of the first.

All started well. The charges against Mick Plunkett were dropped on the second day, 11 October. Plunkett had not signed a confession but was being held on the basis of an identification by Conal O'Toole, that he was one of the men who took over the O'Toole house near the rail line before and during the mail train robbery. Conal O'Toole failed to identify Plunkett when he first saw him lined up in an identity parade at Harcourt Terrace Garda station. He identified him later when he saw him in a corridor at Harcourt Terrace being escorted by two gardaí. Plunkett was released.

For the rest, the "trial within a trial" continued to deal with the question of the admissibility of their confessions, the only evidence against them. The defence lawyers argued against the confessions being accepted by the Court. They argued that the defendants had been forced to sign statements concocted by the gardaí.

In a normal court the jury would be asked to leave until the judge decided whether a statement/confession was admissible, depending on the circumstances in which it was taken. If it was decided to admit it the jury would then be recalled to hear it. In the Special Criminal Court both functions are performed by the same three judges, who literally act as judge, jury and sentencing body.

The court decided it would first hear each case vis-à-vis the admissibility of each confession, and make a decision on each one when all three had been heard.

Brian McNally's case was first heard, then Osgur Breathnach's. Nicky Kelly's case began on 10 November. All gardaí testified that he was a most agreeable, co-operative fellow. All of them.

"A very nice fellow to talk to," testified Det Garda A. He spent almost 12 hours (according to the Garda's own figures) with Nicky Kelly – more than any other garda – during the interrogation period. "He [Kelly] wasn't rude or ill-mannered in any way. He was a fellow that was easy to speak to," continued Det Garda A, "not the normal villain."

At all times, apparently, the atmosphere between him and Nicky Kelly during the interrogation period was friendly, he said. So friendly, he told the Court, that he even brought Kelly cigarettes in Fitzgibbon Street station after lunch on Monday 5 April 1976. Seamus Sorohan put it to him that Kelly would swear this was not true. But Det Garda A could not agree.

Inspector A (by then promoted to Superintendent) agreed with the Court that he was the person in charge of Nicky Kelly's questioning. He too testified about the friendly, relaxed atmosphere. As did Det Garda B, who was with Kelly for six and a quarter hours during the interrogation period. "He [Kelly] appeared to wish to assist as far as possible . . ." he said. And Special Branch Det Garda N found Kelly "pleasant, calm, collected", in the two hours he was with him during the interrogation period. They all found Kelly agreeable.

Kelly's decision to admit to the robbery was not at all unusual in Inspector A's experience. "In my experience", he testified, "that is human nature. It is human nature for a person to deny his guilt and they come to a stage where they sort of put . . ."

" . . . for many reasons, conscience, get it off their chest . . .?" interjected a helpful Seamus Sorohan. "They come to that point. That is what happened in this case," said Inspector A.

The prosecution case against Nicky Kelly took almost seven days to present. Fifty-one witnesses testified against him, including the three prison doctors, from Mountjoy and Portlaoise, who simply gave their medical reports, and a prison officer in Portlaoise who had written down a doctor's notes there. The other 47 prosecution witnesses were all gardaí, headed by Inspector/ Superintendent A. The Superintendent was in court everyday, hand rested on head listening to proceedings, and as often as not emerging from a side ante-room with individual gardaí before they took the stand.

Nicky Kelly took the stand for the first time on 18 November 1978. He was there for two days. In giving his evidence, he could not always have been described as being "pleasant, calm, collected".

His anger at what had happened, and what was happening, broke through, particularly when confronted by the adversarial style of the prosecution counsel. His demeanour was awkward, edgy, self-righteous, irritable. He was not at all the friendly fellow described by garda witnesses – not that it was his intention to appear so contrary to their descriptions. It led to strained exchanges between himself and prosecution counsel Robert Barr.

When he finished testifying, Nuala Dillon was called to the stand. She was followed by Doctors O'Cleirigh and McGee, who had also examined Kelly at Mountjoy. There followed a summing-up by both sides, Noel McDonald for the prosecution and Seamus Sorohan for the defence.

Great play was made by the prosecution of the chair incident, where Kelly had testified that both his palms were pinned under the front legs of a chair during the interrogation while a garda sat down on it. During the hearing itself this was challenged by the prosecution, as the incident left no visible marks, even though there was medical evidence to support the view that such an incident would not necessarily break bones or leave a mark.

The submissions were completed by Monday 27 November, the thirty-third day of the trial. The Court was adjourned to the following Thursday. On Wednesday however the judges returned to say they could not give a decision before Friday, 1 December.

That day they ruled that the confessions were admissible as evidence. The fate of the accused was sealed.

In Kelly's case, Judge Hamilton had this to say: "The Court has carefully assessed all the evidence; has had regard to the demeanour of the witnesses, and the manner in which they have given evidence; and is satisfied beyond all reasonable doubt that the garda witnesses are truthful, and have given a truthful account of what transpired during the different interviews with the accused in Fitzgibbon Street, the Bridewell Garda station, on the journey to the scene of the alleged robbery, Ballymore Eustace, to Bray, and in Harcourt Terrace Garda station.

"The Court is satisfied beyond all reasonable doubt that the statements alleged to have been made by the accused were made by the accused voluntarily, and were not made as a result of any assaults, ill-treatment or improper methods employed by members of the Garda Síochána or any of them, and that the injuries of which he [Kelly] subsequently complained were not inflicted by any members of the Garda Síochána."

He also announced that the Court found that "the injuries that they [the defendants] had suffered at the time of their respective medical examinations were self-inflicted or inflicted by collaboration with persons other than members of the Garda Síochána".

It was further found that Kelly's account of ill-treatment at Fitzgibbon Street was one "of quite savage brutality, at times of a horrific nature" which "if true" the judges considered as "inconceivable" that ordinary gardaí going about their ordinary duties at the station would not have been aware of something going on. They were also satisfied that Kelly had never asked for a solicitor.

It was remarkable. The judges reached their conclusion, to all intents and purposes, because they preferred the "look" of garda witnesses. "Demeanour" had won the day.

The implications of the finding, where the confessions were concerned, were that the defendants had beaten each other up when remanded overnight by District Court Justice Riobard Ó hUadaigh to cells in the Bridewell, after they were formally charged in connection with the mail train robbery on Wednesday

7 April 1976, the day after they had signed the confessions. It is believed this unusual remand to the Bridewell was at the request of Inspector A.

It was normal for prisoners to be remanded to Mountjoy, but Justice Ó hUadaigh never queried the request. It meant that a medical examination of the prisoners, which would have taken place on the arrival of the defendants at Mountjoy, was delayed until their admittance there at four o'clock the following afternoon.

Further and against regulation, as emerged during the Special Criminal Court hearing, the defendants were placed in cells together at the Bridewell. The regulations stipulated that defendants charged with the same offence should not be held in cells together there. Nicky Kelly shared a cell with Mick Plunkett that night. Brian McNally shared with John Fitzpatrick.

The implication of the Special Criminal Court finding that they had beaten each other up while sharing cells that night should have presented a difficulty where co-accused Osgur Breathnach was concerned, but didn't. Breathnach spent the night in the Richmond Hospital and was not charged in connection with the robbery until the following day, Thursday 8 April 1976. At no time was he held in a cell with anyone else. When he was detained in cells during interrogation it was always alone. Otherwise he was in the company of interrogating gardaí. The implication of the Special Criminal Court finding in his case was that he had beaten himself up, and so badly he had to be hospitalised.

After the Special Criminal Court had given its ruling in the trial there was a move by the prosecution and the gardaí to have the defendants detained in custody. This was refused.

Kelly was deeply depressed. He recalls, "We were devastated. Not least our lawyers." This showed in counsel's relationship with the judges, which suddenly become very tense. An example was the exchange between Seamus Sorohan and Judge Clarke after the ruling was given.

"The [judges'] ruling", Sorohan said, "contains reasoning and astounding findings of fact . . ."

Judge Clarke interrupted him, "I beg your pardon, Mr Sorohan. What do you mean by that?"

Sorohan: "What do you mean by that? Surprise . . ."

Clarke: "Are you surprised?"

Sorohan: "Yes . . ."

Clarke: "Then kindly do not make any insinuations beyond that."

Paddy McEntee asked that a copy of the ruling be made available to the defence. His request was refused.

The trial was adjourned to the following Monday.

THE DEFENDANTS AND THEIR LEGAL TEAMS were not the only ones taken by surprise when the Special Criminal Court decided to admit the confessions as evidence. Indeed, the fact that 17 months later two of the (by then three) defendants would have their convictions in the case – based on their confessions – quashed by the Court of Criminal Appeal underlined the very shaky grounds for that ruling.

Part of the surprise at the decision was that, up to then, the presiding judge, Justice Liam Hamilton, had been seen as a no-nonsense but fair man.

He died on 29 November 2000, aged 72, after a sometimes controversial career on the bench, where he served for more than 25 years. The eldest of five children and the son of a garda, he was born in Mitchelstown, County Cork, on 30 January 1928. After attending the local Christian Brothers' school he joined the civil service as a clerical officer. He spent time in the Department of Justice before being assigned as a clerk to the High Court offices, where he also read for the Bar. He was called to the Bar in 1956.

He specialised in labour law and became a senior counsel in 1968. In 1970 he acted for Neil Blaney when he was charged along with Charles Haughey and others in the district court with conspiracy to import arms. Hamilton's plea that there was insufficient evidence was accepted and the charge against Blaney was dismissed.

A member of the Labour Party, Hamilton stood unsuccessfully in the Rathmines ward in Dublin at the local elections in 1967. When six years later Labour entered coalition government with Fine Gael he was their main legal adviser and in 1974 was rewarded with the vacancy in the High Court after Tom O'Higgins was promoted to Chief Justice.

In 1976 Hamilton succeeded Justice Denis Pringle as presiding judge of the Special Criminal Court and as such, in 1978, presided when that Court convicted Osgur Breatnach, Brian McNally and Nicky Kelly of taking part in the mail train robbery.

It has been speculated, perhaps unfairly, that his doing so was possibly influenced by career ambition.

In 1985 he was appointed President of the High Court by the then Fine Gael/Labour coalition government. In 1991 he headed a tribunal of inquiry into allegations of malpractices in the beef industry. It lasted two and a half years and uncovered a litany of malpractice, tax evasion, frauds regarding public funds and government patronage towards the Goodman International beef company.

Hamilton's report in August 1994 set out great wads of evidence as presented to the tribunal but then failed to draw obvious conclusions. He confirmed there had been widespread and planned evasion of tax and abuse of regulations, and that the State had been exposed to a £100 million risk for export credit insurance cover, but found no one responsible.

It had been speculated that the tribunal report conclusions would have implications for some members of the then Fianna Fáil/Labour coalition government, which also had to decide shortly afterwards who should succeed Thomas Finlay as Chief Justice.

Within weeks, in September 1994, that coalition government nominated Liam Hamilton as Chief Justice. The Labour ministers, who had made the allegations that had led to the beef tribunal, were said to be greatly displeased but agreed to his elevation, with reluctance.

He was Chief Justice for six years. Ironically, towards the end of his term events occurred which called into question the repute of the judiciary and whether it could be relied upon to police itself. In March 1999, the government asked him to inquire into the conduct of two judges over the early release of Philip Sheedy, who had been sentenced to four years' imprisonment on a charge of causing death by dangerous driving.

Justice Hugh O'Flaherty had been involved in having the case relisted while Judge Cyril Kelly had quashed the sentence without affording a proper hearing. In his report, Liam Hamilton concluded that what Justice O'Flaherty did was "inappropriate and unwise", and had "left his motives and actions open to misinterpretation". As a consequence, what O'Flaherty had done was "damaging to the administration of justice". Of Judge Kelly, Hamilton concluded he had behaved in a manner unbecoming of a judge and had compromised the administration of justice. Both judges resigned.

Hamilton's own performance as a judge came into focus around the same time when it was revealed that the government, having been sued before the European Court of Human Rights, had agreed to pay damages arising out of a bankruptcy case in 1987 where he had failed to deliver judgment for six years after he had heard it. But nothing happened.

IN THAT WEEK FOLLOWING the Special Criminal Court decision to admit the confessions as evidence, Nicky Kelly's mind was hardly on the trial at all. The predictability of what was to happen stunned him and his feeling of grievance ran very deep. But he was certain on one thing – there was no way he was going to jail for something he did not do, whatever about the possible outcome of an appeal. Over and over, he asked himself, how could he have faith in a legal system that could do something as outrageous as he had just witnessed?

The trial resumed, but on those last days he was present in body only. On Thursday 7 December the prosecution completed its case, the thirty-ninth day of the second trial. Both Seamus Sorohan and Paddy McEntee began their submissions on behalf of the defence. There was a row when the defendants insisted with their counsel that more witnesses be called in their defence. Eventually only the three themselves were called.

Nicky Kelly took the stand and corroborated Brian McNally's account of the robbery night, but by then he had come to the conclusion it was all a waste of time. Seamus Sorohan asked him if he had anything to add to the evidence already given and he said, "It doesn't seem that it is worthwhile adding on to, one way or the other."

That was at 4.00 pm on Friday, 8 December 1978. The Court adjourned and he was due to take the stand again the following Monday for a cross-examination by prosecution counsel Robert Barr.

Kelly was in desperate straits. "Sitting there in the witness box that Friday, 8 December 1978, it was clear as day to me we were going to jail. Through the previous days I had listened with deepening depression as prosecution witness after prosecution witness repeated the same stories they had told during the 'trial within a trial'. But what they were saying now seemed so much worse now than before, in the light of the Court's decision to accept our confessions as evidence.

"It was hard to sit quietly while hearing other people swear your good name and life away, or a great part of it. It has to be bad enough if you are guilty, but for me it was just impossible. I felt like exploding at the lot of them, but everyone else seemed so calm."

He has also begun to wonder who really believed him. "Was even my own counsel convinced I was telling the truth? And if they were, how could they continue to go along with this charade. Were they not outraged by it too? It was not the first time that I found the professional detachment of lawyers hard to take. Their unquestioning acceptance of the rules, even when faced with blatant injustice, is something I have never been able to take on board.

"During the trials I used to wonder, as they engaged in endless legal arguments, whether 'guilt' or 'innocence' was really important to them at all. Whether they just preferred the system and the performance to the substance of a trial. Even, whether I or any of the others were to be absent, whether we would we be missed by them at all. Were we just an excuse for all this show?"

None of which helped his ebbing confidence in the system of law. His belief in it was at a very low ebb. He had given up hope and did not know who to trust or what to do. "I was becoming paranoid. Or maybe that should be even more so."

The stress was telling in other ways too. There were ongoing panic attacks, nightmares, insomnia and numbness down the side of his head. His hearing and balance were affected. He was uncomfortable with the public attention the case had attracted from the beginning, but now that it looked like a "guilty" verdict was about to be brought in, he just wanted to get away from it all.

"It must have been hard for those close to me to put up with my behaviour. I was totally self-absorbed and thought I was going to have a breakdown. And I was faced with one of the most important decisions of my life. Should I go or should I stay?"

As the week wore on to that Friday, more and more people urged him privately to disappear. He was beginning to think that way himself. "It was pointed out to me again and again that I had fewer family ties than either Osgur Breathnach or Brian McNally, both of whom were married with children," Kelly recalls. Of the three, it would be easiest for him to go.

By then, too, it was a foregone conclusion that all three faced prison sentences and few held out hope those sentences would be quashed on appeal. Such was the climate in the country at the time, and the attitude of the judiciary to the case. "It was also suggested I could be more useful out of jail, maybe by starting a campaign on the case."

After the court adjourned that Friday evening, a friend pushed £8 into Nicky Kelly's hand and said to him, "Put that to good use now". "The meaning was clear and although I assured him I'd do with it as bid, I still wasn't certain. I dithered. There was my then girlfriend to think about. We had been going out for just over a year. And there were my parents at home in Arklow, as well as a feeling that I was letting down Osgur and Brian by leaving them to take the rap alone. We had been through a lot together," Kelly says.

It was the following Sunday evening before he made a decision. "Then, as so often happens after a long period of thinking something through, I acted as though on impulse. I just walked out of the flat in Richmond Gardens, off the North Circular Road in Dublin, and I was on the run."

10

ON THE RUN IN EUROPE

H<small>E DID A LOT OF MOVING AROUND</small> Dublin in those weeks before Christmas 1978. "At first I stayed in a house on the
south side of the city. The owner was a personal friend and a
staunch Fianna Fáil supporter. His wife probably knew who I was
but never pretended and I had little contact with their children.
By then I was known as Barry Ryan and had shaved off my mous-
tache. I hardly went out at all."

A warrant was issued for his arrest on Monday 11 December
and a garda search got underway. Word came through to him that
the gardaí had been to the IRSP offices looking for him and to his
parents' house in Arklow. Hospitals, ports and airports were also
checked out but it was soon clear the gardaí were not overextend-
ing themselves in their search.

"I concluded they were pleased I had skipped bail, as it might
lend credence to the view that I was guilty after all."

That bail money would be confiscated by the courts so he borrowed the amount from two businessmen to pay it back. A further
£2,000 was raised for his "escape fund". He would need every
penny of it. But the following Thursday, 14 December, his "freedom" was little consolation.

"Watching TV that day and listening to the radio was a bleak
experience. Hearing the sentences given Osgur (12 years' penal
servitude) and Brian (nine years' penal servitude), and then
seeing both on TV being led off to Portlaoise was one of the
darker moments of my "exile". The following day I was myself

sentenced, 'in absentia', to 12 years' penal servitude. The severity of the sentence shocked me as much as its reality."

Any thoughts he had about starting a campaign on the case in Ireland now went out the window. Between the warrant and the sentence it was clear he'd get no further than the first press conference before being arrested. It began to sink home.

"With it I sank still further. I was kept going only by a determination that, come hell or high water, our names would be cleared. There was also deep down an unshakeable belief that truth would out eventually. For a man with my views on the cynicism of the establishment and the lengths to which it would go to protect itself, this was a surprising realisation for me. But it was so, and it would rescue me from the depths many times in the years ahead."

He was beginning to find the claustrophobia of his new lifestyle in Dublin hard to take, but there was a frightening diversion one day. A garda called to the house.

"I was in a garden when I spotted the uniform coming up a path to the front door. I just ran. I lay low until it was dark and then I made my way during the night to another friend's house. I didn't knock on his door until morning. We had breakfast. He was an artist and asked me to give him a hand with a mural he was painting that day."

He asked the artist friend to call him "John", just in case. They decided it was safest for John to return to the house he had been staying in. "We pushed his car till it started and off we went. He drove me crazy that day, slipping into 'Nicky' nearly every time he spoke. In the evening he brought me back to the house I had left 24 hours earlier."

It turned that the garda who provoked the flight had just been on a social call. "I was getting tired of all this edgy confinement in Dublin and thought I badly needed time away to sort out my head and decide what I was going to do."

His weight had shot up since he absconded, and his hair and beard were growing. It was around then that Clairol first entered his life, and over the following months they became inseparable.

"I become an expert at using it. It dyed my hair and beard a reddish/auburn type colour."

Coming nearer to Christmas, he became more anxious to get out of Dublin. "In the country I believed there would be more freedom, more wide open spaces where I'd be less likely to be recognised." So he contacted a friend who arranged to take him to Clare.

"On the drive down we came on a garda checkpoint. I don't know why it was there, but sitting in a queue of cars inching slowly towards it in the dark, I was sorely tempted to make a run for it. But with the rain pouring down, and with the beard, longer hair and extra weight, I decided to take my chances. We were just waved through."

Their destination was West Clare, where he ended up staying in an isolated farmhouse with a Dutch couple in their thirties who had become born-again Christians. They offered their home as a type of sanctuary to people suffering from stress or recovering from breakdowns.

He was introduced to them as Barry Ryan from Kilkenny, who needed time away from it all, as he was recovering from a nervous breakdown. "They were genuine people, very religious, and ran a self-sufficient house. Their guests – I was the only one there at the time – contributed whatever they could, though nothing was ever asked for. It was a quiet place, very quiet."

This was good and bad. "It left me with too much time to think. During the day I would go for long walks through the countryside, and struck up a friendship with one old farmer in his seventies who lived on the side of a hill. He was on his own in a small three-roomed house with a galvanised roof. He had an open hearth, with a side of bacon – from his own pig – curing in salt in a corner. Outside, a couple of empty tar barrels collected rainwater from the drainpipes.

"He owned a few cattle, a jennet, a small sheep dog and he had a cat which he abused something terrible. Every time it sneaked into the kitchen he'd grab it by the scruff of the neck, shake the living daylights out of it, then throw the poor creature back out the door again. I think he was afraid the bacon might be tampered with.

"He had a radio, which he only turned on for GAA matches and the news. He had no TV. A relic of ould Ireland, he'd sit there every day sucking his pipe talking about the weather and the football or running down the politicians. A favourite topic was the bad old days and the awful times they went through, whether working on the bog or ploughing with a horse. Sure we didn't know what hardship was at all now, or so he said."

Gradually the isolation of the place began to get to Kelly. He rang a friend in Dublin to come and take him away before he cracked up altogether. "I said that if I was to stay there any longer I'd be more likely to end up in a mental hospital than jail." The friend came and took him to a house in Shannon.

"It was early on Christmas morning 1978 when we arrived there and everyone was still in bed. Everything was laid out for the Christmas dinner. So, to be useful, I cooked it." He stayed there for about two weeks. "It was not a great place from my point of view. A lot of people were coming and going all the time and this added to my uneasiness. During the day I stayed inside, reading and watching TV. At night I would go for walks by the Shannon River."

He began to realise that, contrary to his expectations, he was more obvious in country areas than he had been in Dublin. Strangers stand out in rural parts, which was not always the case in a city.

"Galway, I thought, might be a better spot. It was bigger for a start. So my Dublin friend came down once more and drove me there. I stayed just one night, in a Salthill hotel. After a walk on the prom I decided it was time to return to Dublin. There would be less heed on me there."

This time he stayed for a while with a family in one of the northside's middle-class areas. These people were more personal than political friends, though they shared similar views. Again he stayed inside most of the time, going for walks at night.

"In an attempt to bring some normality into my life I went into a pub one evening when who walked into the same premises but a detective I recognised. I froze to the spot. I could not be certain, but I was sure he was looking at me. In fact I convinced myself he recognised me. So I left by a back door."

He stayed on the northside for a couple of weeks before moving to the home of a businessman on the southside. "I remained indoors all the time now. The weeks passed. Nothing was happening, nothing seemed likely to happen. I was up against a wall at the end of a cul-de-sac, and I could see no way back."

He knew he couldn't go on like that. Sooner or later something would give and he felt increasingly sure it would be himself. There was only one thing to do.

"I had to leave the country. England was out of the question. It was too close to home and, being a young single Irishman, the police would be suspicious of me anyway. Getting a visa to go to America would be very hard in the circumstances. I thought that would be pushing my luck too far. The continent seemed the best bet. A passport was secured for me by another friend, using the name of someone who had died young and would have been about the same age as myself, had he lived. She [the friend] had spotted the name in a graveyard."

TOWARDS THE END OF MARCH 1979 his driver friend took him to the ferry at Rosslare. "I must have looked peculiar, dressed in a three-piece suit with blue shirt and tie, topped off with a mop of red hair and the beard. But I thought I looked like any other business man with a small suitcase. Passing through Arklow on the way to Rosslare, I dithered over whether I should call in to see my mother and father, but thought better of it."

He had had no direct contact with his parents since "disappearing" but let them know through intermediaries that he was OK. "In fact, I avoided contacting anyone but the people I stayed with and my driver friend."

Some people from around Arklow worked on the ferry to Le Havre and he was afraid he would be recognised. "I retreated to a dark corner where I need have no contact with anyone, and remained there for the journey. It was also a good vantage point from where I could see everyone who approached the bar, as well as the queue in the restaurant close by."

The crossing was smooth but he didn't sleep. The first signs indicating they were approaching France were small fishing boats they passed. Soon they could see cliffs and, to their right, Le Havre. "A bleak place, it seemed then. More like a working docks than a ferry port."

There were no problems with either customs or passport control. He got on a bus for the railway station. His destination was Paris, from where he intended going to Amsterdam. "I believed it would be easier to 'get lost' in Holland, where I planned to say I was a mature student, and they spoke more English there."

He kept his head down on the bus, out of habit. At the station he stayed by himself, watching and listening, and began to relax. "This was the first time I had been in a public place for over three months and where I didn't feel I had to keep looking over my shoulder. It was a good feeling, sitting there watching the passers-by and listening to their chatter, though I didn't understand a word."

The train was full of young backpackers, mostly American. He got talking to some of them who told him about the places they'd been to in Ireland and how they were now planning to tour the Continent. "I remember being struck by the innocence of their attitude to life."

As they sped through the flat countryside, passing picturesque villages, "I thought about the events which had forced me there and began to think of the many thousands, millions of Irish people forced into exile before me for political and economic reasons – back as far as the Flight of the Earls at the beginning of the seventeenth century."

They arrived at St Lazare station. There were small cheap hotels near the station and he booked into one of them, using a mixture of sign language and facial expression. The old man in charge wanted money in advance, and his passport. Since the days of Napoleon all residents in French hotels must surrender their passports and the innkeeper must inform local police each night how many lodgers he has staying.

The room was basic: an iron bed, wash-hand basin, wardrobe, and a toilet in a little ante-room to one side. He locked the door. Even on the way there from the station he kept his head down and avoided any eye contact. "And though my mind told me this was not necessary, I couldn't help it. I was determined not to attract attention to myself."

In the room he decided it was time for the Clairol treatment once more. He had become very careful of the stuff since he nearly damaged himself with it during a session in February. He had been too generous and his skin reacted, with pimples on his face and his scalp itching.

But his roots were beginning to show and new treatment was necessary. The ritual was always the same. Put on white plastic gloves; wet hair; apply Clairol; rub it in; put on plastic cap; and leave for a while – the longer the better. His beard had to be touched up, as well as his eyebrows and eye lashes.

"I sometimes forgot to do the eyebrows and eyelashes. One day I was out and about when I caught sight of myself in a mirror, with my dark brown eyebrows and bright red hair. I looked like a refugee from the Sex Pistols."

Then, after a while waiting for the Clairol to do its thing, there was the washout, despite which he always managed to leave stains on pillows. "At times, because of this, I sometimes thought that the same Clairol which helped hide me might also one day betray me. I often wondered what the people who discovered these stains thought. Or the bin men collecting all those plastic gloves, plastic hats and bottles of Clairol."

After that treatment he went for a walk through the streets near his hotel. It was a run-down area of Paris, but just to be able to walk about without fear of being recognised was a pleasure. His feet were killing him. "I had put on three stone since skipping bail and my shoes no longer fitted me. I went back to the room and to bed. Next morning I returned to St Lazare to check train times to Amsterdam. I booked a ticket, then travelled by Metro to Gare du Nord station for the connection." The journey to Amsterdam was unremarkable.

He walked from Amsterdam's Centrum station to Dam Rak, the city's main street. It was a lovely day. The city looked good, all those canals with waterbuses carrying tourists and attractive old buildings everywhere. He liked the atmosphere of the place, so much so that he sat at an outdoor café for coffee, not realising then how much more everything costs if you sit at such places.

"I felt more relaxed in Amsterdam, though I was aware of a large Irish population in the city." He enquired about hostels and The Kabul was recommended to him. It was a big place with good facilities. Most of the residents were British and American students. He booked in, had a shower, and ate at the canteen in the hostel.

"As far as I remember it, Nottingham Forest were playing in the European Cup Final on the television there that night, and everyone was cheering like mad for them in the hostel's snooker room. Only two were not involved with all this support, myself and another guy. He was sitting alone reading magazines in a corner by himself. We got talking eventually. He was a Romanian refugee in his twenties, who had applied for political asylum in Holland. A student radical, he had become involved in protests against Ceausescu and his regime, and had to flee the country. His English wasn't good. We talked about Romania and how socialism worked in practice. Anything to do with Eastern Europe or socialism interested me then. Through that and other discussions later we became friendly."

He did not tell the Romanian who he was, though. He remained Barry Ryan, who was getting away from a broken marriage and was trying to sort himself out. "One thing he did say, though, put me on edge. He had to register at a police station every day while his political status was being considered. The police station he used was right next door to the hostel. I passed it nervously later, on the way to buy a new pair of shoes."

He also discovered he had to have his passport stamped at a police station before he could start work in Amsterdam. That limited his options drastically. There was, for instance, no point going to the VVV state employment agency then. "Whatever chance I had of getting work was in quick turnover service jobs such as bars and the like, where staff came and went fairly regularly."

He stayed three nights at The Kabul. He heard of a cheaper hostel, "and besides I could hardly go a yard of the road without the Romanian following. The guy was probably lonely like myself but I was in no condition to carry or support anyone else, considering my own state of mind."

One night there was an incident. "We – the Romanian and myself – had been on a tour of Amsterdam's breweries, with plenty of free beer, and afterwards continued with more drink at a cheap pub near the Heineken brewery. We got drunk and were coming back to the hostel via the red light district.

"I had already passed through the area on a walk around the city and the eyes nearly popped out of my head at some of the sights in the windows there. Scantily clad women, some not dressed at all, sitting there in all their glory giving the wink and the nod.

"But that night, as myself and the Romanian made our way home through the streets, he started to throw stones at the windows where these women sat. I don't know what made him do it, and there was no time talk about it. We were chased by a few guys, pimps probably, and took off helter-skelter back to The Kabul. I expected police and the pimps to come into the hostel after us." But no one did. It was time to leave there.

He had been talking at The Kabul to three young Dubliners from Raheny, all in their late teens/early twenties. They were penniless and hadn't enough to pay for themselves. He loaned them 80 guilders. They told him about another, cheaper hostel.

"They didn't know who I was and cared less. They were on a strictly sex and drugs and rock'n'roll trip to Amsterdam, and had a friend who was coming from Ireland with all the money in the world, who would pay me back pronto. I knew I'd never see the 80 guilders again, but I liked them."

The other hostel was a bare affair with poorer facilities. He gave a roundabout explanation to his Romanian friend, and moved 200 yards away. "We exchanged heartfelt goodbyes, which did not make me feel so good."

He slept on his suitcase, as did everyone else in those hostels. Even going to the shower, he'd hide it somewhere safe. During the day he'd take it to Centrum station, where he'd put it in a locker until evening. It contained all his money and worldly goods. That done, he'd go to a café near the station where breakfast was cheap. Then the search for work would start again. "I remember trying a tea-packing company, a bakery and an Indonesian restaurant, for instance, but there was nothing doing."

Still, all was not black. He got to know Amsterdam well and even went on a couple of tours of the city's canals, by waterbus. He enjoyed the freedom of being able to walk around, despite wariness when meeting any Irish tourists or members of the Irish community there.

"Wandering around that city I saw some things which will always stay with me, such as Dam Square where there seemed to be concerts or protests going on all the time. Queen Beatrix passed by in a cortege every day and was jeered by hundreds. It was incredible. Mostly squatters and anarchists. Then there were the jugglers, buskers, and fire eaters.

"One morning I saw something there which summed up for me the spirit of Amsterdam. The Queen's cortege was making its way out to the usual jeers, flanked by police outriders. One of the outriders, a young policeman with long hair that stuck out from beneath his helmet, veered away in a loop from the others, cut across to a footpath and kissed a young woman standing there, before veering back into line again. The crowd cheered and shouted. I couldn't help wondering when, if ever, a member of the gardaí would attempt such a thing while in an escort at home."

He had a couple of scares in Amsterdam too. Once he was standing in a taxi queue when he heard a voice say, "They don't cut much turf here, Kelly, do they?" He recognised the face from Dublin. "Kelly" wasn't long making himself scarce.

Another time he went to O'Henry's, an Irish bar on Dam Rak. It was risky going into such a place but he had to be somewhere there were Irish people. Standing beside him at the bar he recognised a fellow from Arklow, an engineer with NET. "I don't know if he recognised me, but I left straight away."

Neither experience did much for him. Amsterdam was getting too small, and it was becoming clear with every passing day that he had arrived at another cul-de-sac.

At the beginning it seemed a major step away from being cooped up in a house in Dublin or discussing how to salt a pig in Clare. Now, though, the differences seemed slight enough. But what was he to do next?

There were barges coming in from Germany, which people would hitch rides on to that country, and he thought about going there for a while. But he soon dismissed the idea because of the language problem.

Money was being wasted and he felt he was getting nowhere. Then an incredible incident spurred him to get out of the Amsterdam. "I was staying in my third hostel, a cheaper one again. It was full of bunk beds and student types. It didn't have the facilities of the others but it suited a man who was watching the guilders. One night, at about four or five in the morning, I woke up to find police searching the dormitory. I was sure I'd had it then, and froze still in the bed.

"But it was not me they were looking for but the killers of an Iranian student who had been stabbed to death in his bed, not too far away from my own, during the night. Everyone was searched and questioned, including myself. The police soon left." That experience shattered him. He decided to return to Paris and left Amsterdam with regret, because he liked the city.

๛   ๛   ๛

ON THE TRAIN JOURNEY BACK to Paris he was sitting opposite an elderly American couple and their big overweight son, a computer executive of about 30. They were "doin' Europe" and the father was showing his wife and son all the places he had been during the Second World War. He had served as a gunner with General Patton and described the "scorched earth" policy they employed, killing every living thing in every village they passed through and destroying all the property, leaving nothing that might be useful to the enemy. His "Barbie-doll wife" listened in admiration, as did their son.

Patton was never a favourite of Nicky Kelly's and it was soon obvious. "I asked about the 1968 My Lai massacre [by US troops in Vietnam] and it really hit a nerve with the old man who became very annoyed as he explained how these things had to be done in war. I said any country that believed that had to be warped. It was red rag to old bull time. I left him going on about all the Irish who had fought in the war, and how he had no regrets and how I 'gotta understand', while his wife and son nodded in agreement. But I didn't understand."

After arrival at Gare du Nord station again, he found a cheap hotel and booked a room there from a very friendly *maitre d'*. The room, as in all these places it seemed, was spare, but adequate.

He followed the same routine as in Amsterdam, leaving the area to find the cheapest cafés. His money situation was holding up and he was budgeting to live on £10 to £15 a day. It meant buying bread, salami and cheese, and eating out, on a park bench usually. And, just as in Amsterdam, he discovered that the farthest you went from the centre, the cheaper was the food and everything else.

He began to think there was something strange about the hotel he was staying in. Furniture would be moved in the room while he was out and he spotted small holes drilled in the walls. One evening he noticed that a window in the room had been cracked during the day while he was out. It was time to establish what was going on. "So I challenged my landlady." She changed instantly from charming hostess to Gallic harridan. "Nothing" was going on. What did he mean? The window was always cracked like that.

Eventually it became clear the place was being used as a brothel during the day. "I can't remember how I found this out, whether she told me, which seems unlikely, or someone else did, but that's what turned out to be the case. And it seems the small holes in the wall were used to watch couples at play."

A brothel is hardly the sort of place a man on the run would feel safe in. Police, after all, seem to take a great interest in them. So he left, bag in hand once more, and found a nice, cheap, "respectable" hotel in Montparnasse.

He went out that evening to get more Clairol as his supply was running low. He had shaved off his beard in Amsterdam after a rash and pimples took hold of his face and chin. His roots were beginning to show again and needed further treatment.

He stayed three weeks in Paris this time, mostly spent walking around from morning to night. Work was in short supply, not least for a pidgin-French speaking Paddy, and it was a highly policed city. He would traipse down the Left Bank of the Seine, through the Luxembourg Gardens, across to San Michel, St Germain, through Montparnasse, and the Champs Elysées.

He went to see Oscar Wilde's and Jim Morrison's graves, spent a lot of time in the Pompidou Centre, which was like Dam Square in Amsterdam with all its street performers etc., and spent so much time in the Louvre he could easily have handled a job as a guide there. During this period, for obvious reasons, he was reminded often of George Orwell's book *Down and Out in Paris and London*. A wandering exile he, going nowhere with nowhere to go.

AROUND THIS TIME, he began to get a recurring nightmare. "I was in a cell and I could hear steps coming towards the door, closer and closer, and I would hope and plead they would pass by, but they stopped outside the cell door, and I would wake up in a panic and covered in sweat." In later years he would seek psychiatric help for this, but in Paris he still could not accept he had been psychologically damaged. It seemed a reflection on his own strength to admit such a thing. He had always believed he was made of tougher stuff than that.

He made weekly phone calls to his contact in Dublin, which he always looked forward to, but which as often as not left him homesick and heartbroken. "After one call I remember leaving the phone box in tears and walking along the Seine, past five or six bridges, and crying like a baby. That a 28-year-old man, who still had ambitions to save the world, could be reduced to that did not do much for my self esteem."

One of the great sources of comfort to him in those days were memories of his childhood in Graiguenamanagh. He would remember climbing Brandon Hill when he was four or five, and the great satisfaction when he got to the top; or catching sprats in the river down by Cushen's mill near their house. They were as good as salmon or trout to him.

He made some unexpected friends in Paris, particularly two American women. One ran an art shop in an old forge near Montparnasse. "I was passing by one day, saw something that caught my eye, and went in for a look. She came over to talk and noticed my accent. That's something else I discovered in Paris; when they discover you are Irish they are usually warm and interested. I told her I was getting away from Ireland for a while following the break-up of a relationship. She told me about places where you could get good food for good value. After that I often called in to her for a chat.

"The other lady I met in the Shakespeare and Company bookshop one day. She was small and attractive, with black hair. I can't remember how we got talking, but she was very friendly. We went for something to eat and she told me she was based at the US Embassy, where she worked for the CIA. That took the wind out of my sails. The CIA was not on my list of most admired organisations. After eating we called to see the other American lady in her art shop, and went for a walk.

"However daft the situation may seem, Irish fugitive and attractive CIA lady, by now I was beginning to feel this could be the beginnings of a beautiful friendship. But, with all the complications in my life and in my head, I felt it was the last thing I could handle. We went our separate ways."

ഐ   ഐ   ഐ

FATE WOULD FREE HIM FROM PARIS. He was walking down a side street there near the Opera House one day when he saw a Japanese travel agency. They were offering special Air France fares to Montreal and Toronto. He went in to enquire, more out of idleness and curiosity than anything else. The Japanese man behind the counter spoke English and told him, to his great surprise, that people travelling from France to Canada did not need a visa.

It was clear to him immediately what he should do. He would go to Canada, get into the US somehow and launch his campaign at the Irish authorities from there.

On the spot, he booked a return ticket to Toronto – it looked closer to the US on a map – for the following day. It had to be a return ticket or he would be refused entry. But at £160, even that was a bargain. His story was that he was going on a three-week holiday. "I rang my contact in Dublin to tell him what I was up to and he gave me the address of personal friends of his in Toronto. Next day I got a taxi to the airport."

Looking back on that spell in Paris, he has often been reminded of the wisdom in the saying that "beauty is in the eye of the beholder". "I've been back to the city many times since and have retraced my journeys over those three weeks. Everywhere I have been struck by the great beauty of the place. But then, I saw none of it. My sight was inward, my vision blocked. What is that saying about the two prisoners looking through a cell window? One sees bars, the other sees stars!"

The taxi man left him to the wrong terminal in Charles de Gaulle airport, so he had to walk about a mile to the right one, carrying two bags and wearing his three-piece suit. Passing by all the officials and police, as he went through check-in and security, he was extremely nervous and expected a "hey-you" tap on the shoulder at any minute. But nothing happened.

He was sweating so much, it had to show. But uniform always recognises uniform in this world and the most acceptable uniform to officialdom everywhere, it seems, is "the suit". So if they noticed him sweating at all it was probably put down to executive stress.

No sooner had he got by them than he faced another, greater worry. Flying frightens the life out of him. "I am terrified of heights. When I was younger I was not at all, indeed up to my interrogation in April 1976. I remember working on Urney's chimney stacks at their factory in Tallaght. It didn't cost me a thought. I even used to make a point of doing jobs at a great height because you got extra money for that. One job involved working at 200 feet. We got up so far by hydraulic lift, and the remaining 20 feet by swinging ladder." He can't even think about that now.

So in the departures lounge at Charles de Gaulle he had a few Chivas Regal to help him board the plane. It did the trick. He had a few more drinks on board, checking regularly that the wings were still on the jet, while making sure he didn't look towards the ground below.

He had brought *The Wall Street Journal* and *The Herald Tribune* with him for distraction. It was a long flight, seven or eight hours. He got chatting to a woman sitting beside him. She was a doctor, from Ottawa, and was returning from a conference in Paris. She told him about her family and about Canada. When she found out he hadn't been there before she recommended a clean, cheap hotel in Toronto.

He was afraid she might have noticed he was agitated or that he might seem merrier than he felt, so he spilled the beans about his fear of flying. She laughed and said it was a silly phobia, before explaining that flying is the safest form of travel and that there was nothing at all to fear; all very rational but it made not one bit of difference to him.

"I had read my papers by then and she passed me a book she had just finished. I don't think she realised what she was doing. She didn't comment either way. The book was *Alive* by Piers Paul Read, the story of a plane crash in the Andes which some people survived by eating the flesh of dead passengers. Just what I needed! Being the polite Irishman I can be sometimes, I actually read a good part of the book before we arrived in Toronto. But of all the books in all the world . . .?!"

They said their goodbyes at the airport and she gave him her address in Ottawa, with an invitation to stay should he ever be there.

11

ON THE RUN IN AMERICA

IT WAS VERY HOT IN TORONTO, which surprised him as he had always thought of Canada as a cold country. It was sweltering. He got a taxi to the Dundas area of the city, where the hotel was situated that the woman on the plane had told him about. It was, as she had said, clean and cheap. There was a TV and shower. He just went to bed, jet-lagged and exhausted, as much by the ordeal of the flight as its length.

It felt good to be in a country where everyone understood what he was saying and where he understood everything he heard. Next day he called his Dublin contact's friends in the city, whom he knew nothing about. He was Barry Ryan, a friend of their friend in Dublin and they were delighted to hear from him. They invited him over for a meal and very shortly afterwards the woman of the house arrived at the hotel in a big station-wagon to collect him.

She was Irish-born and her husband had an Irish background but was born in Canada. They were in their forties, comfortable upper middle-class people. Their house was huge, sprawling and luxurious, with a swimming pool.

They talked for a good while, then after the meal it was suggested all go for a drink. So they headed to an Irish bar called The Old Sod. "I'm almost certain a bouncer at the pub recognised me. He was Irish." Afterwards they went on to the Irish Centre where a Rose of Tralee Festival heat was taking place. He got talking to a couple of Donegal lads. They were working in banking. One of them was from Carndonagh and asked him whether he knew a solicitor from that town who worked in Dublin. The solicitor in question had been on Kelly's own legal team.

"I was sure that lad recognised me too. I just passed off his remark somehow. After those encounters I had a 'feeling' – was it instinct or paranoia? I could no longer tell. But it didn't matter. I could not afford to ignore it."

His hosts wanted him to stay the night and he agreed. There was a big bean bag in the bedroom they showed him to and he sprawled out on that rather than on the bed, it was so comfortable.

He woke early the next morning but already the husband had gone to work. He had breakfast with the woman of the house and was invited to stay a few days until he got himself organised. Then he went for a walk. "I had a hangover, which wasn't surprising as not since the night in Amsterdam with my Romanian friend had I had so much to drink. I had brought my jacket, cash and passport with me. Don't ask me why; instinct, maybe."

The house was detached and in a cul-de-sac. "I was walking away from it when two big cars with tinted windows passed by. A window in the second car was down and through it I saw four burly policemen wearing sunglasses. The cars pulled into the driveway of the house I'd just left. I ran to a motorway and flagged down a taxi which took me into the city centre."

Someone must have recognised him the night before and called the police. He never found out. Downtown, he thought about ringing the house he'd stayed in, but decided against it. He has not been in contact with that couple since. It was not possible for a long time, and then it became a case of, "What do I say?"

His two bags were left behind, so he bought new clothes in Toronto, including t-shirts. What he had brought with him was far too heavy for the weather. He did not waste time but got to the nearest Grey Line station and took a bus to Niagara Falls, about a hundred miles away; it was the border and gateway to the USA.

The journey took about two hours. "Niagara Falls is small and a very commercialised town, with billboards everywhere. 'Bliss-land . . .' read one as we arrived '. . . the honeymoon capital where all love stories are cemented', or something like that. It had the biggest Ferris wheel in the world. Biggest and best, here we go. I was getting closer to the US, alright."

Kelly booked a room in one of the cheaper motels, which was a bit out of town. He changed motel nearly every night he stayed there, just in case. For some reason he had thought it would be a doddle to get across the border into the US, maybe because he had got into Canada without any fuss. But he soon realised this would be a tough job.

The Falls were magnificent but, as with Paris, they didn't really interest him at the time. Overlooking them was a tower from where he could look through a binocular-type apparatus for a quarter a time. From there he would spend hours on end studying the US customs post below, with the patience of David Attenborough investigating the behaviour of a rare exotic species of animal or bird. His binoculars always pointed in one direction while all the others were swivelled the opposite way so viewers could see the Falls close up. No one took a bit of heed, even when he would ask for $10 worth of quarters or returned day after day. He became so well known that when he left a pair of sunglasses behind once, someone in a shop nearby found them and kept them for him until the next time he dropped in.

What he saw through those binoculars was not encouraging. Everyone was stopped and checked going through. Even bus passengers had to get out and walk through one way, while the bus was driven through another channel. He saw arrests being made. The hair stood on his head and his heart sank at the sight.

There was a railway track crossing through another checkpoint and he began to wonder. He would act on that later. But first there was the guy he met in a bar, one of those pin-ball machine places. They got talking. Somehow he felt he could trust him. Maybe he was just desperate, but they got around to discussing ways of crossing the border.

"No problem," he said. He had brought lots of people across already, in the boot of his car. "It was agreed he would take me across next day, and we arranged to meet at a particular time. He never turned up, and I started to panic. This guy now knew what I was up to and might report me to the authorities. So I got away from that spot fast, and avoided the pin-ball bar from then on."

It was evening when he went down to check out the local railway station. There was a freight train stalled there with no one about, its engine facing towards the US. Some of the cargo holds had a tarpaulin cover. He climbed under and waited; finally the train began to move.

They were travelling for a good while before the train stopped. They were stalled for a good while. He looked out from under the tarpaulin. It was nearly dawn and they were in a large rolling-stock type of railway yard. There was no one around. So this was America!

It was alright, but it was not the US. Looking around at advertising hoardings, he realised he was in Hamilton, Ontario. The train had gone "the wrong way", further into Canada. The engine had pushed it, not pulled it. He was disgusted. Cutting his losses, he searched around, found a diner, had breakfast, went in search of a bus station, and headed back to Niagara Falls.

It was wits-end time. He was desperate. Money was very low, and there seemed to be no way he could cross into the US. All sorts of hair-brained ideas came into his head. For instance, you could fly over the Falls by helicopter for $10. It flew across to the US side. He wondered about making a jump from the helicopter into the US – this from a man who needed almost a half bottle of Chivas Regal inside him before he could get on a plane.

He returned to Toronto, as it was more anonymous, a few times during those two weeks to ring Dublin. He had an arrangement with his contact there to ring either Jurys Hotel or the Burlington every second Tuesday evening at 7.00 (Irish time), and have him paged under an alias.

There were times when he got the Tuesdays mixed up. Then he'd go back to the Falls again. "I remember seeing the fireworks and crackers for the Fourth of July celebrations on the US side, and wondering whether I would ever get into that country. Hope was running out as fast as my money. Niagara Falls is an expensive place, even when you are staying in cheap motels, and I was nearly two weeks there by Independence Day."

Then, deliverance. God, Fate, the Force, whatever it was, intervened.

IT BEGAN WITH A BALL GAME. Sitting on a bench in a green patch near the Falls one day, he saw a group of young people play ball. They were friendly and happy-go-lucky in that American way. The ball came in his direction a few times and he would kick it back to them. Once he kicked it too hard and sent it over the edge into the Falls below. Feeling stupid, he stood up to go to the shops to buy another, but they wouldn't hear of it. They had another. They got talking. There were about eight of them altogether, equally divided between men and women, and all were in their late twenties early thirties. Their leader was a bit older again. They took out sandwiches and insisted he share their meal.

It turned out they were Mennonites, a charismatic Christian group who had broken away from the more fundamentalist Amish community. The Amish, who mostly live in rural Pennsylvania, refuse to use any modern conveniences and dress in a seventeenth-century style. He had seen a lot of Amish families at the Falls, in their long black clothes. The women wore bonnets, the men were in black suits and black hats, and their mannerly kids were like small copies of their parents. They never bought anything but there was something decent about them all the same, though sometimes he wondered if they were not too strict with their children.

These Mennonites also came from Pennsylvania, the leader being from Yorktown. They were on their way to a charismatic conference in Stratford, Ontario, and were going to record the proceedings in their travelling recording studio, a bus which was decorated to make it look like a church on wheels, with a crucifixion scene and gothic-type windows painted on. When Kelly told them he was Irish they were very interested as they believed it

was a religious country. They talked to him about the moral col-
lapse of the US.

He told them he was in Niagara Falls on holiday, and that he
was from Washington, where he lived in Potomac Street, an address he made up. On a map somewhere he had noticed the Potomac River ran through Washington.

He liked the Mennonites; they were friendly and sincere. But
he also saw them as a route into the US. They asked him if he
would like to go to Stratford with them. He said yes. They were
delighted. Stratford is over 100 miles from Niagara Falls. It is a
lovely town, modelled on Shakespeare's Stratford, in England.

The conference was being held in the Bull Ring there, a huge
place with a capacity for thousands. When they arrived – a day
early, to set up the equipment – there were already hundreds of
trailers parked about. Kelly was introduced to the elders. He felt he
must have been introduced to hundreds of people that weekend.
The elders were mostly middle-aged and older men who again
talked about Ireland. They knew some people there. There was
singing of hymns and clapping of hands and then it was bedtime.
They gave him a sleeping bag and the group all slept on the bus.

There were six or seven thousand delegates there the following day, Saturday. The meeting was very intense, with chants of
"amen" and "alleluia" as each preacher drove home a point. "It
was very emotional, frightening even at times." Kelly helped out
by pulling leads and cables here and there and would escape from
it all every now and again just to wander in the calm of the fields
that ran down to the river nearby.

The conference ended early on the Sunday afternoon to allow
for people travelling great distances. They had come from all over
the US and Canada. Kelly and the group packed up and had a
meal outside the bus before setting off for Niagara Falls, on their
way back to the US. They pulled into a service station a few miles
from the Falls. "The others got out but I stayed on board with the
group leader. I had decided to come clean, so there and then I told
him I was an illegal trying to get into the US. He seemed shocked
and I thought I was done for. He left the bus, got the others

together outside and told them. They were now all as troubled as he was. 'That's it then,' I thought to myself.

"They called me outside and formed a circle around me, each one with a hand touching my head. The leader prayed to God for guidance as to what they should do. They then broke up and headed for a hot-dog stand. After a while meditating, the leader said he felt God wanted them to take me along with them to the US. It is hard to describe how I felt when he said that. I could not believe what I was hearing."

They hit the road again. At the US checkpoint two customs officers got on board. Kelly pretended to be asleep. "'It's OK buddy,' one customs officer said to me. 'Hi buddy,' I said back in my best Wicklow accent. He didn't notice." They were cleared and headed into the US.

His Mennonite friends were still troubled. They pulled in off the highway, a few miles from the border checkpoint they had just come through. They prayed again, hoping they had done the right thing. Then they got back on board and were soon on the way. They wanted him to stay in Yorktown with them.

"I explained I had to go back to Potomac Street, that there was a place for me there. 'Yorktown is a very historic place,' they said, 'especially to do with the Civil War.' But I couldn't be persuaded. My destination was Baltimore. I had an address there, given to me by my Dublin contact during one of those Toronto phone calls."

Arriving in Yorktown, he was struck by how shabby and run-down it looked. They parted there. They gave him numerous addresses and insisted he come and stay with them sometime. Then they were gone.

HE GOT A TAXI TO BALTIMORE, not realising it was still so far away; he was down to a few hundred dollars and the journey was to cost $130. In Baltimore he headed straight to the address he had been given. "As soon as I got there it was clear the people I was going to meet were very wealthy. The house, in the suburbs, was huge and set in its own grounds. The owner was a man in his fifties. He was third- or fourth-generation Irish-American and had made his money in construction. He was married with two children. I was Barry Ryan once more, illegal immigrant. He was not aware of my circumstances beyond that. I could do no wrong in his eyes."

The man took him under his wing and brought him with him nearly everywhere. He treated Kelly like a son and with great generosity. "I was with him about three weeks. I had not worked and I began to feel he preferred it that way. He could not be accused of employing an illegal, and it gave both of us time to sort out my status. Meanwhile I was like his aide-de-camp or chaperone!"

This man was something of a kingmaker in the Democratic Party locally and so Kelly was introduced to nearly all of Baltimore high society while there, including the Mayor and state Attorney General. Both socialised heavily.

"He was a classic case of the work hard/play hard type of guy. Being with him was like a holiday after what had taken place getting there. I suppose I let my hair down a bit for a while and just went along for the ride. However, I also made valuable direct person-to-person contacts at that time. It was also from this base in Baltimore that I made my first contact with Congressmen in Washington, and the two men who were to be the great champions of my case in the US – lawyer Paul O'Dwyer and journalist Jack McKinney."

Other things happened as well. There was, for instance, the weekend at his host's summer house at Ocean City, Maryland. As dawn approached after an all-night session, Kelly decided to take out a speedboat on the bay. It was easy to handle and he tore along the coastline at full speed, had his fun, and was coming back to base. But as he was mooring the boat, he crashed into the pier, which was on wooden stilts. The boat was ruined and he ended up being thrown into the water. Within minutes he was picked up by boats coming to the rescue, and by a harbour policeman dressed like a sheriff. He detained Kelly while preparing a report on the incident.

"This was all I needed, I thought. My illegal status would be exposed and I'd be back in Portlaoise the following day. But he never asked about my legal status. He just concerned himself with the incident. That done, I went to a diner for something to eat before contacting my host about what had happened, something I dreaded having to do." An Irish girl working in the diner came over to him laughing and asked, "Are you the fella we heard about this morning?" He said he was. It was a change to be known for something else.

He returned to his host and told him the story. The man was very angry for a while and then they both went for a drink. It was soon forgotten.

HE SPENT A FEW WEEKENDS AWAY. "On one of them I first met Paul O'Dwyer. He was a man with an incredible human rights record in the US. He supported Martin Luther King back in the early 1960s and defended blacks in the Deep South at great risk to himself. He was held in high regard right across the political spectrum. I went to see him at the New York offices of O'Dwyer and Bernstein, massive plush rooms 17 floors up." Despite its obvious success, no legal firm was better known for the amount of free work it did on civil rights issues.

An impressive-looking, tall, white-haired figure in his seventies then, Paul O'Dwyer already knew the details of the Kelly case from reading Irish newspapers and from his own contacts in Ireland. He was disgusted with the way it had been handled, and the way things had deteriorated there on a human rights front during the 1970s. He said that the only way to deal effectively with the situation was through international exposure. "Then he brought me around the offices and introduced me as 'Nicky Kelly' to his staff. It was a strange feeling to be introduced as myself again, and by a man like this. It made me feel good."

But he still continued to use aliases elsewhere in the US for some time, only reverting to his real name when his case became better known and then only with politicians and the media. With work colleagues, he was whoever he said he was at the time.

Paul O'Dwyer's own office was decorated with photographs of himself and well-known people like President Kennedy, Martin Luther King and Jesse Jackson. There was even one of himself and Gandhi. He introduced Frank Durcan, one of his colleagues. "We discussed the case and what might be done. I was given the names of people in human rights organisations and the media throughout the US who might be helpful. Paul O'Dwyer himself contacted Jack McKinney at the *Philadelphia Daily News* and a meeting was arranged for the following weekend. Frank Durcan set about preparing an information pack about my case which he and I later distributed to the media and human rights groups throughout the US."

To many people Jack McKinney was Mr Philadelphia. He knew everyone there and everyone knew him. From high society to the ghettos, he was welcomed everywhere. His popularity was a result of his column in the *Philadelphia Daily News*, which appeared three times a week, and particularly of his courageous defence of ordinary people, as well as his outgoing personality and his sense of humour. McKinney knew Ireland well and had spent time there, both North and South, as well as in Beirut and El Salvador.

Kelly met him at the railway station in Philadelphia. With a strong stocky build, McKinney, who was 50 at the time, looked fit and every bit the professional boxer he once was. He had been a professional singer too at one stage. In fact, in restaurants, often instead of giving him a bill they would ask for a song. He had won several local awards, including an Irishman of the Year Award from the Emerald Society of Philadelphia.

"He brought me to meet the *Daily News* editorial board to discuss my case. Any phone calls I wanted to make or photocopying that needed to be done, I could do from Jack's office. Eventually I was to become well known in that paper's newsroom."

Kelly also became friendly with a crime reporter on the paper by the name of Byrne. "He used to wear his Press ID in his hat band. We went on the tear together. He knew all the senior police in the city, mostly Irish Americans, and introduced me to them. Many knew about my case and were very supportive. The irony of the situation was something that always struck me."

Jack McKinney brought him to football games and boxing matches in an attempt at entertainment and distraction. "But I don't think I really appreciated all he was doing for me. A policeman friend would bring me fishing near Camp David but I could never work up any enthusiasm for it. Looking back on all the things so many people did for me during that spell in the States, all the money they spent bringing me here and there as well as helping out in the case, I must have seemed ungrateful at times.

"My Baltimore host could not do enough for me either. Then it became too much. He wanted to buy me an apartment which I could pay him back for, in instalments. One day he even decided we should go out to buy furniture for it. I tried to get it across to him I was only passing through, but couldn't. It was never my intention to stay in the US."

He felt he had to do something before things went any further. He still could not tell his Baltimore host the truth. Even though there had been some publicity about his case in the US by then, nothing had broken about it yet in Baltimore and he still felt too unsure of his ground there to go public.

"So I had to invent another story to discourage yet another generous benefactor. I had seen one of those benefactors, the Mennonite leader from Yorktown, in Baltimore one day and was nearly killed trying to cross the road before he saw me. There would be too much explaining to do. I told my Baltimore host I had to go home to Ireland. He took me for a meal and offered me money if I was short. I said I was OK. He insisted anyway, and gave me $5,000, a fortune in 1979. I left there feeling pretty bad."

Washington was just 30 to 40 miles away from Baltimore and Kelly had often paid visits there when in Baltimore, lobbying support among Congressmen. He had met members of the

Congress Ad Hoc Committee on Ireland, to whom he always introduced himself as Barry Ryan who wished to discuss the Nicky Kelly case in Ireland. The accessibility of American politicians in Washington then amazed him and he took full advantage, usually meeting Congressmen or their aides in The Dubliner or The Irish Times pubs.

Kelly was invited to stay for a while in the Washington home of one prominent Irish American, whom he had met during one of these trips. He stayed with this family for a couple of weeks while he got himself organised. A job was a priority, and eventually he got one as a driver with a Jewish delivery firm some distance away, in Maryland. They delivered as far south as Virginia, and to a lot of army bases.

He decided to move nearer to work. "Fourth person wanted to share house. Own room, sharing kitchen and living room", went the ad. He rang up and called around to see the house, a two-up/two-down dormer. It suited him fine and the rent was cheap. "The landlord, Yogi, was a small round Greek man who ran a restaurant close by and only came around to collect his money. My three cohabitants were two guys and one girl, all in their twenties. A lively crew."

IT WAS AUGUST OR SEPTEMBER by then and he still knew very little about the US, though he didn't realise that at the time. Before this he had been sheltered from the mainstream by the Irish. None of his new housemates were Irish or had any Irish connections. "My education proper about the US was about to begin. If the Mennonites represented one strand of American life and the Irish Americans another, this gang were probably closer to the core. Or so it would seem, when similar experiences elsewhere were taken into account."

It took him a while to realise his housemates were all grass heads. They smoked it morning, noon and night. The girl used stronger stuff. Every morning she'd drop a couple of duck-egg shaped pills of some sort. Marijuana was cheap and common-place, and widely tolerated. Shops offered various accessories for sale, particularly pipes, and bakeries had "munchie specials". Everywhere Kelly went, even among the most settled middle classes, people offered grass, and before going out at night nearly everyone had a few "hits".

One of his housemates had a close relative in well-known rock band The Eagles. "He was shocked to discover I had never heard of The Eagles, and invited me to a party to meet them after one of their concerts. I went along, and met them but was not at all aware of the significance of being able to do so. All I could think was that I had never seen as many pointed boots or steel-tipped collars in my life before. It was when I told the guys at work next day where I had been the night before it dawned on me, from their reaction, that I had been in the company of gods."

The other man in the house worked in a store downtown and played guitar at night, while the woman was a Texan and worked in finance. She moved in trendy circles, and picked up some trendy habits. "I seldom saw her as she went to work at about 5.30 am and always got home late. Her mother used to worry about her and her lifestyle, and talked to me about this. Once she told me I was the only sane person in the house and asked me to please keep an eye on her daughter. At the time I was the only one in the house seeing an analyst."

Generally they all lived separate lives. Kelly lived privately and frugally, telling them he was saving money to return to Ireland, and he was away most weekends. The others only got worked up at the prospect of having Ronald Reagan as President. The 1979 Presidential election campaign was in full swing and they had a poster in a window of the house, with a picture of Reagan on a horse with the slogan, "Would you trust this cowboy to run your country?"

Kelly's job involved delivering garden supplies to supermarkets and shops in marine and army bases at Arlington, Norfolk and other centres in Virginia, as well as to hospitals, factories and Woolco department stores. The company also delivered salt purifiers for water when the snow came and mulch – broken up tree bark – in the spring. The warehouse they operated from was huge. The employees were a mixed bunch, black and white. Kelly's wages were $240 a week, hardly a fortune even then, but enough to get by on.

Most of his colleagues were Vietnam veterans and nearly all were on drugs, cannabis mainly, which they'd smoke through water-pipes during the day. "Then they'd have races in forklift trucks up and down the aisles. It was crazy. Very early on I noticed they were very suspicious of me. I couldn't understand it. One white driver in particular seemed to be leading them on. 'Don't fuck with that man,' I was warned one day. Then one morning I was walking down an aisle at the warehouse when three or four of them rushed at me from behind, pulled a bag over my head, and beat me about the body with brush handles while they shouted and roared."

He wasn't badly hurt but it was a frightening experience, which sparked off a few vivid memories. It was time to take a stand or leave. The opportunity came on one of the following days. "I was reversing into the loading bay when I saw my chief persecutor in the warehouse behind me. I reversed with greater speed, pulling up hard just short of him. He got the message and I was left alone from then on."

It was a few weeks later when he discovered what all the suspicion and hostility was about. One morning a small army of plainclothes police, some wearing bullet-proof vests, arrived at the warehouse. "Typically, I thought they were coming for me. But it was a drugs bust. A search got underway and they discovered a massive quantity of cannabis, for supply to the marine and army bases. Some of the drivers were arrested and taken away. It seems that because I didn't smoke and was something of a loner, they thought I was an FBI undercover agent, sent in to investigate what was going on."

After that raid they knew he was not and he became one of the good guys. "The blacks were probably the ones I took to most. They were easy-going and not as stressed or driven as so many of the whites, including myself. They were also always late for work, turning in at 8.00 or 8.15 for a 7.30 am start. And straightaway they'd be into the water pipes. They had little, were socially near the bottom of the heap, and lived in what were not much better than shanty town conditions."

But their patriotism was fierce. That always fascinated him, no more so than one morning during early November that year, 1979. "I was at a garden fete on 4 November when at 3.00 pm news came through that Khomeini had taken American hostages in Iran. People were so down on hearing the news that it looked like the fete would be called off. But it wasn't. I arrived at work early the following Monday – I had always been a good time keeper – when I heard shouting inside one of the trucks. I recognised the voices of some of my black colleagues.

"I looked into the truck and in the gloom, literally, all I could see were the whites of their eyes. 'What's going on?' I asked, and teased them about being early for once. But they were in no mood for jokes. All of them were Vietnam veterans, they explained to me, and they were going to re-enlist so they could rescue the hostages and 'nuke that commie fucker [Khomeini]'. They'd show him. And they did go off to re-enlist, but they were too old."

It was a very emotional time in America. Walter Cronkite started to cry on TV when he was talking about the hostages one day. "In Washington I saw about 5,000 police protect around 60 Iranians who were taking part in a protest march outside the White House. Tens of thousands of livid Americans stood on the sidewalks nearby, itching to get their hands on them."

KELLY WAS FOREVER GETTING LOST when making deliveries, taking wrong turnings on Interstate highways. He would radio back over the CB and get guidance to where he should be.

He found other uses for the CB too. Sometimes on the Interstates he would come on a convoy of trucks, usually 40- to 44-footers, about twice the size of his. "I'd get in among them and over the CB totally confuse all with my accent and 'rubber- duck' call. Then I'd hear these guys asking one another who I was. No one would know, and it'd be 'check him out' time. Usually two of those massive things would pull up alongside me, one each side, as we drove along. Once they established I was no more than a messer they were OK."

The truckers considered themselves "Kings of the Road" and didn't welcome any impostors elbowing in on their turf. They had their own world, pulled in at the same stops all over the US, talked about the same women and even speaking their own coded language.

One wrong turning off an Interstate was to lead to an unexpected encounter. Kelly was driving through West Virginia delivering to a series of Woolco stores and admiring the scenery when he realised he was lost. His young helper wasn't too bothered, but said he wanted to stop at a shop.

"'Mean John Mean' they called him. He was anything but. A lovely guy, he was just passing through life. I often wondered whether there might not be a policy at some level in the US to allow these young black guys easy access to soft drugs. It kept them sedated. 'Mean John' had the munchies and wanted ice cream."

Looking at the needle, Kelly realised the truck was low on gas. He pulled into the next gas station. The pump attendant was a middle-aged man in a plaid shirt and dungarees, like a refugee from umpteen films or TV ads. "'Fill her up,' I said in my best American accent. I always spoke in that accent when out and about. It helped my disguise, I thought, and I felt the practice was useful. 'Where ya from?' he asked. 'Minnesota,' I said and he laughed. 'Were you ever in O'Donoghue's pub in Dublin?' he wanted to know. That knocked the stuffing out of me."

He was a Cajun fiddle player who had been to Dublin many times and had been at concerts by the Chieftains, the Bothy Band, and Planxty. "He recognised my Irish accent, despite 'Minnesota', and we started talking. I knew some of the people he had met and soon I had forgotten about gas, about being lost in West Virginia, being on the run in the US, being 'Nicky Kelly'. I was, of course,

Barry Ryan to this man, but the name didn't matter to him. I was Irish. I knew most of the people he talked about and I was right there on his doorstep. He wanted me to come inside for a beer. I explained about 'Mean John', and went back to the cab to get him. But he refused to come in. So I returned for 'just one' beer."

The Cajun man introduced Kelly to his wife, who took over the gas station, as they went inside to drink beer and go through his record collection of Irish music. "After a couple of beers I began to feel very cosy, and all this talk about Ireland and things Irish was a tonic. So I went outside again and succeeded in persuading Mean John to join us this time. I think he was afraid of meeting some Ku Klux Klan-type or the like. We stayed until the night was on us and we were merry. Our host invited us to stay and we did."

Next morning the man directed them to the Woolco store they had been heading for when they had got lost, and hearty farewells were exchanged. At the Woolco store management were mad as hell and refused to take the consignment because it was a day late. Kelly rang the base and they were just as angry.

"'Where were you yesterday?' they wanted to know. I said I met a guy from Ireland, as though no further explanation was needed. 'Where's Mean John?' they asked and I explained he was with me. We were ordered back to base and grounded for three days as punishment. No more was said about it."

The fact that his employers had asked "Where's Mean John?" was, for Kelly, a reflection of their attitudes. "They were just not used to the idea of whites and blacks socialising together, and they did not like it. They couldn't figure me out on that score at all. Though I didn't socialise very much with any of the guys at work, mainly because of my circumstances and because I was away most weekends anyhow, but I did do so on the odd occasion. One evening myself and one of the black guys went to a pub near the warehouse. It was full of whites. The place went silent when we walked in. My black friend read the situation immediately and walked out. When I followed him, one of the white guys, who also worked with us, said to me, 'What ya doin with them niggers?' I just kept going."

After the shaky start at the warehouse they soon accepted Kelly as he was. He didn't bother them, he got on well with everyone and worked hard. The managers were impressed. They wanted to know whether he knew any other Irishmen who might be looking for a job. "I said I didn't. What they couldn't have known was that my work rate was dictated more by a wish to distract myself than because of any great passion for the work ethic."

In Virginia one day he got soaked in a downpour and it dried into him. Two days later he collapsed and was taken to hospital by the policeman friend who used to bring him fishing.

"He was very decent to me always. His wife was a psychiatrist, and by now both knew who I was and were familiar with my case. He had won a purple heart in Vietnam and was very much the outdoor type. He was into white-water surfing and was always on to me to take up some sport. Both of them tried to persuade me to integrate more into the US and settle down there. But I couldn't. I had to borrow the money from them to cover my stay in hospital. It came to a couple of thousand dollars. Money was always a problem. I couldn't keep a bank account because I was illegal and couldn't get a credit card for the same reason, and I could cash my pay cheque only in a pub where I made myself known for that purpose."

He was in hospital for just a few days. He wanted to pay back the money borrowed as soon as possible. That gave him a clear if short-term purpose, which helped. Christmas was coming, and so there was a lot of extra part-time work available. He got two extra jobs, along with the delivery work. One was in telephone sales. It operated from a big open-plan office where they got together every evening and were each handed about ten pages photocopied from a phone directory. Their job was to ring every number, trying to sell subscriptions to magazines. It was usually dinnertime when they'd call. Then they could be fairly sure of getting people at home.

"My accent was a problem. Not many could understand it, especially on the phone. That, combined with the time of day, meant I got a good share of abuse. 'Cocksucker' was a word that often came my way, particularly when on the third or fourth attempt the person I called still couldn't make out what I was saying. Then it was 'fuck off you' and 'listen motherfucker you just burned my dinner'. The managers even picked out Irish names from the directory for me. As for the others, they thought the whole thing was just hilarious. And whenever I got a sale they all stopped what they were doing and cheered like mad."

His third job was at a toy warehouse where they packed miniature custom-built motorbikes for spoilt children, which cost over $3,000 each. They'd also drive them around the warehouse, into the small hours. He often felt it was a miracle no one was killed.

At that time he was rising at 6.00 am to be at the delivery warehouse by 7.30. He'd finish there at 3.30, to start on telesales by 4.00. That finished at 10.00. At 10.45 pm he would begin at the toy warehouse and be there until 2.00 am.

❧   ❧   ❧

THAT CHRISTMAS, HE HIT A WALL of deep depression. "It was my first time ever to be away from Ireland for the season. I missed home desperately. In the gap created by the holiday and the ending of those part-time jobs I was tormented by memories of happier days."

He stayed with Jack McKinney in Philadelphia for the New Year. It was a lovely apartment overlooking the river, where McKinney lived alone. He was divorced and his three children were adults by then. "As far as I was concerned it was do or die time. Despite all my efforts up to that point I had a feeling of no more than running to stand still. I did not seem to be pushing the campaign forward one bit. Jack wrote a piece about my 'enforced exile' and it was published in the *Philadelphia Daily News* in early January 1980. That was the real beginning of my going public in the US. No one knew what it might lead to, even whether I would be arrested and deported back to Ireland. Myself, I was beyond caring. Anything was better than the limbo in which I found myself."

Other articles followed in *The Philadelphia Inquirer*. Local radio and TV sought interviews. Then the story was taken up through syndication in Los Angeles and San Francisco to the West, in Boston, New York and Washington to the East. It was beginning to get noticed. Through Jack McKinney he had access to the journalists' club in Philadelphia, where he met Bill Stone, deputy editor of *The Philadelphia Inquirer*.

He also met Pete Hamill of *The New York Post* and Michael Daly of *The Boston Globe*. Meetings took place with the Lawyers Guild of America, the US Union of Civil Liberties, and in New York with The Brehon Law Society. In Washington he met more Congressmen's aides as well as Congressmen Hamilton Fish and Bill Bryden, who were concerned about Human Rights issues generally. In Philadelphia lawyer John Corcoran took an interest in the case. And Kelly began to receive invitations to all sorts of civil rights/human rights functions and cultural events.

One led to a peculiar situation. "I was in Washington at a poetry reading which was introduced by the then Irish Ambassador to the US, Sean Donlon. As he spoke I was right in front of him. He could not have missed me, but did not make any eye contact. After that I began to wonder whether my being in the US might not be just another 'Irish solution to an Irish problem' for the authorities at home. It probably suited them better to have me out of the way."

The campaign was moving at last. But nothing seemed enough and Kelly became convinced he was heading for a breakdown. Jack McKinney later described his spells staying with him as "a horror show". "I could not sleep for more than a few hours at a time and then would wake up hysterical from nightmares. I had constant headaches and was desperately agitated, anxious and homesick. My hearing also seemed to be getting worse. I went to New York often, just to be with Irish people, taking more and more risks now as the publicity mounted and my own concern for the consequences diminished. I saw a lot of people I recognised and I even recognised a few guards at Gaelic Park once. They were over playing football."

One experience convinced him he was flipping over the edge. He was having a drink in the Archway pub in the Bronx one night. He couldn't sleep and stayed there tippling till the morning. Then he took a subway to 213th St and Broadway. There was a shop there, Jennie Campbells, which sold the Irish papers. The area around was poor and most of the residents were old Irish men who worked in menial jobs in the city.

"Passing the Cork Club, where a lot of these old men were, I heard the voice of Mícheál O'Hehir doing a commentary on a match, and I suddenly thought I was in Croke Park again. It was a very real feeling, as though it was actually happening despite the New York traffic and streetscape all around. I thought I'd cracked up then, but I didn't. All I did was cry at the sound of that familiar voice and all the things it brought back to me. I cried and cried. I could not stop. I had lost control."

Eventually it subsided. Inside the Cork Club he saw these old men sitting around listening to a cassette tape replay of a Cork/Limerick League Championship match. He had seen these same poor old devils many times before. They would get together every Sunday evening at about 10.30 to talk about the football results from home, usually in that club or in a park nearby because they couldn't afford to go to a pub. All they talked about was home. None of them would have looked out of place at any crossroads in Ireland, except for the trilby hats they wore.

Observing them Kelly gained an insight into the "returned Yank syndrome". Nearly all of them had been at home on holiday at some point, and splashed money about right, left and centre, impressing the neighbours at how well they were doing. It was a great show of confidence that took them years to pay off on returning to America. Now they were trapped, and would remain so for the rest of their days. For Kelly, they were the sad underside of the great Irish success story in the US.

❧   ❧   ❧

DR ROMA FIELDS WAS A RENOWNED psychologist living in Alexandria, Virginia. She had treated a lot of South American torture victims and had written a book about the psychological effects of the Northern Ireland conflict, titled *A Society on the Run*. Paul O'Dwyer brought Kelly to see her in February 1980. He visited her every week after that. Under her observation he re-lived the interrogation and attempted to come to terms with it. She would conclude later that he was suffering from anxiety and connected psychosomatic disorders including insomnia, headaches, gastric problems and psycho-motor inadequacies.

In her view, though Kelly's physical problems may have been caused by assaults, such as blows to the head, these had since become exacerbated by a declining mental state brought about by the strain of a lengthy trial period; the strain of being on the run in Ireland; and the extra strain of being on the run abroad.

She referred him for a complete neurological examination to investigate whether his difficulties were caused by problems in the brain or the central nervous system. This examination was to take place at a New York hospital in April 1980.

The urge to go home became stronger and stronger as time went by. "Everyone discouraged me. All advised caution. But it was really beyond being a choice for me. No matter how bad things were for me in Ireland, even if I had to serve out the whole sentence, however unjust the scenario, it would have some meaning for me there. Abroad, I was living at a distance from myself."

So many people in the US wanted to help him and look after him. And if he had stayed there for the 12 years of his sentence he could then have gone home a free man as, under the law, once you are given a penal servitude sentence you are deemed to be serving it automatically from the day it is pronounced, even in absentia.

All these things were true and possible, but they did not matter to him. "I had to go home. It was a need, not a choice. By the end of March my mind was made up. The timing was helped by the fact that in a couple of weeks my neurological tests would take place and I thought it would be better if I didn't return before

Osgur and Brian's appeal was heard in mid-May. I picked a date in early June for the homecoming."

At the warehouse they did not want to accept his notice and tried to convince him to stay. He said he had to go home. So a big party was organised, for around 7 April, and they had a ball. His co-workers still knew him as Barry Ryan. They had to travel seven miles before finding a place that would accept a mixed company of blacks and whites for the party.

IN MID-APRIL 1980 THE PROVISIONAL IRA issued a statement in Dublin saying they had been responsible for the mail train robbery in 1976, "for which a number of completely innocent people have been convicted and jailed," it said. It described "Breathnach, McNally and Nicky Kelly" as "completely innocent victims". The statement had been issued, they said, to "formalise" what was "common knowledge throughout the country for years".

For Kelly "this was even more encouragement to go home. Here, after all, were people claiming they robbed that train. Surely it was now only a matter of time before our sentences would be quashed and our names cleared."

Paul O'Dwyer arranged for his hospital treatment in New York. It cost $600 a day. For three days he was prodded and poked; wired up to just about every type of medical machine; injected with dyes; x-rayed at all angles; and had fluid and tissue samples taken from his spine, under local anaesthetic. After that he was told they wanted him to stay on for five more days.

"I discharged myself thinking, 'Ah, come on now, enough is enough.' I left hospital on 23 May and stayed that evening with acquaintances in the Bronx. The next day I heard Osgur and Brian had won their appeals and were already out of Portlaoise. That was it. Now nothing would stop me from going home."

He rang his solicitor Pat McCartan in Dublin, who pointed out that the Courts had yet to give reasons for allowing the McNally/Breathnach appeals. Paul O'Dwyer advised caution, everyone advised caution, but Kelly was listening to no one. "To me it was as simple as it was clear; truth had won out, however the authorities at home might dress it up, and I would not listen to older and wiser counsel. I could not. I just had to go home."

John Corcoran, by then effectively acting as his lawyer, announced that Nicky Kelly would be returning to Ireland to clear his name. On 2 June, Jack McKinney wrote in the *Philadelphia Daily News* that Kelly was returning voluntarily. Kelly rang RTÉ and did a radio interview with Shane Kenny announcing his return. On 3 June he set off for the Irish Consulate in New York. Jack McKinney paid for his the tickets.

He had been in contact with the consulate before and was told that they were not in the business of "apprehending fugitives". He needed a temporary passport to get into Ireland. Again there was little enthusiasm when he arrived at the consular offices, but eventually they agreed to give him a single sheet form which he filled in, attached two photographs, and paid over $9.50.

Then it was off to JFK Airport by taxi. "I had a few quick drinks in the Departures Lounge with Jack, to settle my nerves before flying, and was the last man on the Aer Lingus plane. It was 8.00 in the evening. On board I had a few more 'steadiers' and read *The Irish Times*, where the paper's Washington correspondent Sean Cronin had a story about my return headed 'Mail train man to return?' A few people recognised me on board, including a hostess. I asked for a drink and took out a note to pay for it. She said it was 'on the house'. I insisted she take the money and have a drink for herself. She said she would, but only if I autographed the note. I did."

As the plane approached Ireland, Kelly worked up the courage to look out a window. The morning was clear with the sharp red light of a rising sun welcoming them to a new day and to Ireland. "In the distance I could see the green fields and soon was able to make out stone walls. I was overcome by a powerful surge of feeling. Ireland never looked so good."

At Shannon, four gardaí came on board the plane and escorted him off to a small room in the terminal. There he met Pat McCartan and they had a short consultation before he was escorted to a squad car and driven to Dublin. The gardaí were brusque and businesslike and didn't have a lot to say. When they arrived at the Special Criminal Court in Dublin he was held for about an hour in the cells below before the hearing took place.

"By now I was convinced I'd either be freed immediately or at worst be detained in custody until an appeal would be heard. The court appearance was brief. The judges simply ordered that I be taken to Portlaoise to serve the remainder of my 12-year sentence. I was brought downstairs again and handcuffed to a prison officer. Shortly after that I was taken under military escort to Portlaoise prison with four or five or sullen prison officers in my van, another van behind, two army jeeps and two to four outriders, who stayed with us until we cleared the city."

At Portlaoise he was escorted from the van through a series of checks and searches, including a strip search and medical examination, before being brought inside. Four levels of tiered cells rose in the grey gloom to the ceiling. He was taken to the second tier.

His cell was of the standard size, twelve feet by eight feet with a metal bed, sheets, army-style blankets, and a pillow. There was a plastic knife and fork, a cup and plate on a small wooden locker, with a pot under the bed. The walls were grey and the floor wooden.

A barred window made up of several small panes, some broken, looked out from a height onto the prison yard. From the ceiling a bare bulb hung down. The switch was outside. The door had a "Judas hole", so prison officers could keep an eye on whoever was inside. The door closed.

Alone again. Kelly just lay on the bed and thought to himself, "Well, here I am."

12

To be Free Again

NICKY KELLY COULD NEVER ACCEPT being a prisoner and from the beginning in Portlaoise every fibre in him was concentrated on just one thing – getting out! But, he says, it could not be just any "out". It would have to be in circumstances which cleared him totally.

In those early weeks he did not think that would take too long. He was confident an appeal would succeed. After all, the circumstances of his conviction and those of Osgur Breathnach and Brian McNally were the same. So he reconciled himself to a temporary stay in jail.

Were he to serve his sentence he would be in Portlaoise until December 1990; maybe until 1986, when he could be released with remission of a third of the sentence for good behaviour. But he never seriously considered either date.

He was held in "E" wing. There were about 100 to 120 prisoners there at the time. The wing was rectangular and four floors or tiers high. In the middle was a stairwell connecting all floors. There were just narrow walkways opposite the rows of cells on each level. On every tier, and at both ends, there were washrooms, toilets, a recreation room and a laundry. The two top tiers held prisoners convicted of being members of the Provisional IRA. In the bottom two, where he was, they were a mixed bunch.

Prison life was dominated by two things, tension and routine. The tension existed between the prisoners and prison officers, known always and without regard as "screws". They operated a brutal regime, Kelly remembers. "As a bunch, the majority were bad, nasty and vindictive. Some more so than others," he recalls.

One thing they used to take great delight in was tearing up letters or photographs sent to prisoners, as a reminder that "inside" there was no such thing as personal property. As his stay there progressed he got letters from people and organisations all over the world, which he would like to have kept, but all were destroyed by the screws in this way. All, of course, would have been opened before he got them as well, and every letter he sent was opened before it was posted.

At the 1984 Prison Officers' Association conference in Cork, there were complaints from members that those willing to beat prisoners in Portlaoise were getting more overtime and were more likely to be promoted. The beatings eased after that.

Between the prisoners themselves, however, there was no tension. Relations generally were good, and probably better because of the sort of regime under which they all lived. "It bred solidarity against what was believed to be an organised attempt to humiliate, degrade, and dehumanise each and every one of us," Kelly recalls.

This "bonding" was necessary too, if only to ensure the prisoners' psychological and emotional survival, he says. Differences they may have had outside, political and otherwise, did not manifest themselves much in the prison. The prisoners were also particularly supportive of him because they were aware of his innocence, he remembers.

Still, he did not become close to anyone during the four years he spent at Portlaoise. There were reasons for this: his own preoccupation with fighting the case, which soon became an obsession; his state of mind, which was not good and which tended to drive him inward rather than out towards people; and the "different" status conferred on him by the widespread knowledge inside that he was innocent.

He was not in good shape mentally at all during most of this period. He could not sleep at night due to a combination of bad headaches, anxiety, insomnia and nightmares. As a result, during the day he was on edge most of the time, intense and usually on his own. As a way of surviving all of this, and in an attempt to tire himself out so he could sleep, he began to run, whether round and round the yard, or on the spot.

It was a way of calming his mind too. After a certain point in running, he realised he would hit a sort of "high", which would help him to relax. As he was not able to concentrate long enough to read or watch TV, he ran, he answered letters, he planned strategies for his release campaign, and he survived.

THERE WERE MANY TIMES during those four years in jail when he regretted having returned to Ireland at all in 1980 and having ignored the advice of all those who had warned him to be cautious. Eventually even, and to his surprise, the loneliness of America seemed a better option than incarceration in Portlaoise.

Fundamentally, Nicky knew one of two things would happen: he would die or he would be released. He had decided there was no way he would serve out his sentence. Anyone who has been wrongly accused, he feels, or even just misrepresented or misunderstood, would know this frame of mind. As the accusation, misunderstanding or gossip begins to "set" and spread, a sort of stubborn anger makes itself felt. It gets deeper with time and gives birth to a single-minded determination that living this way is not an option.

For him to "settle down" and serve out his 12 years' penal servitude was tantamount to throwing in the towel, letting "them" get away with it, and accepting a guilt that was not his. At its most basic, the issue was a matter of self-respect. He, Nicky Kelly, was not going to lie down and "die" before this crazy situation. If he died, it would be in fighting his case. It was, he says, a matter of being able to look himself in the eye.

Later, he would discover that his reaction was not unusual. Talking to the Guildford Four, the Birmingham Six and Judy Ward in the years that followed, he came to realise that if you are innocent you simply cannot live with being in jail. Deep in your heart there is always a great anger that you are there at all, and this makes it impossible to settle down to or accept prison life.

The other thing they all discovered was that in each of them – probably in everyone – there were reserves of strength none would have suspected until put to the test. It was this more than any other single factor which helped him, the Guildford Four, the Birmingham Six and Judy Ward to pull through, he observes. It was something for which none of them willingly takes credit. It was almost as if it came from outside, that it was not part of them as individuals at all.

In Portlaoise routine was the bane of his life. He did not take to it readily. "By nature I am more of a free-range person, who prefers to go with the moment rather than be dictated to by a clock." In Portlaoise there was no debate about routine; you simply followed it. "Beginning at 8.30 am, when the cell door would be opened. You would get up and go to the washroom/toilet. There was a trolley for each tier, with cereals, bread, jam, and tea. You helped yourself to breakfast from this. Afterwards you could have a shower. There was TV in the recreation room, the library, a walk in the yard, or a visit to the workshop."

He usually went to the yard or the workshop. He made a bodhran there once which he gave to singer/songwriter Christy Moore, a regular visitor and great supporter. On a Planxty album they printed his name in the list of credits – "Bodhran by Nicky Kelly, Portlaoise". Afterwards he got a letter from a music wholesaler in Germany, addressed to "Nicky Kelly, Portlaoise, Ireland", inquiring about the price of 100 bodhrans. The letter writer had no idea he was dealing with a prisoner in a jail; he must have thought he was dealing with "Nicky Kelly, Supplier of Bodhrans Ltd"!

Apart from the bodhran, they made things like wooden harps, Celtic crosses, leather wallets and belts in the workshops, and these were usually given to family and friends.

"At about 12.30 you returned to your own floor/tier; collected dinner from the trolley and ate it in your own cell. Then it'd be back to the yard or workshop, library or recreation room, until

4.00 pm when there'd be a cup of tea. Then back to the yard, etc. until 8.30 pm, when you'd be locked up in your cell for the night."

Radios were allowed in the cells. Nicky listened to the Dublin pirate station, Sunshine Radio, mostly as he felt it had none of RTÉ's hang-ups about dealing with his case, he says. He would write letters, or just lie back and think until sleep came, if it did.

On top of that deadening routine there was the same dull colour everywhere, a sort of battleship grey, inside and outside. "On cloudy days it seemed to seep into your soul. The only relief was a single tree that grew outside the prison wall. It and the sky, on a clear day," he remembers.

The worst times for him in Portlaoise were not always the obvious ones, such as all those failures in court, or the hunger strike later, or even the beatings. "The worst times were the Christmas and New Year's Eve period, and not for sentimental reasons. No, it was that they underlined the fact that I had spent another year there and it brought home to me, hard, that I was facing into still another New Year with no hope of release. There was never a New Year in Portlaoise when I knew I was going to get out, or had any concrete hope of doing so. All I had was the determination that I would.

"It was always a 'down' time, when I usually cried and talked to myself. It was something I got into the habit of doing in Portlaoise, and I would remind myself that there were a lot of good people out there who were helping me and would not stop until I was free."

At the beginning, however, he had been confident it was only a matter of time before the Courts released him. His main frustration in those first months, was with the slowness of the Courts process and the apparent lack of urgency on the part of all those directly involved, except himself.

His most regular visitors those early months were his sisters Breda, Margaret and Stella, and his lawyers. He was allowed two visits a week. His parents did not come. "I did not want my mother to see me there. It would have been too much for both of us. She had to be sedated when she heard of my arrest. My father, who would drive my sisters to the prison, could not bring himself to pass through those gates for a long time. The entire situation was hard for my family. But it would be years before I would hear just how hard. For instance, after my arrest the guards began to raid our house in Arklow at all hours of the day and night. As it was, my father was not a great sleeper. He had developed an asthma problem over the years and breathing often kept him awake at night. My mother says it all started with the wettings he got while out with the Forestry. There was no wet time when he started with them.

"Many people also believed I must be guilty of the robbery or, if not that, then something as serious. To most people, in those more innocent times, the guards just did not arrest people for nothing. At school, my sister Margaret didn't answer a question one day and her teacher shouted at her, 'Of course, you wouldn't know, you're only interested in robbing trains.' And there was name calling. My father always told the girls to 'never answer back. Walk on and say nothing, otherwise people like that know they have upset you. And that is all they want to do.'

"My father was very strong about the situation, and in his own solid, quiet way was always one of my staunchest supporters. 'If it wasn't this family,' he would say, 'it'd be someone else's.' He was always convinced right would win out in the end, and that I would be freed and cleared. It grieves me still that he should have died in November 1991, just months before I was exonerated of all involvement in the robbery. It would have been an occasion of great satisfaction for him."

Breda had been in to see him soon after his arrival from America. He was wearing gaudy American clothes and looked thin, she said. She and Margaret had been at the trials almost every day. They would take it in turns, sometimes. Then, when he went on the run, they had no idea where he was for a long time. It was a while before he could get word to them that he was OK. He could not make direct contact with them because he believed they were probably being watched by the Special Branch. Around then too a body was found in the Wicklow mountains. He heard afterwards that not a word was said in the house until it was identified three days later, when they knew it wasn't him.

They brought him clothes in Portlaoise, which had to be striped, as no plain, navy, or blue colours were allowed. They'd always bring him in a copy of the *Wicklow People* newspaper, and all the news, as well as things he might want from the shop such as envelopes, pens and writing papers. They were searched every time and had to remove all loose clothes, and while they sat chatting with him each side of a grille, a prison officer stood close by within earshot.

Of all the visitors he had during his stay in Portlaoise their's were the ones he looked forward to most – their's and Christy Moore's. Christy was a good friend to him during those years and a great letter writer. He would write and drop in to see him at Portlaoise. They even corresponded about the words of the song "Lisdoonvarna", which Christy was writing at the time. He sent Kelly drafts of it as it came along. Later he wrote "The Wicklow Boy" about the Nicky Kelly case, which was banned by RTÉ.

TD Tony Gregory was another regular visitor and always among Kelly's staunchest supporters. He was the only TD to visit him in jail. He too had been an admirer of Seamus Costello and had been a member of the IRSP for a while.

He also looked forward to visits from the Release Nicky Kelly Committee. "All these people who gave me hope," he recalls. He needed it.

ON THE DRIVE FROM SHANNON to the Special Criminal Court, following his arrival back from the US, one of the guards had said something to him about making sure to get in an appeal before the summer recess. At the time he wasn't sure what this meant, but he soon found out.

His expectation of an early release was quickly brought down to earth. Indeed, it looked like his appeal might not be allowed at all, as it had not been lodged within the specified seven-day period after his conviction. His lawyers set about preparing a case to petition the court for an extension of that time.

The psychiatrist Professor Robert Daly of UCC examined him shortly after his arrival in Portlaoise. Prof Daly was an influential figure in that he had acted for Ireland in the torture case against Britain, which was taken to the European Court of Human Rights. He concluded that Kelly was suffering from "a traumatic neurosis resulting from his experiences during interrogation four years ago" and further explained that Kelly exhibited both neurological and psychological symptoms of an ongoing underlying disability.

Kelly swore an affidavit, explaining the psychological background as to why he went on the run; treatment by psychiatrist Dr Noel Browne (who he had attended before the Special Criminal Court trials) and Dr Roma Fields; as well as giving details of their findings. He explained that it had always been his wish to return to Ireland and clear his name and that this was the case irrespective of the Breathnach and McNally appeals.

Pat McCartan swore an affidavit pointing out that he had entered an appeal on Kelly's behalf on 15 December 1978, well within the legal limit stipulated, but that this had been refused. He also added 14 other grounds for appeal relating to the conduct of the case.

However, despite the rush, they did not succeed in having the petition for a right to appeal heard before the summer recess. So he had to readjust his expectations.

"Home for Christmas, I thought then," Kelly remembers.

13

JUSTICE, BEING DONE

O N 11 NOVEMBER 1980 SENIOR COUNSEL Seamus Sorohan and
Paddy McEntee presented Nicky Kelly's application before
the Court of Criminal Appeal. The three judges presiding were
Justice Weldon Parke of the Supreme Court, and Justices Mella
Carroll and John Gannon of the High Court. They reserved judg-
ment, giving their decision on 18 December.

They rejected the application, saying that Kelly had "failed to
show even the contemplation of dissatisfaction with his trial or
the intention to challenge the verdict of the court at any time prior
to 29th of May 1980". On this application, they said, "he has failed
to adduce evidence of facts or circumstances to which his inaction
can be attributed".

Basically the Court was criticising his lawyers for not presenting them with all the facts, as though they were attending an actual appeal hearing rather than making an application for a right
to appeal. The judgment was widely regarded as strange.

It was established they could appeal to the Supreme Court, but
first they had to get permission to do so from the same three
judges who had already rejected Kelly's right to appeal. It was not
until the following March of 1981 when he appeared before them
again, seeking permission to go to the Supreme Court.

Two months later, on 29 May 1981, they said "yes". Throughout this long drawn-out period he was becoming more and more
frustrated. Every time he would go to court the prison officers
would send along all his things with him, expecting he would not
be coming back. There'd be the usual rigorous strip search as he

was let out to be taken the 50 miles to Dublin, with military escorts and wailing sirens.

They would be met at Newlands Cross by a garda motorcycle escort as well. He would console himself every time by believing it was the last occasion when he would be given such high security treatment. But it never was. Afterwards he'd be brought back to Portlaoise in the same style, rigorously strip-searched again and put into his cell. Until the next time.

His case was receiving little or no attention outside. Following the Breathnach and McNally appeals most people thought it was only a matter of time before Kelly too would be released. He was fed up with the delays between court appearances and the passive acceptance of this slow process by everyone else except himself. His faith in the outcome was evaporating with every long day.

It was in early 1981 that he considered going on hunger strike for the first time. He decided against it after talking to some people. The H-Block hunger strikes were about to start in the North and it was felt that one by him in Portlaoise would be a distraction and of lesser benefit to him.

He was also very annoyed with his lawyers, believing that had they approached the case differently he might have been released by the Court of Criminal Appeal for Christmas 1980. He argued a lot with his legal team. He asked that some other barristers be approached to see whether they might take on the case. Sean McBride expressed an interest, but when he saw the amount of trial transcript he realised he couldn't take it on and fulfil his other commitments as well.

In June 1981 there was a general election and again Kelly decided to go on hunger strike. Again, he was persuaded not to. The appeal would probably succeed in the Supreme Court, he was told. But he was not so sure. His instincts told him there was something strange at work, something that was beginning to take on a pattern where he was concerned.

To him it seemed the judiciary had set their faces against him. After all, he had been before many judges in several different courts – charged at the District Court, convicted by the Special

Criminal Court, refused appeals by the High Court, Supreme Court, and the Court of Criminal Appeal (in "the sleeping judge" action). He believed that every major decision handed down in his case was odd, no matter how reasonably it was put. His faith in the courts was nil to non-existent by the time he won his first case – the right to appeal the Court of Criminal Appeal rejection to the Supreme Court. It was a boost but he did not hold his breath.

The Supreme Court hearing was in July 1981. In the meantime there had been a change of Government. Another Fine Gael/Labour Coalition took office, this time led by Garret FitzGerald, but it survived only until February 1982 and made no impact on his case whatsoever. Kelly decided to present his own appeal at the Supreme Court this time. However, the night before the hearing he was informed by court officials that he could not do this. His case was then presented by his usual legal team. A week later he was granted leave to appeal.

Six months later again the Supreme Court gave its reasons. The Court of Criminal Appeal had taken "a slightly blinkered view" of his case, it decided. Most extraordinarily of all it also found that he could have submitted his appeal in the normal way, as of right, to the Court of Criminal Appeal rather than being bogged down in technicalities.

"So there I was in January 1982 being told I need not have spent the previous year and a half in jail pursuing the right to appeal, when I could have simply appealed directly and maybe won my freedom long before. The news did not improve relations between myself and my lawyers."

So it was back to the Court of Criminal Appeal again. This time the judges were the President of the High Court Thomas Finlay, who presided, Judge Seamus Henchy of the Supreme Court and Judge Donal Barrington of the High Court – the same three judges who had heard the Breathnach/McNally appeals.

The case was presented by Seamus Sorohan. He argued that the Special Criminal Court was wrong to find Kelly's confession was not caused by violence or unfair methods and that his detention was unlawful at different times during which the confessions were made. The hearing lasted four days, from 15 February 1982 to 18 February. The judges retired to consider their decision. It was a long retirement.

Forty-three days later, on 2 April, they rejected the appeal. Judge Finlay and his two colleagues ruled in accordance with their colleagues on the Special Criminal Court – in accordance with the "facts", as had been established by that Court. It was a similar situation to the Courts' findings in the first Special Criminal Court trial when judges on the High Court and the Supreme Court found, in accordance with the finding of fact of their colleagues on the Special Criminal Court, that their colleague Judge John O'Connor had not been sleeping.

What was most intriguing about the Kelly appeal, compared to those of Osgur Breathnach and Brian McNally, was the difference in weight the court attached to the same circumstances which prevailed in all three cases. Some of those circumstances were enough to allow both Breathnach and McNally be cleared, but in Kelly's case this was not so. He was now convinced there was no will on the part of the judiciary to free him.

IT WAS 1982, THE YEAR OF GUBU, when murderer Malcolm McArthur was discovered at Attorney General Patrick Connolly's residence in Dalkey, County Dublin. But the "Grotesque, Unbelievable, Bizarre, and Unprecedented", as then Taoiseach Charles Haughey described the episode, was not confined to happenings in the political arena alone.

"True men of the system, my lawyers' reaction to this latest judgment was predictable – they decided to appeal, to the Supreme Court again. I didn't care anymore. It just seemed another waste of time."

That Supreme Court appeal began on 13 July 1982, before Chief Justice Tom O'Higgins, Judges Brian Walsh, Frank Griffin, Anthony Hederman and Judge Herbert McWilliam of the High Court. It lasted six days.

Kelly was not there. Once more judgment was reserved. It was given over three months later. On 29 October Chief Justice O'Higgins announced that the Supreme Court had rejected the appeal. He used the opportunity to praise the Irish judicial system in ringing tones. "It is seldom that the appellate jurisdiction of our courts has been so fully exercised . . ." and he went on, and on, in praise of an excellent system of justice which had just, for the umpteenth time, upheld the "guilt" of an innocent man.

He accepted as "undisputed fact" that Kelly was "bruised" when remanded to Mountjoy, and that, except in one instance, this "bruising" was found to be consistent with the allegations Kelly had made. It was this exception, though, rather than all the consistencies, which intrigued Chief Justice O'Higgins most. This was the chair episode, which he decided was probably "evidence" of invention. It, he implied, never happened and was really a figment of Kelly's imagination. That being so in one instance, he postulated, could not Kelly therefore just as easily have concocted all the other stories about how his injuries had been sustained? The learned judge had come up with a theory, treated it as fact, and on that basis had decided that all Kelly's evidence was false. QED.

He based this implication on the observation that, following the chair incident, "no marks or injury or bruising were found on his [Kelly's] hands, however". This ignored the medical evidence presented to the Special Criminal Court. There, Dr O'Cleirigh had told prosecution counsel, Robert Barr, that it would be necessary to put a lot or weight "suddenly" on the hands to cause serious damage to the palms. Otherwise it would not necessarily cause an abrasion, he said. The Supreme Court had picked out just those elements in the medical evidence which suited its judgment, and ignored all the rest, which was heavily loaded the other way.

But it was at the suggestion of perjury by the gardaí and the implication by Kelly that the Court of Criminal Appeal should have found accordingly, that Chief Justice O'Higgins got really fired up. The Supreme Court was being asked, he said, in an appalled tone, to decide from a reading of the trial transcript that the gardaí named by Kelly had committed perjury.

"This drastic conclusion . . ." was how Chief Justice O'Higgins described it. He compounded his own outrage at the suggestion by noting that this drastic conclusion was also expected to be arrived at by a Court which "neither saw nor heard any or the witnesses involved but which nevertheless was to feel itself at liberty to brand as untruthful those witnesses who by their manner, demeanour, and evidence had satisfied experienced judges at the trial that they were telling the truth."

Ah, "demeanour"! It was the "demeanour" of garda witnesses which had convinced the Special Criminal Court they were telling the truth. Not what they told the Court, but how they told it. So Justice Liam Hamilton had said in announcing the decision to admit the mail train robbery defendants' confessions as evidence. But demeanour, like beauty, is in the eye of the beholder. By now Kelly was beginning to believe that so, too, was truth.

Chief Justice O'Higgins continued: "If such [the drawing of 'this drastic conclusion'] were truly within the powers of a Court of Appeal", he went on, "one wonders what would be the function of a Court of trial?"

Now there, at last, though for very different reasons, lay common ground between Kelly and the Chief Justice. It was a topic to which Kelly had given a lot of thought over the intervening six years since he had been charged at that special late night sitting of the District Court on 7 April 1976. What really was the function of a court of trial? Was it, in practice, really only there to enforce the prejudices of the establishment in society?

His Supreme Court appeal rejected on all grounds, he had now exhausted every legal avenue of appeal open to him. The only good thing about the situation was that he was now finished with it all. The charade was over. On with the show.

TOM O'HIGGINS WAS OF QUINTESSENTIAL Fine Gael stock. According to former Taoiseach Garret FitzGerald, he would have become leader of that party had he not withdrawn from politics in 1973.

It is impossible to escape the conclusion that his judgment and comments in the Kelly case were influenced by his own history. His father Tom and his uncle Kevin, who was murdered by the IRA in 1927 – as was his grandfather in 1922 – were both government ministers and his brother Michael served with him in the Dáil for many years.

Tom O'Higgins was born in Sunday's Well, Cork, on 23 July 1916. His father Dr Thomas F. O'Higgins, was then director of the army medical service, and the family later lived in Dublin's Portobello Barracks. While there Tom O'Higgins attended the nearby St Mary's College in Rathmines. He finished his schooling at Clongowes.

His father was a founder member of the Army Comrades' Association in the 1930s, better known as the Blueshirts, which claimed to have been set up to protect Cumann na nGaedheal (later name-changed to Fine Gael) candidates during election campaigns of the period while being ideologically inspired by the corporatist philosophy of papal encyclicals and of the Italian fascist leader Benito Mussolini. In later years Tom O'Higgins defended his father's role with the Blueshirts saying that it was "a time when people forget that the right of free speech was everywhere in danger in Ireland". He recalled that when his father fought a by-election he was "several times nearly killed", while the gardaí were "confined to barracks".

Tom O'Higgins gained first class honours at UCD in legal and political science, winning first place in Ireland in his final Bar examination at the King's Inns in Dublin. He was called to the Bar in 1938. In 1943, he stood unsuccessfully for Fine Gael in Dublin South but he won a seat in Laois-Offaly in the 1948 general election. The O'Higgins family roots were in Stradbally, County Laois. That same day, his father was re-elected in Cork City and his brother Michael was elected in Dublin South-West. His father was appointed Minister for Defence and later for Industry and Commerce in that first inter-party government.

In the 1954 general election, also the year he was called to the Inner Bar, O'Higgins was re-elected and became Minister for

Health in the second inter-party government. His father was Minister for Defence in the same government. In 1957 he set up the VHI shortly before that government fell.

Back in opposition, he combined legal practice with efforts to modernise Fine Gael, where he helped found a study group called the Research and Information Centre which eventually led to the "Towards a Just Society" document. When Liam Cosgrave took over as leader of the party in 1965 he appointed O'Higgins as spokesman on Finance and Economic Affairs.

In 1966 O'Higgins was chosen by Fine Gael to oppose Eamon de Valera in the Presidential election that June. He almost won, coming to within a percentage point, or 10,717 votes, of defeating de Valera. In the 1969 general election he moved constituency to Dublin South, was elected, and subsequently became deputy leader of Fine Gael to Liam Cosgrave.

Early in 1973 O'Higgins was selected again as the Fine Gael candidate for the Presidential election that June on the retirement of de Valera. However, Taoiseach Jack Lynch suddenly called a general election which obliged O'Higgins to announce that he would not seek re-election to the Dáil because of his plans to contest the presidential election. Before that general election he played a major role in agreeing an advance programme for government with the Labour party, which helped defeat Fianna Fáil. He was defeated by Fianna Fáil's Erskine Childers in the presidential election.

In November 1973, Liam Cosgrave, now Taoiseach, appointed him a High Court judge. Within a year, with the sudden death of Chief Justice William Fitzgerald in October 1974, the Cosgrave coalition appointed O'Higgins Chief Justice. He held the post for ten years. In 1984, when Ireland's representative on the European Court of Justice, Andreas O'Keeffe, resigned, the then Fine Gael/Labour government appointed O'Higgins to replace him. His term expired in October 1991. He was 86 when he died in Dublin on 25 February 2003.

If it is not unreasonable to infer that Tom O'Higgins's own history played a part in forming his judgment when addressing the

Nicky Kelly case; no such inference is required when it comes to seeing how his personal beliefs, if not prejudices, influenced his judgment.

To illustrate this one only has to look at his reasoning when delivering the majority verdict against a Supreme Court action taken by Senator David Norris in April 1983. The Senator and gay activist was seeking a declaration that sections of the Offences Against the Person Act, 1861, and of the Criminal Law Amendment Act, 1885, were unconstitutional. The first made male homosexual intercourse punishable by life imprisonment while the second, under which Oscar Wilde was prosecuted, made other forms of homosexual sex between consenting adults in private punishable by up to two years in prison with hard labour.

Norris argued that, as he was not sexually attracted to women, marriage was not open to him. He believed that he had, nevertheless, a right to love and companionship, and that these rights ought to be upheld by the Constitution's guarantees of equality before the law, of privacy and of bodily integrity.

O'Higgins rejected Norris's case on grounds that were overtly religious, but of a type. "From the earliest days, organised religion regarded homosexual conduct, such as sodomy and associated acts, with a deep revulsion as being contrary to the order of nature, a perversion of the biological functions of the sexual organs and an affront both to society and to God," he said.

He cited the preamble to the Constitution as proof that, in adopting it (the Constitution), the Irish people, "so asserting and acknowledging their obligations to our Divine Lord Jesus Christ, were proclaiming a deep religious conviction and faith". Since Jesus, in O'Higgins's view, was against homosexuality, it followed that the Constitution could not protect homosexual acts.

However, Jesus's views on homosexuality are not known as nowhere in the gospels does he make reference to the issue. He did, however, have plenty to say on adultery and extra-marital sex, but O'Higgins did not go on to suggest the law should punish such acts also – the logic of his argument in the Norris case. The inconsistency was recognised in a dissenting judgment by Justice

Niall McCarthy, who argued in more practical, modern terms about the inconsistency in the law on homosexuality.

Such a judgment by the Chief Justice could not even be discussed publicly in 1983, or thereafter. Writing in his "Irishman's Diary" column with *The Irish Times*, shortly after Tom O'Higgins died in 2003, Kevin Myers pointed this out. He said that some years previously he attempted to write a column "attacking O'Higgins's famous defence of the laws against male homosexuality. But I was prevented from doing so on the legal opinion that to criticise a ruling of the Chief Justice as I was doing could be considered contempt of court or libel, with predictable consequences. And that opinion was unquestionably right. So no column."

On the judgment, Myers said that O'Higgins "had not merely uttered it; he had pronounced it *ex cathedra*, and it was essentially immune to non-legal criticism, not merely for the decade that it remained the law in Ireland, but for the ten years succeeding, until its author was dead."

14

FREE NICKY KELLY

A S KELLY'S APPEALS FAILED in the Courts, time after time, interest in his case began to grow "outside". Still, it was hard for supporters to muster any sort of campaign as the appeals meandered through the never-ending, labyrinthine ways of the legal process. There was nothing for it but to wait.

Still, there were some other things going on. In April 1982, for instance, Nicky Kelly initiated a civil action against Ireland, the Attorney General and 18 gardaí he had encountered while in custody.

However, it was what was happening in the political arena which seemed to offer most hope. In January 1982 the Coalition Government fell when the then Minister for Finance, John Bruton, failed to get his budget passed because of a proposed tax on children's shoes. In the general election following, Fianna Fáil, led by Charles Haughey, took office in what was a minority Government. It was heavily dependent on the support of three Workers' Party TDs, but above all the vote of Independent TD Tony Gregory. This vote was secured by Haughey through what became known as "The Gregory Deal". It involved a multi-million pound plan to improve poverty-stricken parts of Dublin's inner city, which made up the greater part of Tony Gregory's constituency. Tony Gregory became the most powerful TD in Dáil Éireann, even more powerful than the Taoiseach, it was said, as Haughey needed Gregory far more that Gregory needed Haughey.

Tony Gregory, who had known Kelly for years, had no doubts about his innocence. Gregory made inquiries of the new Minister for Justice Sean Doherty about the Nicky Kelly case, and got a sympathetic response. Doherty was concerned, particularly following the release of Breathnach and McNally. Doherty also expressed doubts about the Garda investigation leading to the confessions. It gave rise to "a lot of questions", he said. In later conversations with Kelly supporters Doherty would go even further, saying he believed Kelly had been "brutalised" while in custody, and that "convictions should not have their origin in unacceptable police methods". It was the first time a senior political figure, not least a Minister for Justice, had expressed concern about the handling of the case, albeit privately. However, Doherty, felt unable to act on the case as the appeals process was taking place.

Tony Gregory went to see Kelly in Portlaoise in August 1982. He said he would talk further to Doherty, and to the Taoiseach as well, about the case, if the Supreme Court rejected the appeal. He did just that. Haughey gave him the impression that Kelly would soon be free.

But the Government was in deep trouble. An election was called and Fianna Fáil lost. In early December 1982, at one of its last Cabinet meetings before leaving office, the Kelly case was brought up by Doherty. He was advised to get further information before any action would be taken. The Government left office and Kelly stayed in Portlaoise.

Another coalition took control, with Garret FitzGerald as Taoiseach again. The new Minister for Justice was Michael Noonan. At the beginning, at any rate, he was preoccupied with exposing the phone-tapping of journalists Geraldine Kennedy and Bruce Arnold by his predecessor. Where the Kelly case was concerned, Noonan seemed reluctant to do anything for fear it might be seen as a reflection on the judiciary.

The Supreme Court rejection of Kelly's appeal on 29 October 1982 had a liberating effect on Kelly's supporters. A Release Nicky Kelly Committee had been set up earlier in the year. It was made up mainly of young people who had taken a keen interest in the case from a human rights perspective. During the summer they organised protests and pickets outside the Dáil and Department of Justice. Graffiti began to appear on walls and hoardings all over the country. At an earlier stage the group itself was called the "Free Nicky Kelly Committee", but this was changed when some wit adjusted the slogan on a graffiti-laden wall in Blackrock to read "Free Nicky Kelly . . . with every packet of cornflakes", which was soon imitated everywhere.

Amnesty International were also taking a greater interest. On 26 October, three days before Chief Justice O'Higgins gave the Supreme Court judgment, Amnesty expressed concern that Kelly should be imprisoned purely on the basis of a confession extracted after a long period in police custody and that he should still be in prison when two others convicted with him had been released. After the Supreme Court announced it was rejecting the Kelly appeal, Amnesty announced it would be writing to the Government about the case.

The Irish Council for Civil Liberties called for Kelly's release. RTÉ began to sit up and take notice. The *Day by Day* programme on RTÉ Radio One dramatised excerpts from Kelly's trial. This led to a protest from the Knights of Columbanus, who said the broadcast had helped "undermine and belittle the institutions of the state". Within a year those same Knights of Columbanus would be among Kelly's staunchest supporters.

Early in 1983 the Release Committee decided to change its tactic and broaden its appeal. From offices loaned to them, they launched a new campaign seeking the support of people from a wide range of backgrounds. This soon began to pay dividends. By spring they had the open support of leading trade unionists such as Phil Flynn, Matt Merrigan, John Mitchell, Noreen Green, Des Bonass, Michael Brennan and Kevin McConnell. Also publicly supportive of Kelly's release were journalists such as Vincent Browne, John Mulcahy, Eamonn McCann, Paddy Prendeville, Con Houlihan and Des Fennell. Other supporters included Kadar Asmal, lecturer at Trinity College Dublin, Eastern Health Board chief psychiatrist Professor Ivor Browne, artist Robert Ballagh, musicians Christy Moore, Donal Lunny and Keith Donald, as well as author and playwright Ulick O'Connor. Among the clergy his supporters included prominent Catholic priests such as Frs Denis Faul, Donal O'Carroll, Raymond Murray, Des Wilson and Piaras O'Duill.

The Committee prepared an information pack on the case which was distributed in Ireland to the media, politicians and local authority representatives, and abroad to a wide range of human rights groups. The results were good. Soon County Councils in Roscommon, Wicklow, Clare, Tipperary and Longford had passed motions calling for Kelly's release. Abroad support groups were established in the US, Canada, Britain, France, Germany, Holland, Belgium and Australia.

Kelly got an indication of just how active these support groups were when he heard the story of a young Irishman who was arrested for being drunk and disorderly in Greece. When the police heard he was Irish they asked him if he knew Nicky Kelly.

Someone sent him a letter from Bulgaria enclosing a photograph of a "Free Nicky Kelly" poster on a wall in Sofia, the country's capital. He got many similar letters with photographs from Ireland of the various unusual places where the "Free Nicky Kelly" slogan was spelled out, one on Ben Bulben mountain in County Sligo.

Throughout all of this he was kept abreast of what was going on through regular visits from Caoilte Breathnach, brother of Osgur and PRO of the Release Nicky Kelly Committee. Despite the Committee's success in getting widespread support among influential people, nothing seemed to be happening at Government level. They would have to be forced to confront the case, Kelly decided. The time had come for more serious action.

As already explained he had thought about going on hunger strike many times after arriving at Portlaoise in June 1980, and as recently as Hallowe'en 1982 when the Supreme Court rejected his appeal. Each time he was talked out of it. Supporters argued that he should wait and see what would happen at the next stage of the appeals process. That process was exhausted at the end of October.

Then it was said the Haughey Government might be prepared to do something but it had left office before anything happened.

By the early months of 1983 it was clear to Kelly the new Government was not interested in his case and that he believed he could rot in Portlaoise for all it cared.

His options were limited. He could serve out his sentence in silence, hoping Amnesty and the Release Campaign might sway the Government through mustering public opinion. Or he could take action himself, which might galvanise public opinion and force the issue on the Government.

15

SALT AND PERRIER

NICKY KELLY WAS WELL AWARE that the record for the success of hunger strikes is not good, particularly after the H-Block deaths less than two years beforehand. He also knew the Government was unlikely to give in to him. But they might, at least, look at the circumstances of his conviction. Besides, he felt he had to do something active. He had to take control of his situation and not be forever at the mercy of a system that continued to fail him so spectacularly.

On 1 April 1983 he let people know that, as of 1 May, he would be refusing all food. This was greeted with scepticism, which wasn't surprising, as they had heard it all before. He didn't think people believed he would go through with it. What they did not know were the reasons why he had not gone ahead on other occasions.

He asked to see his family. He told them what he planned to do and asked them not to put pressure on him to take food once the hunger strike started. He knew that relatives of the H-Block hunger strikers had come under a lot of pressure to make their sons, brothers or husbands eat. The family agreed to his request.

Not surprisingly, it was an emotional meeting. He had not seen his father or mother since going on the run in December 1978. Much later, he heard that they did not believe he would survive the hunger strike. Leaving the prison after that meeting, his father said to his mother, "He's not coming out of there, except in a box. He'll never beat the blooming system. What kind of country is this?" His father became ill on the way home and hardly spoke a word on the journey. His mother was very upset. "I would write to her regularly during the strike, to reassure her, but she was always a worrier."

A week before the strike was to start he issued a statement explaining what he intended to do and why; it read:

"On the 1st of May I am embarking on a hunger strike to highlight my continued incarceration for something I did not do. Over the last three years I have pursued all legal and judicial channels to gain my rightful freedom, to no avail. Also, continuous efforts of international human rights and civil liberties organisations to gain justice on my behalf being treated with seeming contempt by the authorities have convinced me that I have no option but to take this extreme action to gain my rightful freedom.

"I feel there is a fundamental principle involved in my case, and feel morally obliged to fight this blatant cover-up, denial of human rights and civil liberties. Should the authorities be allowed to substitute honesty and justice with political expediency in my case, they can cover up the activities of the 'Heavy Gang' and the perverse judgment of the non-jury Special Criminal Court. While it's Nicky Kelly today it would be someone else tomorrow, were they to succeed in my case.

"I am sure that all fair-minded and freedom-loving people will understand my position and support me in the struggle that lies ahead in my quest for my rightful freedom. Finally, considering what had been covered up by the duplicity and political expediency in my case, the possibility of my demise being allowed cannot be ruled out. There can be no doubt that there are people in high places who have a vested interest in the truth being prevented from surfacing in this case and they will go to any extreme to prevent this truth from coming out.

"My hope is that there are enough people out there who are interested in honesty and justice and will not accept or allow this cover-up to continue".

On the morning of 1 May Kelly refused breakfast. He asked to see the prison Governor and informed him what he proposed to do. Then he was brought back to his cell and locked in. Over the previous few days he had psyched himself up for this moment and was resolved he would go all the way, to death if necessary.

About an hour after he was confined to his cell a hot meal was left in, one such as he had never seen before in Portlaoise. Bacon, eggs, sausages, served on a tray, hotel-style, with orange juice. "A pleasure not just to smell but even to look at. It proved to me that when they really wanted to prepare food properly in Portlaoise they could do so."

The breakfast lay there on the locker beside his bed, filling the cell with its smells for the next two to three hours, when it was replaced by another inviting dish – a hot lunch of roast beef, potatoes, vegetables and tea, which was served as stylishly as its morning predecessor.

This would be the pattern while he was on hunger strike at Portlaoise. Every carefully prepared meal was left there until it was replaced by an equally well-prepared one at the next meal time. The cell was never without food, and good food at that. "Most of what we were given to eat ordinarily was barely edible and rarely well prepared," he recalls. He was also given bottles of Perrier water, which he drank constantly, with regular pinches of salt. As someone who liked food, he did not find fasting easy.

It was a hard battle, and the temptation to eat remained great. But he reminded himself constantly of just how important the exercise was, for himself and maybe for others. The strike quickly became, for him, a one-man moral crusade to expose what he felt was the rottenness in the system.

He was kept isolated in his cell for 23 hours a day. When the other prisoners were locked up in the evenings, he was let into the yard to exercise for an hour. That would be one of the few reference points in his day. Another was the arrival of the Governor or his assistant every morning to check whether he planned to continue. This was usually followed by a visit from the prison doctor, who would examine him briefly.

Within two or three days he began to develop pains in his stomach. He was cold all the time, and his joints began to get sore and stiff. His stomach rumbled loudly, so much so he thought his body was eating itself, which it would begin to do later. Asleep, he dreamt of food – "great big American pancakes with loads of golden syrup".

After a week he was feeling weak, but continued to go for exercise in the yard until the eleventh day. By then he wasn't able to do so. He would spend subsequent days lying or sitting on his bed in the cell. By then, too, the authorities had stopped Caoilte Breathnach from going to see him. Tony Gregory tried to visit him on the fourteenth day but was refused permission by the Department of Justice, as was the former Minister for Justice, Sean Doherty.

He had no access to newspapers, TV or radio. There were just the visits from his sisters to keep him in contact with the world. For a while his fellow prisoners were able to shout bits and pieces of information to him through the "Judas hole" in his cell door, but they were stopped when a guard was stationed outside.

It was clear the authorities hoped that isolation would break his spirit. He believed the only reason they allowed his sisters continue to visit him was because they felt the girls would put pressure on him to stop. After two weeks he was feeling very weak and his headaches were becoming severe.

The hours dragged by as he lay there, thinking about the crazy situation in which he was and wondering when or how or if it would end. Fish and chips replaced American pancakes as his favourite food obsession. Even though he had trained himself to suppress thoughts of food while awake, he could not control his dreams. Even when awake he often found himself unconsciously eyeing the latest meal left into the cell.

Coldness was permanent by then, particularly after taking water. He began to get sick, and would vomit after drinking. This vomiting became more and more regular, and he could feel himself deteriorate physically. Strangely though, as this happened his mind seemed to become more lucid and alert.

The pain in his joints got worse. His sleeping pattern was disrupted, so that he would sleep at any hour of the day, or be awake for long periods at night, and the isolation would get to him.

જ઼   જ઼   જ઼

MEANWHILE THE RELEASE CAMPAIGN was busy lobbying support outside, putting up posters, issuing statements, organising public meetings, and mounting pickets on various Government buildings. Pickets were mounted on Irish state and semi-state offices abroad. There were pickets on Bord Fáilte offices in London, Glasgow, Brussels, Paris and outside the UN in New York. Aer Lingus offices in Frankfurt and Copenhagen were also picketed, as well as Irish embassies or consular offices in The Hague, Washington, Montreal, Vancouver and Toronto. A 48-hour fast took place in San Francisco.

A Free Nicky Kelly Committee was set up in the US, and included in its membership people like Fr Daniel Berrigan, former US Attorney General Ramsey Clarke, as well as Fr Sean McManus of The Irish National Caucus.

On Sunday, 22 May, Taoiseach Garret FitzGerald was heckled by members of the Release Committee as he opened a community week at Sandymount in Dublin. Three of the hecklers were arrested and brought to court the next day. They were fined £2 each and bound to the peace for a year.

The Irish Council for Civil Liberties were also active, and politicians such as then Senators Michael D. Higgins (Labour), Brendan Ryan (Independent), Paschal Mooney (Fianna Fáil). Dublin Fianna Fáil MEP Niall Andrews publicly expressed concern about the Kelly case.

Behind the scenes the Catholic bishops Irish Commission for Justice and Peace (ICJP) had also become involved. This body, chaired by the Auxiliary Bishop of Dublin, Dr Dermot O'Mahony, and which also included his colleague and fellow Dublin Auxiliary Bishop, Dr James Kavanagh, was set up in the early 1970s and had made serious attempts to negotiate an end to the H-Block hunger strikes. They attempted to do something similar in Kelly's case, particularly as the Department of Justice was suspicious of members of the Release Committee.

During the third week of the hunger strike 62 solicitors – the figure would rise later to 150 – in the Dublin area signed a petition calling on the Michael Noonan to release Kelly, as justice had not been seen to be done in his case.

The following day Minister Noonan told political correspondents that he could not intervene. To do so would be a snub to the courts, he implied. If anyone came forward with new evidence, then that might allow for a reconsideration of the case, he said. He called on Kelly to end the hunger strike. Indications were, he said, that if Kelly were to do so at that time there would be no permanent damage done to his health.

In response the Release Committee issued a statement saying that by ignoring the facts surrounding Kelly's arrest and detention Michael Noonan was effectively sentencing Kelly to death.

Later, on RTÉ's *Day by Day* radio programme, Noonan expanded on his reasons for refusing to act in the case, during a discussion with programme presenter John Bowman. "First of all", he said, for "a Minister to intervene and release Nicky Kelly would be acting beyond his powers. He would also be saying, . . . either directly or by implication that the seven at least of the principal judges in this country acted incorrectly or incompetently or both. And thirdly, he would he saying that 15 or16 members of the Garda Síochána had gone into the witness box and had committed perjury if he was to imply that what Nicky Kelly said was the truth and what the Garda Síochána said was not the truth. And that is the crunch issue which is referred to in the Supreme Court judgment when they say that there is a clear conflict of evidence and that the court had to decide where the truth lay."

On 27 May Kelly was moved from Portlaoise to the Curragh military hospital. He was very weak by then and was carried by stretcher to an ambulance, while handcuffed to a prison officer. They travelled under a maximum security garda and army escort to the Curragh. There he was brought to what looked like "a big, run-down Victorian-type dormitory", a grey and bleak place where they had set up what was a make-shift cage at one end. Kelly recalled that it looked like a rabbit hutch cobbled together by a bad carpenter. This was surrounded by lines of sand bags, piled on top of one another, and about half a dozen armed soldiers. Inside the cage was a bed.

He was now barely able to move. The hunger pangs were so great he forgot all the other pains. He often had stomach cramps and his headaches were as bad as ever. His sight was beginning to go. At times his vision would disappear entirely. He had to make a deliberate effort to focus his mind on anything. Soon it would begin to drift in and out of consciousness. "There were a couple of times when I thought I had died. I would be lying there alert and conscious, the next minute I would have drifted away and then I was back again. This was so confusing that there were times when I wasn't certain whether I was awake or asleep, alive or dead."

The hardest part was seeing the reaction of others when they saw him, particularly his sisters. The shock on their faces was all too obvious.

The Catholic bishops' ICJP was now playing a central role between his side and the Department of Justice. They had established contact with both, and negotiations were going on. They asked the Committee what the bottom line was. "Release," they were told and conveyed this to the Department, who said it was just not on.

It ended there. The Department refused to negotiate further and stopped all meetings with the ICJP. Officials said there would be no concessions as long as the hunger strike continued and that this needed to be brought home directly to Kelly.

On 3 June 1983, Jose Zalaquett, secretary general of Amnesty, wrote directly to Michael Noonan expressing deep concern about the case and its conduct. He asked for immediate action on it. The Minister had already refused to meet Zalaquett, who would later comment that his dealings with the Irish Government at the time were only equalled by his experiences with the authorities in Chile and South Africa.

The hunger strike was now receiving a lot of attention internationally. Pickets were mounted again on Irish offices in the US and Canada. While President Hillery was on a state visit to Denmark, two Members of Parliament presented him with a letter calling for Kelly's release. The Minister for Foreign Affairs, Peter Barry, who accompanied President Hillery, was furious. He complained to the parliamentarians that they were interfering in Ireland's internal affairs.

Ramsey Clark of the US Free Nicky Kelly Committee went further with such "interference". While on a visit to Ireland he called to see Kelly accompanied by Jose Zalaquett of Amnesty.

Kelly's sister Breda had called to the Papal Nuncio, Archbishop Gaetano Alibrandi, at his residence in the Phoenix Park to see what he could do to help. He told her he believed in her brother's innocence but he did not want to go public on the matter. He did, however, write to Michael Noonan and received the standard reply that it was "being brought to the Minister's attention". He then sought a meeting with the Minister, but was refused. Archbishop Alibrandi later told Kelly's mother he felt he was treated by Noonan and his Department "like a meddling old man who should mind his own business".

Breda was now visiting her brother as often as twice a day and kept him informed about what was happening outside. She also liaised for him with the Release Committee. She usually brought in pen and paper in case Kelly might want to send messages.

Everyone was trying to buy more time. Kelly was looking for concrete answers and they were not coming quick enough.

Other groups began to come out in support of him – journalists, members of the Catholic hierarchy, Fr Sean Healy of the Conference of Major Religious Superiors (now CORI), the Knights of Columbanus, as well as old stalwarts Christy Moore, Donal Lunny, and Keith Donald from the music world, and people from the arts world. Lawyers and politicians became more vocal.

Channel 4 TV arrived to make a documentary about the case, which would later be transmitted as *Open Those Gates*. Marches took place around the country and Release Nicky Kelly concerts were performed, some outside the walls of the prison itself.

Breda brought him a silk dressing gown. His skin had become so thin against the bone that it seemed the rough army blankets would tear his shoulders, elbows and knees. Despite all this, but true to her word and in line with his earlier request, she never put pressure on him to take food, though he could see she was finding his decline hard to take.

ON 1 JUNE THE ICJP issued a statement suggesting Kelly take his case to the European Commission and Court of Human Rights. They also suggested Noonan should re-examine his position on the case, particularly in the light of conditions in the country during the mid 1970s. The proposal that Kelly take the case to Europe was further explored between members of the Release Committee and the ICJP. It seemed Kelly would have had to make such an application within six months of exhausting all local legal avenues, which meant 29 April 1983. However the ICJP said he could apply at any time as long as there was a "continuing disability". Solicitor Garret Sheehan began the preparations for taking the case to Europe. Senior counsel and then Senator Mary Robinson and Kevin Boyle, Professor of Law at University College Galway (now NUIG), agreed to act for him.

The army chaplain at the Curragh was getting on Kelly's nerves. "Every day it'd be the same thing: 'You're killing yourself . . . this is suicide . . . you must stop it now . . . give it up, give it up, give it up.'" Kelly asked for him to be removed, and he was.

Another visitor in those critical early June days was his old friend from Philadelphia, Jack McKinney. He had written about the case again in the *Philadelphia Daily News* when the hunger strike began and had been following it closely. He became aware the Government was having problems finding mediators who Kelly would trust and who did not compromise them.

McKinney's family originally came from Donegal and he was related distantly to former Fine Gael TD Paddy Harte. He made contact with Harte and offered his services if they were needed. It was suggested they might be, and McKinney came to Dublin two days later. He met Michael Noonan twice, who offered Kelly full remission on his sentence and asked McKinney to advise him to come off the hunger strike. McKinney said he would convey the offer but would not try to influence Kelly one way or the other on the hunger strike. It was not his place to do so, he said. When he went to see Kelly at the Curragh he told him what was on offer, and was fairly blunt in his reading of the Government's determination to hold out. And that was that. Kelly refused to accept the offer or to end the hunger strike.

He and McKinney talked about what was happening in the US, and McKinney left later in a grim mood. Jack McKinney had covered eight of the ten H-Block hunger striker deaths in 1981, and Kelly heard later that his prognosis for his own survival was not great. He returned to America the following day.

A day or two later a priest in Limerick rang Caoilte Breathnach saying Michael Noonan wanted to talk to him, and gave a phone number. It turned out to be Noonan's office. Breathnach told an official he would only meet Noonan if accompanied by another member of the Release Committee. The official rang him back later to say he wanted to speak to him, and asked whether he would go down to the Curragh to see Kelly. He said he would, but that there was no question of him asking Kelly to give up the hunger strike. This was the first time Breathnach had been allowed to visit Kelly since 10 May.

He and solicitor Garret Sheehan both went to see Kelly on 4 June. Kelly recalls how shocked they looked at his condition. He was then propped up in bed with pillows; his skin was grey and his weight was down to six and a half stone. He was having blackouts, and when not in bed sat in a wheelchair.

Seeing their reaction, Kelly asked for a mirror. He remembers looking gaunt, his eyes sunken, the skin transparent. He put away the mirror. They told him about the ICJP European Human Rights proposal and outlined what was involved. He asked for time to think about it. Next day they went to see him again and he gave them the go-ahead, arguing that if necessary the case should go ahead posthumously. The hunger strike would go on.

Pat McCartan had already been to see him. Kelly had asked for him to be allowed visit again for what he believed would be their last meeting. He wanted to make his will and say goodbye.

It was the evening of 7 June. Again, Kelly could tell from the look on McCartan's face how shocked he was too. By then Kelly was not able to get out of bed, and was being given a saline solution intravenously. But he was lucid. McCartan tried to talk him out of continuing the strike. Caoilte Breathnach was with him. Both explained to Kelly the great support there was, both in Ireland and internationally, for his release. The Catholic Primate, Cardinal Tomás Ó Fiaich, who had taken an interest in the case for some time by then, had let some of the Release Committee members know that Kelly's release was likely following a cooling off period of a few months.

They also gave him details of the general content of a Government statement to be issued later that evening, which would point out there was still a further legal avenue to be explored in his case – namely the civil action against gardaí, the Attorney General and Ireland. The statement would point out there was nothing to prevent Kelly from pursuing such an action if he wished to do so and, as he was in custody, the case would get priority. A favourable outcome in such an action, which would take place before a jury – the first time his case would be heard before a jury – "could be adduced as being relevant, even if only indirectly, to his imprisonment," it said.

Kelly was unsure. They talked and talked. McCartan bluntly told him he would not survive much longer and asked what use would be the campaign, further court actions, and the efforts of so many people then. All that would happen is that the authorities would win out, he said. Kelly would be "a dead problem", soon forgotten. McCartan also talked about old times, going to dances in Arklow and Courtown, that sort of thing. The conversation between the three had become very emotional. Kelly knew he was dying but he could not put his faith in further law. Then he thought about the breadth and depth of support from all those people at home and abroad. He became convinced, eventually, to call it off.

Shortly before 9.00 pm, Kelly whispered to Caoilte Breathnach, "I'll come off." Not surprisingly, in such an already highly emotional situation, all three men broke down and wept. "All I could do was cry. I just couldn't stop. I had been so psyched up. But I told them I would go back on hunger strike again if things didn't work out," Kelly remembers. He was as determined as ever not to serve out the sentence. "I'd prefer to be dead," he said at the time.

Army doctors gave him a glucose sweet to suck. They were as indifferent as usual. Every day he had been examined by them and was made to feel more a prisoner of war than a human being. However, the attitude became more compassionate when he began to take food again. He could take very little at first and had severe stomach cramps for some time after doing so.

Both Caoilte Breathnach and Pat McCartan were anxious to get the news out that he had ended his hunger strike before the authorities heard it and put their own gloss on what had happened. A statement was prepared fast and Breathnach was ringing it through to the media from a phone at the Curragh when a prison officer, worried that he should not be allowing that sort of carry-on, stopped him.

They left the Curragh and drove to the home of Nancy Moore (Christy's mother) in Newbridge. From there they rang the statement through to the media. Details of the Government statement were carried on RTÉ's 9.00 News that night. On the civil action, it said, "it is not the responsibility of the Government or the Minister for Justice if no such proceedings were instituted". The statement was openly inviting an action against the State by Kelly, which it indicated would be looked on benignly by the Government.

"Was this a device to release me and get everyone off the hook at the same time?" Kelly wondered at the time. It was nothing of the sort, of course. Later this "invitation" would be described by one of the country's most eminent lawyers as "a most dishonest document". But that was some time away still.

ço   ço   ço

THAT NIGHT IN LEINSTER HOUSE, there took place one of the most bizarre conversations concerning Kelly's case, but which was in itself revealing. Tony Gregory was eating in the Dáil restaurant when Michael Noonan came "bounding" over to him. So anxious was the Minister to talk he knocked over a chair in his way. He was "euphoric", according to Gregory. What made this encounter even stranger is that the deputy and Minister had never spoken to each other before, outside exchanges in the Dáil chamber. Indeed, they had passed one another on Dáil corridors without as much as a nod in acknowledgement. Now here was the Minister, desperate to talk. That was surprising enough, but what he had to say was extraordinary.

He wanted to know if Tony Gregory had heard anything about the so called "big bang" which had been threatened if Kelly died. "What do you mean?" Tony Gregory asked him. Noonan explained that he had been told there were plans to assassinate him if Kelly died. Gregory was incredulous. He pointed out that there had not been so much as an assassination threat, never mind any attempt of the kind, on a Government Minister in the State since 1927, when then Minister for Justice Kevin O'Higgins – uncle of Chief Justice Tom O'Higgins – had been assassinated. He was also amazed the Minister should presume he would have any knowledge of such a plan in the first place.

Noonan had presumed that because Tony Gregory had once been a member of the IRSP he would therefore know all about such a possibility in Kelly's case. Then an old, familiar, almost forgotten explanation began to emerge.

The information about the so-called Noonan assassination plan had come from "garda sources" who had kindly conveyed it to the Minister – probably those self-same unexplained "sources' which had led to Kelly's incarceration in the first place. No doubt such "information" strengthened the Minister's and the Government's resolve in dealing with Kelly's hunger strike. He could have died as a result. He almost did.

16

THE ROAD TO SHELTON ABBEY

NOT SURPRISINGLY, KELLY WAS in a bad way physically after the hunger strike. Among the first to see him on 8 June 1983, the day after he began to take food again, were barrister Tony Sammon and solicitor Greg O'Neill, who were to prepare his case against the State. He had not met Greg O'Neill before and many years later O'Neill would write the following about that visit:

"My first experience of seeing Nicky Kelly was of a frail, dying man being helped into a wheelchair padded with pillows and wheeled to a hatch in a cage constructed inside a military hospital ward – rather like a gigantic bird cage or something which some dangerous wild animal might have been housed in a Victorian zoo.

"This cage was located in a room at the end of a corridor in a hospital in the middle of a compound in the middle of the largest military barracks and camp in the country with thousands of soldiers in the immediate vicinity. The corridor leading to the room was policed by up to 20 armed soldiers, stationed behind no fewer than four sandbagged machine gun emplacements. The building itself was ringed by four circuits of rolled barbed wire, patrolled by half a dozen soldiers with guns at the ready, a military personnel carrier and an armoured car.

"The paranoia of these security arrangements was shocking and revealing. The United States Marine Corps could not have rescued Nicky Kelly without incurring enormous loss of life.

"I became satisfied very shortly that these security arrangements, paranoid as they were, told me more about the mindset of the authorities of the day, rather than that of Nicky Kelly, and were in place, not in any real sense to deter any foolhardy rescue attempt, but were there to give emphasis to the lie that Kelly was a dangerous terrorist despite the fact that he was so weak from his hunger strike that he had to be lifted and carried and that, had his hunger strike continued for even a few days more, he would undoubtedly have died.

"In that regard the vision of Nicky Kelly in a cage has stuck in my mind with the vividness of a recollection from yesterday. In a very real sense Nicky Kelly's imprisonment was there to justify a lie. The truth about what happened could, not in any circumstances, be released. Nicky was a prisoner of that, but in a very real sense, truth, as much as Nicky Kelly, was a prisoner in that cell."

Within a few days of his ending the hunger strike Kelly was able to eat light bland foods. His strength began to return and his sight improved. The cramps had eased a bit by then too, but already there were fears that part of his oesophagus may have been permanently damaged – and it was. His body had begun to eat itself before the hunger strike ended.

He was kept at the Curragh military hospital until he was strong enough to leave. Within a month he was back in Portlaoise prison, but it was about six months before he felt strong in himself again. By then too he had got into a fitness routine and was running many miles every day, whether on the spot or in the yard. Running gave him something to do. As a result, he would soon be fitter than ever before in his life.

He had initiated a civil action case against the State as far back as April 1977 and this was renewed again in April 1982, but it had not been progressed beyond that. Greg O'Neill and Tony Sammon set about preparing the case. Paul Carney senior counsel and Barry White (both now judges at the Central Criminal Court) would also be involved. Meanwhile solicitor Garret Sheehan was processing the case at European level, with Mary Robinson and Kevin Boyle.

On 27 July 1983 the civil action was lodged against the Attorney General and Ireland. It was felt it might proceed at a faster pace, towards both Kelly's freedom and exoneration, if the gardaí named in the original statement of claim were left out, to be dealt with in a later action.

Greg O'Neill also decided to investigate petitioning the Minister for Justice for clemency. Kelly was not at all keen on this latter option. To him it suggested the sort of conditional release he did not want. What he did want was his good name back and an acknowledgement that he had been ill-treated in custody and forced to sign a false confession. Officials at the Department of Justice informed Greg O'Neill that Kelly could petition in the normal way open to all convicted prisoners, and that such a petition would receive due consideration.

The State failed to enter a defence against his civil action within the required time. Kelly's legal team moved for judgment in default. On 24 October both sides agreed to waive this motion, when the State promised to enter a defence within two weeks. Again it failed to do so.

The pattern was becoming familiar – a reminder of the State's carry-on following those first charges in 1976. Again Kelly's legal team entered a motion for judgment in default. Again they agreed to waive this when the State agreed to enter a defence within four days. By then they were confident the State did not have the will to fight. They were in for a surprise.

In the meantime, there was an odd tussle with the Department of Justice, which should have been a warning. Greg O'Neill had arranged for Kelly to see an ear specialist at the Eye and Ear Hospital in Dublin on 11 November, as part of the preparation for his civil action. O'Neill had to write to the Department of Justice to arrange this. There was no response, and the appointment had to be cancelled. A letter dated 1 November, but postmarked 15 November, arrived from the Department saying Kelly would be taken to the hospital if he gave an undertaking to pay within two weeks for the cost of the security involved in bringing him there.

Considering that he had been in Portlaoise for three and a half years by then, this was a tall order. O'Neill wrote the Department a stiff letter pointing out that the stance they were taking amounted in essence to an obstruction of Kelly's rights of access to the Courts. The Department replied that it only paid the costs of such medical examinations and of the security involved when prison doctors recommended specialist examination, but that they would waive payment of whatever costs might be incurred in this instance – estimated at being between £800 and £1,200 – until after the civil action had taken place. By the end of January 1984 that too was waived and no mention of payment was made again. However, the wrangle had delayed Kelly's action, which may have been its purpose. Things were getting more and more bizarre.

On 31 October 1983, John Fitzpatrick – who had also confessed to being involved in the mail train robbery after interrogation – attended a press conference organised by the Release Committee. Fitzpatrick had lived quietly in Dublin for almost seven years, after "disappearing" in December 1976. His appearance at that October 1983 press conference was his first in public since 9 December 1976. He told the press conference he had signed his confession about taking part in the mail train robbery after being beaten and brutalised. Like Kelly, Breathnach and Brian McNally, the confession was the only evidence against him. Plunkett did not sign a confession.

Though John Fitzpatrick had signed that confession admitting his involvement in the robbery, he had a rock solid alibi. He was in Limerick that night and there were witnesses to prove it.

The DPP had considered not charging him but was persuaded by the senior gardaí at the meeting in December 1976 (at which senior gardaí had insisted on the men's guilt) that it could have been possible for Fitzpatrick to drive up from Limerick to take part in the mail train robbery, and to drive back to Limerick again that morning before anyone noticed. The DPP remained sceptical but decided to leave it to the courts to sort out.

The gardaí had other concerns where Fitzpatrick was concerned. He was named as one of those involved in the robbery in Kelly's "confession". It raised pertinent questions. For instance, how could it happen that Kelly in his "confession" had named someone as involved in the robbery who wasn't there? And, if

Kelly had named one man wrongly, what about the others? Was Kelly there at all?

Of course, this never came up in court, as John Fitzpatrick was not found by the gardaí when the DPP instructed his re-arrest, though he had been in Dublin throughout most of the intervening seven-year period before the October 1983 press conference.

It was while Nicky Kelly was on hunger strike that Fitzpatrick decided to set about publicly highlighting inconsistencies in the case.

Following that October 1983 press conference the DPP Eamonn Barnes asked to see relevant gardaí about the issue. They arrived at his office led by Inspector/Superintendent A. They said they wanted Fitzpatrick arrested and tried in connection with the mail train robbery. The DPP was not so sure. The following day, he decided charges against Fitzpatrick would not be pursued. There was no announcement about this. It was let slip away, quietly.

The Release Committee meanwhile argued that Fitzpatrick's appearance and what he had to say constituted new evidence of the sort Michael Noonan talked about in the early days of Kelly's hunger strike.

Tony Gregory put down a special notice question on the matter in the Dáil, but it was disallowed as not being urgent. Later it was taken on the ordinary list of Ministerial questions. Noonan disagreed that either Fitzpatrick or what he had to say constituted new evidence. The lawyers at the trial would have been well aware of all those details, he insisted. It ignored the fact that because Fitzpatrick was not before the Court, as he could not be found by the gardaí, evidence concerning him could not be used.

The Release Committee picketed Portlaoise prison, the Department of Justice, the home of Taoiseach Garret FitzGerald and the Minister for Justice's home in Limerick. Tony Gregory went on a two-week speaking tour of the US dealing with the Kelly case.

Earlier, at the end of October 1983, Greg O'Neill and Tony Sammon finalised Kelly's petition to the Minister for clemency on the basis of "the nature and circumstances of the case". It was submitted on 1 November, with two medical reports. Dr Sean Ó

Cleirigh recommended Kelly be examined by a specialist as he complained of sore eyes and blurred vision. He found Kelly had difficulty moving his head, hips and knees, and suggested this could lead to arthritis later on.

Kelly had complained about deafness in the left ear and numbness on that side of the face, as well as suffering from vertigo and dizzy spells. Dr Ó Cleirigh reported that Kelly complained of nervousness, a lack of self-confidence, anxiety, lethargy, an inability to sleep, severe headaches and generally what he described as "stress" – all of which, he felt, was exacerbated and perpetuated by "the continuing and unique circumstances" of Kelly's imprisonment.

The psychiatrist Professor Robert Daly of UCC, in his report, concluded that Kelly suffered from post-traumatic stress disorder, as the Professor had also done in June 1980. Examining Kelly in June 1983, after the hunger strike, he concluded this condition resulted from severe emotional stress and manifested itself as a depressed mood or as feelings of hopelessness and pessimism. He felt this affected Kelly's perception and judgement, and meant he showed little interest in caring for himself, and was probably one reason why he had embarked on such a damaging hunger strike to begin with.

The petition was received in silence by the Department. There would be a long wait for a response.

WHILE ALL THIS WAS GOING ON Kelly's mother and his sister Breda had been to Rome to see the Pope. Breda had remained in touch with the Papal Nuncio, Archbishop Alibrandi, and as the months passed following the hunger strike with still no immediate prospect of Kelly's release, the Nuncio wrote to Michael Noonan again.

Again he got the standard reply. So he was pretty fed up when Breda met him some days later. "Would you like to see John Paul?" he asked her. At first she thought he was talking about some TD she must have overlooked.

"Who?" she asked.

"His Holiness," he replied. He was planning to visit the Pope the following Wednesday and would arrange it, he said. He would also write – requesting an audience – to the Pope's personal secretary, Monsignor John Magee (now Bishop of Cloyne), who had intervened in the H-Block hunger strikes.

The audience was arranged for 14 December 1983. Funds were raised through friends. Kelly's mother, Stella, and Breda set off. By co-incidence, Archbishop Alibrandi was on the same flight to Rome, on his way home to Sicily for a break. He introduced both of them to the pilot and asked for permission to distribute the "Release Nicky Kelly" leaflet. It was granted and the leaflets were handed out to other passengers on the plane.

On arrival in Rome, and having said their goodbyes to Archbishop Alibrandi, the two women set off for the Hotel Canada on the Via Vicenza, near the Vatican. The following morning they met Monsignor Magee at his quarters, where he explained the protocol for their meeting with the Pope, which would take place the following day.

Monsignor Magee also offered them a choice of interpreters who would speak in Polish to the Pope for them. They were surprised how much Monsignor Magee and the interpreters knew about the case. Monsignor Magee encouraged Mrs Kelly "to keep up heart".

The following morning, there was a huge crowd of people gathered already in the very large room where they were brought when they arrived at the Vatican. Soon the Pope and his entourage of cardinals made their way down the middle of the crowd. Mrs Kelly and Breda were brought to the front, where they held up a photograph of Nicky and a Celtic cross he had made in Portlaoise. The Pope stopped before them. Breda explained about the case and the hunger strike. A bishop alongside filled the Pope in on details of the case. Mrs Kelly was so nervous she could hardly speak; indeed, she didn't say a single word to the Pope. It was Breda who did all the talking.

The Pope listened without question, then he asked how Nicky was and how he was coping. They told him. They presented him with the Celtic cross and explained that Nicky had made it in prison. Pope John Paul accepted it and an aide took it away. Breda then gave the Pope three addresses at which he might contact Michael Noonan: the Minister's home in Limerick; where he stayed when in Dublin; and his office in Dublin. She asked whether he would write to the Minister about the case. The Pope said he would. Then he blessed them and moved along the crowd. They returned to Ireland the following Sunday.

A few months later Mrs Kelly heard that Michael Noonan would be visiting Shelton Abbey, near Arklow. Her husband had worked there many years before it had been converted into an open prison. She went there, introduced herself to the Minister, and asked for a word with him. He got into his car quickly, and said, "I'll see you in my office . . ." But contacting him at his office proved impossible for either the Kelly family or supporters. It had been easier to meet the Pope.

ON 16 DECEMBER 1983, two days after Breda and Mrs Kelly had met the Pope, the State entered a defence against the civil action they had implicitly invited Nicky Kelly to take. It denied that he had been beaten up by gardaí.

But Christmas was coming and the postbag was getting fat. By now he was getting letters of support from all over the world. He tried to reply to each of them, using the same formula of 25 to 30 words, but it was a full-time and often impossible job. That Christmas he estimated he must have received up to 1,000 cards from supporters, which was embarrassing in a place where some prisoners received no correspondence at all.

Some of the letters were strange, such as those from people asking him to pray for them, some with terminal illnesses who believed Kelly was some sort of holy martyr. He was even enrolled as an honorary member in an American group called "The Blue Army", which existed to pray for the conversion of Russia. Other people sent him scapulars, relics and medals.

Christmas Midnight Mass that year was broadcast on RTÉ radio from Sean MacDermott Street in Dublin, with Fr Mick Casey as celebrant. In his sermon he compared Kelly's persecution with that of another 33-year -old, Jesus Christ, 2,000 years before. Nuns and priests everywhere wrote to Kelly.

On the more secular side, there was a lot of support too. Actor Jane Fonda and her then husband Tom Hayden wrote to Kelly; as did Nobel Prize-winning German author Heinrich Böll, who had a house on Achill Island; and author Isabel Allende, niece of the murdered President of Chile, Salvadore Allende.

Kelly was elected an honorary member of various law faculties/ societies in universities throughout the US, and vice-president of UCC Law Society. Zimbabwe's Prime Minister Robert Mugabe visited Ireland during this period and was asked at a press conference whether he would be taking up the matter of Kelly's release with the Government. He said he was not aware of the case, but some time later one of his Ministers wrote to Kelly expressing solidarity.

Meanwhile concerts and marches organised by the Release Committee seemed to go from strength to strength. There had been a lull in activity after the hunger strike, with people believing some sort of release deal had been done with the Government. But when it became clear that was not the case, activity was renewed with even greater vigour and imagination than before.

An Post marked its arrival as a semi-state body on 1 January 1984 with a special penny stamp. Members of the Release Committee used the opportunity to post over 750 letters lobbying support for the case. They wrote to every bishop in the country, as well as trade unionists and members of the Labour and Fianna Fáil parties. As a result, Bishop James Kavanagh, Auxiliary Bishop of Dublin, went public on his concerns about the case, the first Catholic Bishop to do so. Others had been acting behind the scenes.

An example of unusual support from the economic sphere came when Texan millionaire "Big Jim" Delaney, then interested in developing a major site on the Boyne, announced a halt to any investment in Ireland as long as Kelly was in jail.

The group Moving Hearts released a Mick Hanly song about the Kelly case titled "Open Those Gates" and Christy Moore released "The Wicklow Boy", the words of which he and Nicky Kelly had worked on together over many months. Both songs were banned on RTÉ. In live performances Moore sang a much-expanded version of the song.

DESPITE ALL THIS ATTENTION and interest the Government remained unmoved – though not quite. It had, after all, decided at a cabinet meeting in December 1983 to stop Kelly's civil action. The difficulty was in finding a way to do so. But one was found – the infamous 1980 Lord Denning "appalling vista" judgment delivered in the Birmingham Six case and upheld by the House of Lords in 1981.

Lord Denning had concluded that the issue of whether the Birmingham Six had been beaten in custody had already been decided in the Criminal Court, and that a successful civil action by them would suggest "the police were guilty of perjury, that they were guilty of violence and threats". He considered this such "an appalling vista" that their civil action could not be allowed.

It was May 1984 before Kelly became aware that the Denning judgment was to be used to stop his civil action in this State. That month there was a preliminary hearing of the case in the High Court before Justice Liam Hamilton, who had presided at the Special Criminal Court hearing which allowed admission of Kelly's confession as evidence.

The State legal team argued that the case should not go ahead as it had already been heard at the Special Criminal Court and all relevant issues had been decided there. They pointed to the higher level of proof required in criminal cases where the issue must be beyond reasonable doubt, whereas in a civil case it must be proven on the balance of probabilities. As Kelly's case had already been proved beyond reasonable doubt it was therefore "estopped" from being heard again, they argued. Kelly's defence team countered that the State should not be allowed make such an argument as it had itself invited Kelly to take the civil action. Justice Hamilton decided the issue would have to be decided by the High Court, without a jury. And so the Kelly team were off on the legal merry-go-round again.

It was also in May 1984 that Kelly first that heard his case to the European Court of Human Rights had been ruled out of order, as it had not been lodged within a six-month period after the Supreme Court judgment made against him on 29 October, 1982. It would not accept legal arguments by his lawyers that his mental state made it impossible for him to lodge such a case within the required six-month period. He was up against yet another legal wall. It was familiar and depressing territory.

He considered going on hunger strike again but was advised that this time he would not survive very long. By then he regretted coming off the hunger strike at all. He felt cheated and tricked. It was probably his darkest hour.

WHILE ON THE LEGAL FRONT things were again in familiar terrain, the Release Campaign was going well. At its annual conference in April 1983 the Labour party passed a strongly worded motion calling for Kelly's release.

Weeks later, during the Fianna Fáil Ard Fheis, as the party leader Charles Haughey rose to give his address on live television, Siobhan Troddyn of the Release Committee tried to confront him, calling for Kelly's release. She got halfway across the platform towards Haughey before security men succeeded in removing her.

Tony Gregory met Haughey later, along with members of the Release Committee. Haughey told them his Garda contacts said Kelly was guilty, but he added that he "understood things could happen in a police station". He wanted to be sure before committing Fianna Fáil on the issue. A second meeting was arranged, which took place before the Dáil summer recess. Whatever Haughey planned to do, if anything, remained unclear.

In the background to all of this was the Fr Niall O'Brien case. Fr O'Brien, who was from Dublin, and an Australian priest Fr

Brian Gore were being held for trial on what most believed was a trumped-up murder charge by the authorities in a small Philippine town. Six local people were being charged along with them. The Irish Government was very active on the issue and campaigned widely for their release. The Philippine Government said it was an internal matter and refused to meet representatives of Amnesty International in connection with the case. Familiar?

Kelly wrote to the newspapers highlighting the parallels between his case and that of Fr O'Brien, and the extraordinary hypocrisy of the Irish Government in its differing approach to each. In *Magill* magazine journalist Gene Kerrigan wrote about his own efforts to contact Nicky Kelly and Fr O'Brien by phone. He had no problems getting through to Fr O'Brien in the Philippines and talked to him at length. He was refused permission by the Irish authorities to speak to Kelly.

Fr O'Brien was eventually released, as were the others held with him, thanks mainly to political pressure. He arrived home to a hero's welcome on 14 July 1984, and was given a civic reception at the Mansion House in Dublin.

BEHIND THE SCENES the Minister for Justice Michael Noonan was making discreet inquiries. After Kelly's clemency petition was lodged with the Department of Justice, the medical reports were sent to the doctor at Portlaoise for examination. Kelly was not aware of this but he was asked if he would agree to be examined by a psychiatrist nominated by the Department. He referred the query to his solicitor Greg O'Neill, and the matter never went any further.

Apparently Noonan was impressed by the numbers and sort of people who were now privately expressing serious reservations about Kelly's case. Further pressure followed the arrival home of Fr Niall O'Brien, which it was expected would lead to even more calls for Kelly's release. Also of importance was a letter being prepared by the Catholic Primate Cardinal O'Fiaich, of which Michael Noonan had been made aware in advance. The Primate planned to publish it as an open letter to the Government, calling for the release of an innocent man from jail.

It is believed that by early summer 1984, Michael Noonan had decided on Kelly's release. The question was: how and when? It would have to be done at a time when no one could interpret it as a concession to any sort of pressure, and when it could be handled with minimum fuss. The grounds for release would be Kelly's petition, which Noonan had not shown to either the gardaí or the judiciary and of which they were not aware.

On the morning of 17 July, before a Cabinet meeting, Noonan told Taoiseach Garret FitzGerald that he planned to release Kelly. The Taoiseach agreed with the move and, again before the meeting, spoke to the Tánaiste, Dick Spring ,who promised the support of Labour's four ministers – Ruairi Quinn, Liam Kavanagh, Barry Desmond (who voted for Kelly's release but spoke against it) and himself. The other supporter of release, along with FitzGerald and Noonan, was Gemma Hussey who was also a TD for Wicklow, Kelly's home county.

The matter was not placed on the agenda and was brought up at the end of the meeting. Attorney General Peter Sutherland argued against release, saying that it would be seen as criticism of the Courts and could undermine the rule of law. Those who agreed with him and opposed release included Alan Dukes, John Bruton and John Boland. Absent on business elsewhere were the Minister for Defence Paddy Cooney, the Minister for Foreign Affairs Peter Barry, and the Minister for Agriculture Austin Deasy.

After that cabinet meeting a letter was hand-delivered to Greg O'Neill at his offices in Dublin. It said Kelly was being released "on humanitarian grounds".

IN PORTLAOISE KELLY HAD BEEN LOCKED into his cell for the afternoon period. That morning he had run ten miles, as part of his fitness routine. At about 4.30 pm he heard the footsteps of four or five prison officers coming along the walkway outside the cells.

He thought it would be another random strip search, something the prison authorities allowed "out of sheer vindictiveness", he believes. Led by a senior officer they crowded into his cell, where he was lying on his bed. They had a black plastic bag with them and threw it to Kelly with the instruction to "get your things into that".

"Why?" he asked.

"Never mind," was the reply.

"I'm being shifted," he thought to himself, wondering why.

The prison officers pushed clothes into his bag and tried to bring him out. He refused to budge. They dragged him.

He began to shout, "They're shifting me . . .", hoping the other prisoners would hear, ". . . they're shifting me".

"They literally dragged me out roaring," he recalls. "Where am I going? Where am I going?" he shouted at them. They would not answer and pulled him to the reception area.

He was not strip-searched there, as he expected, so he began to realise then that something serious was afoot. They handcuffed him to an officer and he was led out past three gates. All of a sudden there was an eruption of noise from the prison behind him. Doors were beaten hard and the men cheered loudly. They had just heard on the radio that Kelly was being released. But he still knew nothing about it.

He was taken to a security car with two or three prison officers, and no army escort. Now he knew something very significant was going on. He began to get excited. No army jeeps, no armed gardaí. But they still wouldn't tell him what was happening. Then one said they were going to Shelton Abbey.

They got lost en route and as they drove around the Wicklow mountains the car radio was on. The news bulletin began and there it was, top of the headlines – he had been released. He went crazy. "I wanted to have the cuffs removed there and then, and to get out of that car. They wouldn't let me. Their orders were to take me to Shelton Abbey, they said," he recalls.

At about the same time, according to some reports, Minister Paddy Cooney was also very excited, but for different reasons. He had been driving to Dublin when he heard about Kelly's release

on the radio as well. He was furious. Stopping at the next telephone kiosk, he rang Dublin to find out how such a decision
could be have been taken in his absence. He is believed to have
said later that, had he and other absent ministers been at that cabinet meeting, Kelly would have remained in Portlaoise.

Eventually, the prison officers found Shelton Abbey and Kelly
was taken to the Governor. He informed Kelly that he would be
taken home to Tyndall's Lane in Arklow. He was brought by car,
still handcuffed and listening to the radio, where he heard his
mother speaking to a reporter on the early evening news. "It was
a peculiar situation. There she was talking about my release while
I sat a few miles away listening to her from the back of a car
where I was still handcuffed to a prison officer."

When he got home there was already a huge media presence
there. The reunion with his family was as emotional as it was unexpected. "I spent the rest of the evening talking to them, to well-
wishers, neighbours, friends and supporters. It was slowly sink-
ing in that I was free. I was totally hyper and didn't really sleep
for about three days."

There was a crowded press conference in Buswell's Hotel in
Dublin the following day. "I was waking up to the idea that I had
become some sort of celebrity in my absence. It was great to be
free and I was grateful to all who had helped me, but the battle
was far from over. My determination to clear my name was as
strong as ever, as was my intention to fight for an inquiry into
what took place both in Fitzgibbon Street and the Bridewell Garda
stations on the days and nights of 5, 6 and 7 April 1976."

He was also sickened to discover he had been released "on
humanitarian grounds". This was further political expediency as
he saw it. "If I had known those were the reasons for my release I
would have refused to leave Portlaoise. But I was out now, and
there would be a break before I'd enter the fray again."

17

FREE AT LAST

T HAT FIRST PERIOD OF FREEDOM was crazy. Kelly found the crowds hard to deal with at first and he was still wary of people. "Looking at old videos and TV film from the period covering my release from jail I am struck again and again by the hesitancy with which I respond to questions. It's as though I'm wondering, 'What is this reporter's agenda? What is he or she really getting at?'" he says.

He was finding it very hard to trust people or accept they were as they appeared at face value. This was hardly surprising. It was over five and a half years since he had been able to walk about freely in Ireland – since he went on the run in December 1978 – and there was still a cloud over his name which no "humanitarian grounds" got rid of.

Still, the great goodwill of so many people helped relax him. But there was a long way to go before he could really be at ease. He was also unused to such celebrations and high good humour. "There had not been much *craic* in my life for years and I had to almost relearn how to take part in things. Fortunately, there was plenty of help at hand on that score."

He based himself at home in Arklow for the first while, then moved to Dublin. "The day after my release there was an earthquake there. I don't think my release was related to that event, but there were times in Portlaoise when if someone had said to me, 'You'll be here until there's an earthquake in Dublin', I'd have believed them."

Just as surprising was the price of everything. He went into a shop in Blackrock for three choc ices and handed over 50 pence. "Where have you been . . . ?", the assistant asked. Looking closer, she continued, ". . . I know where you've been!"

Two nights after Kelly's release Christy Moore was performing at the Wexford Inn on Dublin's Camden Street. When Kelly arrived there the place was packed, and Christy belted out "The Wicklow Boy" under a banner which read "Free(d) Nicky Kelly". The place went wild.

After a few whirlwind days in Dublin he went to Spanish Point in Clare and stayed for a few weeks with Christy's sister Ann and her husband Davog Rynne. "I spent the time there doing nothing, listening to the sounds of the waves in bed at night, visiting the Burren, the Ailwee Caves, and McGann's pub in Doolin." Christy Moore arrived down and invited Kelly to go to a few gigs with him. He was touring around the south-west and thought it might get Kelly out of himself if he accompanied him.

"We joked that we were 'The Wicklow Boy and Christy Moore on tour'. The song, when he sang it, would bring the house down. In those live performances he would of course add plenty of extra verses. When he performed 'The Wicklow Boy' I'd have to join him onstage. In at the deep end, for a man who had gotten so used to his own company, and I would end up signing autographs. Christy used to joke that people were more interested in my autograph than his."

He remembered another night at Friel's in Milltown Malby. "The *craic* was so good a French film crew wanted to put it on video. But they got so caught up in the atmosphere themselves they forgot to put video cassettes in their camera. Next day they asked us would be mind doing it again. We made our apologies."

That September there was a major thank-you party at the Spa Hotel in Dublin, as a gesture to all those who had helped in the campaign for Kelly's release. It was a huge success with music by Moving Hearts – including Donal Lunny, Keith Donald and Mick Hanly – Christy Moore, Mary Black, her sister Frances and brother Martin. That month also saw the launch of the book *Round up the Usual Suspects* by Derek Dunne and Gene Kerrigan.

It was the first time a lot of people became aware of all that had happened to Kelly. The book led to Kelly's appearance on *The Late Late Show*. Derek Dunne and Gene Kerrigan were also on the show the same night. *Late Late* host Gay Byrne gave the book a rave review and said "it should be read by everybody in the country".

In general Gay Byrne had done more to draw attention to the Kelly case than anyone else at RTÉ, certainly more than most of the station's then current affairs producers. Many of those apologised to Kelly later for the station's lack of coverage of his case. In fact the pirate radio stations, and later the new independent radio stations, took a greater interest in the Kelly case.

Towards the end of 1984, another book on the case was published. *Blind Justice*, co-authored by Joe Joyce and Peter Murtagh, was a highly informative detailed account of what had happened to the mail train robbery defendants. Both books that year highlighted the miscarriages of justice at the heart of the mail train robbery story. They also reminded people that, although Kelly was "out", his name had not been cleared and there had been no inquiry into the case. "This was no harm as, following my release, a lot of people thought, 'Well, that's it'. I knew it would be hard to overcome that attitude, now that I was 'freed Nicky Kelly'," he remembers.

However the Unions of Students in Ireland (USI) remained very active. A former president of USI, Joe Duffy (now of RTÉ Radio One's *Liveline* programme), had been a staunch supporter of Kelly's throughout his stay in Portlaoise. In 1983, when Duffy was jailed himself for occupying offices during a student protest, he corresponded with Kelly in Portlaoise. Duffy's successors as leaders of USI, Giolliosa Ó Lideadha, Trish Hegarty and Mark Little, were as supportive of Kelly and organised speaking tours of the various universities and colleges around the country to raise interest of the case.

A new group, the Justice for Nicky Kelly group, was set up to forward his campaign. Its chairman was filmmaker Tiernan

McBride and it included people like Declan Turnbull, Peter Graves, Brian Judge, Helena Caulfield, Rosa Meehan, Trish Hegarty and Giolliosa Ó Lideadha. It focused on securing support for a pardon for Kelly from among trade unionists, civil rights and Church groups and politicians. Among supporters in politics were Tony Gregory, Pat McCartan, Brendan Ryan, Joe Costello, Michael D. Higgins, Emmet Stagg, Niall Andrews, Neil Blaney and Senator Joe O'Toole.

Kelly also met the man whose own arrival back in Ireland co-incided closely with his own release from prison – Fr Niall O'Brien. "I visited him at his home in Monkstown (Dublin). He was very friendly and was delighted I had been freed. He had heard about my case while in the Philippines. I met him again before he returned to the Philippines and we continued to meet down the years."

Later in 1984, Young Fine Gael invited Kelly to their party's annual conference. "I attended and got a good reception, from most. Many there seemed more interested in me being there, than in what was going on."

He also attended that year's Fianna Fáil Ard Fheis. The party press officer, PJ Mara, approached Kelly quietly to inquire, "Will Charlie be mugged when he comes out for the speech?" which Kelly interpreted as a roundabout way of asking whether he planned a protest similar to that staged by Siobhan Troddyn at the previous year's Ard Fheis. He assured PJ he was "only there for the beer".

After those first lively months it was time for him to address basics. His long-term objective was simply to clear his name. But there were the practicalities of living to think of too: what to do with himself, where to set up base, how to make a living?

He stayed for a while with friends in Monkstown, Dublin, to begin with. "I wasn't fit to go back to my old work on the sites. I couldn't cope with heights. Physically I may have been fit but I was not up to too much manual work, and mentally I was still nervy and anxious."

It was Tim Pat Coogan, then editor of the *Irish Press*, who first suggested he try journalism. Tim Pat, along with Vincent Browne, then editor of *The Sunday Tribune* and *Magill* magazine, and John Mulcahy of *Hibernia* and *The Phoenix* magazine, had been among Kelly's firmest supporters among national newspaper and magazine editors.

He began by writing articles for the *Irish Press*, usually on social topics, such as unemployment in Arklow. He also wrote a column for *Hot Press* magazine, as well as articles for *In Dublin* magazine and, for a brief period, he was Snooker Correspondent for the *Magill TV Guide*.

He did a lot of work for the *Tribune* and *Magill*. "People in general, and in particular Gerald Barry, then news editor at the *Sunday Tribune*, were generous and a lot of work was made available to me. Eventually I got an NUJ card. But I found journalism tough. Derek Dunne, then working for the *Tribune* and *Magill*, was a great source of ideas and became my typist too. I had no practice at typing and would write out all my pieces longhand, which Derek would then type up."

He even won an award for a travel piece he wrote for the *Tribune*, "Down and Out and Living in Paris". It dealt with seeing that city cheaply, something he had became expert at in his stay there while on the run. "I revisited Paris before writing the article, which I thought was a terrible piece of journalism. There were those who liked what I wrote and those who maintained I couldn't write to save myself."

He stayed with journalism for about three years, but never really enjoyed it. "I could only work to deadlines, but above all I hated the intrusiveness that often goes with the job. As a result I could never do 'fire-brigade journalism', reporting on disasters, etc. I would prefer to make my living swinging a shovel. There is more dignity in that, if less money."

18

"... SILLY PEOPLE ..."

IN JANUARY 1986 JUDGE Rory O'Hanlon gave judgment in the High Court that Kelly's civil action against the State, as initiated after his hunger strike in 1983, could not proceed. He agreed with counsel for the State that Kelly was estopped from pursuing the case as it had already been heard by the Special Criminal Court. He also rejected protests by Kelly's counsel that the State should be disallowed from entering such an argument as it had invited the civil action to begin with. Kelly's team initiated a Supreme Court appeal against Justice O'Hanlon's judgment.

Justice O'Hanlon had used the 1980 Denning judgment in the Birmingham Six case as precedent for his judgment. It was the first overt illustration of a link between what, to then, had seemed a remarkable sequence of parallels in the Irish State's handling of Kelly's case and the handling of the Birmingham Six cases by the British authorities.

Those parallels are striking – similar stories of police brutality; of confessions forcibly extracted; of alleged conspiracy on the part of police to pervert the course of justice; even to the point where defence counsel in both cases believed or suggested that a senior policeman in both instances had kept a timetable/schedule as a masterplan to co-ordinate police evidence.

In both instances also, and some years after the events which had led to the convictions, the IRA had claimed responsibility for the crimes. In both instances too the IRA said that those convicted were not members and were innocent of the crimes for which they had been jailed. However, it is, above all, the parallels in how the

Courts in Britain and Ireland dealt with the cases which is most indicative and interesting.

This similarity in approach by the judiciaries in both jurisdictions – the broad sweep of agreement in the decisions arrived at and their nature; even the common phraseology used – point to something more than a common heritage of language, legal tradition, shared history and similar use of precedent.

There is more than a suggestion that in arriving at decisions in Kelly's case, the Irish Courts were influenced, whether consciously or otherwise, by the methods employed by the British Courts in their handling of the Birmingham Six cases some years earlier. Crucial in both instances was whether or not the confessions should be admitted as evidence in the light of allegations that they had been extracted by police brutality. In both instances these allegations were backed up by medical evidence.

The judges decided, in Britain as in Ireland, that there should be "a trial within a trial" to decide the matter. The Courts in both jurisdictions found there was a clear conflict of evidence between police testimony and that of the defendants. And both Courts in both jurisdictions decided in favour of the police, essentially for precisely the same reasons – the judges were more impressed by the demeanour of police witnesses.

Giving the Criminal Court's decision on the matter in the 1975 Birmingham Six trials, Justice Bridge said, "All the police officers who gave their evidence of the circumstances in which the statements were taken impressed me as being straightforward and honest witnesses."

Giving the Special Criminal Court's decision on the matter in the mail train robbery trials in 1978, Justice Hamilton said, "The Court has carefully assessed all the evidence, has had regard to the demeanour of witnesses and is satisfied beyond all reasonable doubt that the garda witnesses are truthful, and have given a truthful account of what transpired during the different interviews."

Justice Bridge considered the allegations against the police to be of "a most bizarre and grotesque character". Justice Hamilton found Nicky Kelly's account of ill-treatment to be one "of quite savage brutality, at times of a horrific nature".

Arguing against the Birmingham Six allegations of ill-treatment by the police, Justice Bridge pointed out that the Lancashire and Birmingham police officers were "complete strangers" to each other, and that if a single Lancashire officer was honest he could put all the others' careers in jeopardy. He could not believe the police had put themselves at such risk.

Arguing against Nicky Kelly's allegations of ill-treatment by the gardaí, Justice Hamilton concluded that if they were true "it was inconceivable that ordinary members of the Garda engaged in their ordinary duties at the station [Fitzgibbon Street] would not have been aware of it". Yet all gardaí had denied the allegations, he noted.

Still, the medical evidence presented both Courts with a problem – but not for long. Justice Bridge concluded that the injuries sustained by the Birmingham Six had been self-inflicted "to add colour to the allegations" (of police brutality).

Justice Hamilton concluded that injuries suffered by the men detained following the mail train robbery "were self-inflicted or inflicted by collaboration with persons other than members of the Garda Síochána".

Indeed, in either instance the medical evidence presented to the court did not weigh very heavily with the judges – except where it was absent to sustain a single allegation in both trials.

In the Birmingham Six trials Billy Power alleged he had been beaten over the back of his hand by a policeman using handcuffs as a knuckleduster. There was no medical evidence to sustain the allegation. Justice Bridge considered it "a crucial inconsistency".

Nicky Kelly had alleged that a garda had made him lie on the floor with his hands outstretched behind his head and that the garda then placed the front legs of a chair he was balancing on, in Kelly's palms, while spitting in his face. Though medical testimony indicated that this could have taken place without leaving a mark, it was not corroborated by medical evidence.

In the Supreme Court judgment of October 1982, dismissing Kelly's appeal, Chief Justice Tom O'Higgins drew attention to this "one particular exception", which was not, he said, "consistent with the violence and treatment to which he said he had been subjected".

In neither jurisdiction were the Courts interested in the many consistencies between the medical evidence and the allegations made. Nor were these referred to in judgments. In both instances the acceptance of the alleged confessions as evidence sealed the respective fates of those accused.

On 15 August 1975 the Birmingham Six were found guilty and sentenced to life imprisonment.

On 15 December 1978 the four remaining accused in connection with the mail train robbery were found guilty. Nicky Kelly was sentenced to 12 years' penal servitude.

The Birmingham Six appealed to Britain's Court of Criminal Appeal in 1976. They lost.

Nicky Kelly appealed his conviction to the Court of Criminal Appeal in 1982. He lost.

In 1977 the Birmingham Six took a civil action against the police. The police applied to have the action struck out – that the defendants be "estopped" from taking such action as the case had already been heard. The police failed, and appealed to the Court of Criminal Appeal. It was presided over by Lord Denning, who found the proposition "that the police were guilty of perjury, that they were guilty of violence and threats, that the confessions were involuntary, and were improperly admitted in evidence and that the convictions were erroneous" to be, as he put it "an appalling vista". He ruled in favour of the police. That was in 1980.

In 1982 Nicky Kelly appealed to the Supreme Court. It was presided over by Chief Justice O'Higgins, who found Kelly's proposition "that the various garda witnesses allegedly involved in ill-treatment committed perjury in their denials of the appellant's allegations and that, contrary to the conclusion arrived at by the trial Court, the evidence given by the appellant was true in substance and in fact" to be, as he put it a "drastic conclusion".

Lord Denning, in his 1980 judgment, felt the trials enjoyed by the Birmingham Six proved what a wonderfully civilised country Britain was "where the State had lavished large sums on their defence", and continued to do so in their actions against the police.

Chief Justice O'Higgins, in his 1982 judgment, felt it was "seldom that the appellate jurisdiction of our courts had been so fully exercised", as they had been in the Kelly case. "The appellant," he said, warming to his subject, "although he remained, culpably, out of the country for 18 months, following his conviction and sentence, has nevertheless been afforded every opportunity of establishing that he should not have been convicted and to this end has had his appeal fully heard and considered, not only by the Court of Criminal Appeal but also by this Court".

The Birmingham Six appealed the Denning judgment to the House of Lords. In 1981 a hearing presided over by Lord Diplock upheld the Denning judgment. All legal avenues were now closed to the Birmingham Six.

With the failure of his Supreme Court appeal in 1982, Nicky Kelly believed all legal avenues were now closed to him. But the parallels were about to dovetail, as true parallels never do.

On the last day of his hunger strike, 7 June 1983, the State implicitly invited Kelly to take a civil action against the Garda, the Attorney General, and Ireland.

Seven months later, in December 1983, the Government decided to oppose Kelly's civil action, basing its legal argument on the Denning judgment which was upheld by the House of Lords. Included in that same Government were many who, without irony, had campaigned for the release of the Birmingham Six, while criticising British injustice.

In January 1986, High Court Judge Rory O'Hanlon, in dismissing Kelly's civil action, made explicit reference to that Denning judgment, which had been employed by the State, at the direction of the same Government, to frustrate Kelly's appeal and which had denied justice to the Birmingham Six.

By the time of the O'Hanlon judgment in 1986, 19 of the foremost members in the State's judiciary had dealt with the Kelly case. They included seven Supreme Court judges: Chief Justice Tom O'Higgins, and Judges Seamus Henchy, Brian Walsh, Frank Griffin, Anthony Hederman, John Kenny, and Weldon Parke; seven High Court judges: President of the High Court, and later Chief Justice, Thomas Finlay, as well as Judges Liam Hamilton (later Chief Justice also), Donal Barrington, James McMahon, Mella Carroll, Herbert McWilliam, and John Gannon; two Circuit Court judges: Gerard Clarke and John O'Connor (who died during Kelly's first trial); and three District Court judges: President of the District Court, Cathal O'Floinn, John Garavan and Riobard Ó hUadaigh. Some had been involved in hearings of the Kelly case a number of times.

The use of his judgment to obstruct the Kelly case was a source of some wonderment to Lord Denning himself, when he eventually heard about it. By then he had recanted that "appalling vista" judgment, and had regularly expressed regret about delivering it.

But even that did not prevent the Irish Government from persisting in its use, to stop Kelly's civil action. This was brought to Denning's attention one day by the Labour MP Chris Mullin, as they chatted outside the House of Lords in London. As Chris Mullin later told Nicky Kelly, Denning was baffled. "They were always silly people, weren't they?" Denning commented.

19

CAMPAIGNS

Nicky Kelly was not politically active as such after he came out of Portlaoise, in the sense that he did not join any political party. But in 1986 he was very impressed by the Dunnes Stores strikers who had refused to handle South African oranges, as a protest against apartheid. They ended up picketing the Dunnes Stores premises on Dublin's Henry Street, where they had been employed.

Nicky Kelly was asked to support them and did so, eventually ending up on their support committee. They organised fund raising to cover trips by the strikers to Johannesburg and the UN. The strike generated a great deal of publicity and goodwill.

In February 1987 Kelly went to Belfast to see what was happening there during the Westminster general election that year. Kelly had an interest in that Gerry Adams, along with Bernadette McAliskey, had spoken publicly in support of him at various meetings during his imprisonment in Portlaoise. But he had gone there to write articles about the campaign, particularly the allegations of impersonation being made against Sinn Féin by the SDLP in West Belfast.

What he discovered was that large sections of the population had effectively been disenfranchised by a primitive ID card system. Most of those affected would have been among the working-class poor of the constituency – Sinn Féin supporters in the main. So, rather than the SDLP suffering as a result of the conduct of the vote, as far as he could see the only people affected were Sinn Féin supporters.

He also discovered something else during his spell in Belfast – what he saw as dishonesty from some journalists covering the election, who seemed to be writing to an anti-Adams agenda rather than from what they saw. He believed they persisted in demonising a man who was lionised by his people, the people who in fact elected him as their MP in that election. As far as he could establish, the only exceptions to this type of wilfully distorted coverage were the British quality papers.

One of the most extraordinary moments he ever witnessed happened there on the evening Adams was declared elected. As Adams arrived at the end of the Falls Road, from Belfast City Hall, he was greeted by a huge crowd of weeping men and women who converged on him. Kelly recalls that he never before or since witnessed such a spontaneous outpouring of genuine feeling. That night west Belfast was ablaze with celebration – bonfires and bonhomie everywhere.

৯৹   ৯৹   ৯৹

KELLY ALSO MADE CONTACT with a lot of international media people about his own case, as well as the Birmingham Six and the Guildford Four cases.

By 1988 he was convinced he could no longer combine work with fighting to clear his name. So he left journalism and borrowed money to concentrate on the Justice for Nicky Kelly campaign full-time. It helped a lot that he had access to offices belonging to various bodies such as the Union of Students in Ireland, the ICCL and the Anti-Apartheid Movement. Most of the people who had been involved with the Release Nicky Kelly Committee had re-formed as the Birmingham Six Committee, but remained supportive of Kelly as well. He combined work on his own case with work for the Birmingham Six, the Guildford Four and Judith Ward through that Committee and the Miscarriages of Justice Committee.

Some very good friends who believed in his innocence offered to lend him money over the year. When he received compensation from the Government in the summer of 1993, he returned £66,000 to one man, for instance, money lent him for the campaign over the intervening years. "He told me he always knew he would get it back," Kelly recalls. Support like that provided the means for a campaign which cost over £150,000 in total, and which was so efficient that some politicians believed he had hired a PR agency to work for him.

In 1988 two American friends of his, Brian and Julie Riley, helped him from their Galway home to prepare a comprehensive information pack dealing with the case. Brian was a photo-journalist and Julie a writer. Derek Dunne wrote up the copy. "It is hard to believe Derek and Brian have since died. Both were in their thirties. Neither would live to see me pardoned," Kelly says.

Lawyers looked at the pack and it was of such quality that newsrooms all over the world would later use it as reference material. Two thousand copies of the pack were made and circulated internationally, to civil and human rights groups, political organisations, newspapers, magazines, radio and TV stations, as well as news agencies.

The cost of posting outside Ireland – at between £2 and £2.90 each – was steep, but so was the return. Kelly's hope, and intention, was to embarrass the Government sufficiently that it would have to take action to exonerate him. "I had long since learned that Governments never do the decent thing until they have to. Their concern is not with right or wrong, but what they can get away with," he says.

Throughout this period, from his release in 1984 right up to his pardon in 1992, he continued to be harassed by gardaí, as were members of the campaign committee and its supporters. They were harassed at their homes, on the streets and at their places of work – which could have had serious implications for them, as most were professional people.

"In my own case there were so many incidents it is pointless selecting. Being hassled and frisked by plainclothes gardaí on the streets was normal, and being followed home by a car or cars with lights flashing and sirens wailing was not unusual. It really didn't bother me, I became so used to it. Always throughout there'd be the line, 'You can forget about an inquiry, Kelly,' or some such comment, and things like 'watch yourself'. It was blatant intimidation, but it had little effect. In fact I used to take particular pleasure in letting them know how little it affected me. 'What more can ye do to me?' I'd say, 'Ye've tortured me, framed me, exiled me, and had me wrongfully imprisoned!'"

Despite this close attention the case was getting a lot more notice. Singers like Dolores Keane, Mary Coughlan and Sinead O'Connor all offered their support through special concerts.

One imaginative angle to the campaign came from Rathmines student Enda O'Callaghan. He decided to stand as a candidate in Dublin North West – Taoiseach Charles Haughey's own constituency – during the 1989 general election campaign. O'Callaghan had his name changed by deed poll to Lord Tom Denning and was listed as such on the ballot paper. He campaigned in judicial clothes while wearing a remarkably ugly mask. His slogan was "Vote Denning number 1, and Haughey number 2 – because Haughey supports the Denning judgment" – a humorous exercise in exposing the continuing hypocrisy of Irish Governments in the Kelly case.

The momentum for Kelly's exoneration, which had lapsed after his release from Portlaoise, was beginning to gather again. It would receive a terrific boost from two forthcoming events.

20

OPENING THOSE GATES

NOVEMBER 1989 WILL BE REMEMBERED mostly for the fall of the Berlin Wall. But it was then too that the Kelly campaigners got their first indication that cracks were beginning to show in many walls in these islands.

No one in the various committees expected the release of the Guildford Four that month. "We would have said that it was much more likely the Birmingham Six would be freed first. That case was attracting far more attention and had done so over a longer period. Indeed at the time a big Parade of Innocence was being planned for Dublin, which was operating on the assumption that the Guildford Four would still be in prison," Kelly says. Their release was a powerful moment, heightened by not being expected.

Shortly after that release, Paul Hill and Gerry Conlon both came to Ireland and Kelly was asked by the Miscarriage of Justice Committee to meet them at Dublin Airport. There were also representatives from the Irish Commission for Justice and Peace, the Irish Commission for Prisoners Overseas, the Birmingham Six Committee and various other supportive organisations.

"I had exchanged Christmas cards with the Four – as well as with the Birmingham Six – while in Portlaoise, and a few letters. It wasn't therefore contact for the first time, and they were well aware of my case," Kelly remembers. "I did not know, however, just how aware, until I met Paul Hill that day. We hit it off straight away, and after exchanging warm handshakes, Paul was almost in tears as he told me how moved and upset he had been that I should have had to endure a hunger strike like that under an Irish Government. He said my campaign had given great strength and resolve to himself, his colleagues in the Guildford Four, and all the Birmingham Six. The fact that I had fought injustice and eventually succeeded in being released had been a great encouragement to them all, he said."

Everyone went to the Burlington Hotel, where the Guildford Four were staying. That afternoon Paul Hill and Gerry Conlon went to see Taoiseach Charles Haughey. They asked him to publicly call for the release of the Birmingham Six.

Then the infamous "suits" episode took place. Haughey sent them to an expensive men's shop off Dublin's Grafton Street, where he used buy some of his own clothes, and offered them a present of two suits. When they returned to the Burlington they were teased about being taken in by a man who over the previous ten years had not lifted a finger on their behalf.

That night Paul Hill and Gerry Conlon were on *The Late Late Show*. Nicky Kelly went along too, staying backstage. In his interview with Gay Byrne, Gerry Conlon drew attention to Kelly's case, pointing out the hypocrisy of successive Irish Governments in dealing with it, and saying it was time this country too got its justice house in order.

Back at the Burlington afterwards all celebrated well into the small hours. The following day a public welcome had been organised for Paul Hill and Gerry Conlon outside the GPO. The crowds were huge. Beforehand the two men and Nicky Kelly visited the vigil for the Birmingham Six, which had been staged every Saturday for years outside the British Embassy, now on Merrion Road.

There was a security alert while they were there. Carloads of plainclothes gardaí arrived with sirens wailing, then disappeared again. People on the vigil explained it was probably a false alarm and a further, if minor example, of the harassment they had endured on the vigil from gardaí down the years. During the week, between vigils, some would be visited at their homes or at work by the gardaí. Sometimes they would be stopped on the street for no good reason.

The three men then drove to O'Connell Street. The numbers of enthusiastic supporters were so great that they had major problems getting through to the platform outside the GPO. Once there, both Paul Hill and Gerry Conlon spoke, and there was a tremendous outpouring of goodwill from the people. Both men were overcome by the event. Getting away afterwards was as difficult as arriving. At one stage their car was almost turned over as people tried to get through to shake hands. Eventually a way was cleared and they drove to the airport.

The release of the Guildford Four was a major boost to the other release campaigns, and added an unexpected impetus to the Innocence Parade which took place a few weeks later. More than a parade, it was part pageant, part theatre, with actors and musicians participating, as well as supporters of the various release campaigns. Kelly had been asked to act as a sort of Grand Marshall for the parade, which set out from Parnell Square, led by a Birmingham Six banner.

There was a remarkable turnout of musicians, artists, politicians, clergy, trade unionists, people from various cultural, civil and human rights and political groups. Large crowds watched from the pavements. They marched down through O'Connell Street to Leinster House, then back to the Central Bank Plaza, where there was a concert with Christy Moore. Paul Hill and Gerry Conlon joined him onstage.

The "Birmingham Six" were pulled along in two lion cages that had been borrowed from Fossetts Circus. The Diceman, Thom McGinty, made a particularly obnoxious judge, passing callous sentence on passersby and destroying years with the flick of an eyelid. It was a colourful spectacle, part protest, part carnival. Dublin had never seen anything like it before. It was a great success.

IN FEBRUARY 1990 KELLY was invited, along with Paul Hill and Gerry Conlon, to attend a Human Rights Congressional hearing on Capitol Hill in Washington, dealing with the Birmingham Six case. David Andrews TD represented the Government.

One of the hearing organisers was Congressman Joe Kennedy. Again Kelly was impressed by the openness on Capitol Hill at the time. "Once inside you could call to any representative's office and get a hearing without a problem. I spoke to David Andrews about this afterwards and remember saying to him that if anyone was to try to have access to any Irish politician at Leinster House in the same way, he or she would either be evicted or arrested."

Gerry Conlon testified about what it was like to be wrongfully imprisoned. He made a tremendous impact. He, Paul Hill and Nicky Kelly attracted a lot of media interest in the US on that visit. A one-week speaking tour of American cities, highlighting the Birmingham Six case, was extended to a month. They took in Washington, New York, Boston, Philadelphia, Chicago, Minneapolis, St Paul, Miami, Rhode Island, Vermont and other cities. Everywhere they went there was great interest. They met representatives from various local organisations and authorities, and were interviewed for local TV, radio and newspapers.

Combined with the inevitable "welcome celebrations" and "make-them-feel-at-home" sessions afterwards, they were well washed up at the end of it all. They met Ethel Kennedy, wife of Senator Robert Kennedy, in Washington and she invited them to visit her home at Cape Cod. Nicky Kelly believes it was then Paul Hill met Courtney Kennedy, later to be his wife, for the first time. They also met Senator Ted Kennedy, who was well briefed on all their cases.

One of the people who most impressed Nicky Kelly on that trip was Mayor Dinkins of New York. "He struck me as a very genuine man who had an aura about him which you were aware of immediately. In conversation his frankness and honesty was very refreshing. A good man." The mayor declared that day "Birmingham Six Day" in New York.

Similarly, when they visited Boston, Mayor Ray Flynn declared it Birmingham Six week there. Everywhere they went there was great welcome and great interest, with even further invitations to visit other places. They met Paul O'Dwyer in New York and Jack McKinney in Philadelphia, where they also addressed the Quaker Society.

"All our efforts were geared towards the forthcoming International Birmingham Six Day, which would involve vigils outside British embassies and consulates all around the world. The lead-up to St Patrick's Day was particularly demanding. We were now doing five to six interviews every day for radio and TV, as well as taking part in chat shows and giving talks.

"On the night of 16 March, Paul and myself ended up in downtown Manhattan at a Pogues concert. The group had always been great supporters of mine. Then it was a dash back uptown to a small party organised by Congressman Brian Donnelly, a big imposing man who doesn't mince his words. He told us how he had taken some visiting Irish ministers down a peg or two, when in the middle of applauding him for all he was doing for the Irish in the US, he would ask them about their carry-on in my case. He was going to Savannah, Georgia, for the St Patrick's Day parade there next day and wanted me to go with him and talk to the people there. I was very tempted, but a series of interviews had been lined up for us in New York and I had been invited onto the reviewing stand for the St Patrick's Day parade there too."

One thing the three came across again and again in their various meetings was what seemed like a concerted attempt by staff at the Irish Embassy in Washington and the consulate in New York to "rubbish" their right to speak on behalf of the Birmingham Six. The diplomatic staff insisted they were the official representatives of the Six and that all civic receptions for the three – Kelly, Conlon and Hill – should cease. "They were seriously ignored. Many of the people we met remarked on the hard neck of the Irish Embassy staff in insisting they represented the real campaign for the release of the Birmingham Six. The civic receptions for us continued."

The profile of the three in the US by then was so high that people were recognising them in the streets, and in pubs and restaurants, where they soon felt the effects of so much generosity.

"I arrived back in Ireland on 30 March, exhausted. Such was my relief at getting off that hectic merry-go-round I literally kissed the ground when I got off the plane at Dublin Airport. It was good to be home. And I was reminded of the last time I had arrived in Ireland from the US. That was in June 1980, when I was met by Pat McCartan and four gardaí and packed off to Portlaoise. Things were looking up."

That summer they organised a "Parade of Light", to coincide with an EC (now EU) summit in Dublin. (Ireland held the EC presidency at the time.) It was a candle-lit procession aimed, once more, at highlighting the Birmingham Six case and taking advantage of the large international media presence in Dublin for the summit.

Again it was to be a highly theatrical event. The intention was to march from Parnell Square to O'Connell Street, then turn down Middle Abbey Street to a river pageant opposite Capel Street, which was the nearest they could get to the summit taking place at Dublin Castle. It was the night of Ireland's famous victory over Romania in the 1990 World Cup. The city was wild with celebration.

The gardaí were none too keen on the parade going down O'Connell Street and attempted to divert it via Parnell Street to the quays. The marchers stuck to the original parade route and would not budge. As Nicky Kelly was one of the organisers, a senior garda approached him with persuasion in mind. Who should it be but one of his old "friends" from his interrogation, promoted now like so many of his colleagues from those times.

"Occasionally I did meet some of the gardaí I spent those unforgettable hours with. Dublin is such a small place you could hardly avoid them. We wouldn't exactly run across the street to exchange greetings with one another. But one detective did approach me coming up to Christmas 1987. He apologised 'for all that happened' and said he had nothing to do with 'the cover-up' – as he put it – and that he hadn't been involved in 'the beatings'. We shook hands and he went off. Maybe it was the Christmas spirit."

That summer evening, the Parade of Light marched down O'Connell Street illuminated by candle-light, the numbers swollen beyond all expectations by a crowd emotional about all things Irish. Because of the match as much as the summit, the international media focused on the parade and it was well reported abroad.

In November 1990 Paul Hill and Nicky Kelly spent three weeks on a Birmingham Six lecture tour of US universities and colleges, including Yale, Fordham and Columbia. They also spoke to various Irish Associations and Human Rights bodies.

It was the time of the presidential election campaign in Ireland, which they missed. "It cost me a fortune in phone calls when the Lenihan tapes story broke. By the time I returned we had a new President, Mary Robinson, she who had taken my case to the European Commission of Human Rights in 1983."

One of the most successful events organised in connection with the Birmingham Six campaign was the celebrity prison breakfast at Gallagher's Boxty House on Dublin's Fleet Street early in 1991. The owners, Ronan and Padraic Gallagher, offered the use of their premises. It was converted to resemble the inside of a prison, with actors Brendan Gleeson and Paul Bennett as prison officers. Dried toast and cornflakes were served at £25 a head, to raise funds for the Birmingham Six campaign.

The *Gay Byrne Show* radio programme was broadcast live from the restaurant, with Joe Duffy officiating. The large attendance included celebrities from the arts and entertainment worlds as well as clergy and politicians. At the end Nicky Kelly presented a cheque for a substantial amount raised to Bishops James Kavanagh and Dermot O'Mahony of the Irish Commission for Justice and Peace.

Increasing international interest in his own case meant he was receiving invitations to more and more international Human Rights conferences around the world. However, he deliberately avoided courting publicity in Britain as he did not want anything to deflect attention there from the moral force of the Birmingham

Six's right to freedom, not even the hypocrisy of successive Irish Governments.

There was a lot of interest in his case on the part of the right-wing tabloid media in Britain, who pursued him for interviews, which he always refused. Their interest, he felt, was not in him. "I was just afraid it could lead to a further delay in the release of the Birmingham Six." However, the same newspapers did run some stories about his case, without either his consent or help.

When the release of the Birmingham Six seemed near it was decided to activate a campaign on his case in Britain also. The night before they were due to be released he was invited to address the House of Commons Select Committee on Human Rights, and did so, as did Paul Hill. Next day Wicklow Fianna Fáil TD Dick Roche said he had met a Tory MP who remarked to him "your problem [Kelly] was here addressing us last night".

At home in Ireland Kelly was also attracting more and more support from across the political spectrum. People such as Senators David Norris and Shane Ross, as well as Fr Pat Hannon of the ICJP, were becoming more vocal in his support. Despite this, there was much winking and nodding from the political establishment, but no action. It proved at least that his campaign was embarrassing them into trying to get him to tone things down.

"I did the opposite, of course, knowing now I was getting them where it hurt. Image is so important to politicians, and they would have loved it if they could have basked in the aftermath of a Birmingham Six release and crow about all they had done and boast how it could never happen in Ireland. As long as I was around this just was not going to happen. By now I had little or no respect left for the vast majority of our senior politicians.

"It was even suggested to me from a very authoritative source that if I was to activate my Supreme Court appeal against the 1986 O'Hanlon High Court decision to block my civil action against the State, I would now probably win. But I had been down that road far too often before. To me it was just another cul-de-sac, with a swamp at the end. Experience had alerted me to such 'invitations'.

I would continue with my campaign before the only court left that I could trust: the court of public opinion."

In early March 1991 supporters and family members waited outside the Old Bailey in London for the best part of ten days, expecting the Birmingham Six to be freed at any moment – as soon as legal procedure allowed. Passes to the hearing inside were limited, so the families shared with people like Nicky Kelly and Paul Hill. Hundreds of people were turning up outside every day, mostly Irish people working in London. It became like a vigil. A lot of Irish politicians also dropped by, people like David Andrews, Tom Kitt, Paschal Mooney, Dick Roche and Peter Barry.

Opposite the Courts was Rumpoles, an unremarkable pub where they adjourned frequently for coffee. They had begun to watch the races at Cheltenham on the Thursday afternoon there when word came through that the men were coming out. This time it was certain – there had been a lot of false alarms. The Gold Cup was forgotten in the rush.

A strategy for what was to happen next had been worked out with the families and solicitor Gareth Pierce. The more immediate matter of what would happen when the men came out had been planned that morning between Kelly and the police Chief Inspector involved. The families had asked Kelly to arrange this on their behalf. It was agreed that three vans and two limousines would be allowed through the crowd control barriers to pick up the men and their families. Leaving the Old Bailey the men would go to a spot where three microphones had been set up before a media corral.

Kelly's main problem was in persuading police that the families should be allowed to join the men immediately and not be corralled at the opposite end to the media, as was being planned. Paul Hill and Kelly had passes for the families' corral also. This matter had not been resolved by the time the men were released.

There was a further problem when a police sergeant refused to allow the third van through to pick up the families. "I argued with him that clearance had been agreed, but he wouldn't listen. So I went off in search of the Chief Inspector, who was inside the

Old Bailey. While I was doing this a well-known opportunist TD shoved his way into my place, much to the annoyance of Maggie McElhinney, who made no secret of how she felt. But thick-skinned as ever, the TD would not be moved."

While he was still searching for the Chief Inspector there was a tremendous roar as the men were released. This was followed by a melee as the families broke through the police cordon and ran to the men. So did Paul Hill, rushing through the cordon as if it didn't exist. Kelly held back. "I didn't know these men personally. It was their day, their families' day, and Paul's day – he knew them inside. I had been invited back to join them at a secret location but hung around afterwards with Peter Graves (a long-time Kelly and Birmingham Six supporter), trying to master the emotions aroused by the event.

"A scrum of Irish politicians huddled with the media, giving loads of free comment. Out of the corner of my eye I spotted Sr Sarah Clark and another nun disappearing into the courts, away from the limelight. She had done more for the Birmingham Six than the whole herd of politicians now hogging the cameras put together and was on her way to sit in on another miscarriage of justice hearing which had come under her wing. The young man wrongfully jailed in that instance would be released soon too.

"But while part of me noticed all this, I was in the main overcome by the impact of what I had just witnessed and what it meant. It hit me like a ton of bricks then, now that the pressure was off. Peter wasn't much better. And as the two of us stood there weeping, an English couple came towards us, extended a friendly hand and congratulated both of us on our release!"

Kelly got a taxi to the Columban Fathers headquarters in Hampstead where he knew the men and their families would be and where he had been asked to go. When he got there the place was under media siege. Nearly every news organisation in London had hired couriers to follow the three vans and two limousines as they crossed the city. Soon the Birmingham Six's secret location was the best-known address in London.

"I was pleaded with to sneak in a camera for a reporter, but wouldn't. There was a media 'ban' on the get-together of the men and their families, which most journalists understood and respected. The men had to be allowed a bit of peace and privacy after all those years. The only media present at the release party were from the *Irish Post*, the London Irish paper which had been one of the first to take up the Birmingham Six case." Despite the media black-out, however, a home video of the celebrations appeared on the BBC TV *Nine O'Clock News* that night.

The atmosphere was electric when Kelly got there. Things were just getting into their stride. Fr Bobby Gilmore had organised everything. There was plenty of food and drink, and time for everyone to relax and renew acquaintances. Photographs were taken and speeches were made, with a lot of heartfelt emotion. It was a truly great occasion. Some of the men also visited the Irish Centre in Camden that same evening.

The following day the men and their families were taken by Granada TV to a large hotel in Berkshire. The building and its grounds were completely surrounded by a moat, with access by footbridge only. Kelly had been invited there too and when he arrived it was into another barrage of media people, as anxious as ever to get inside. One journalist nearly drowned trying to get across the moat to the hotel.

A major feast took place that night, sponsored by Granada. They got exclusive interviews in return for all of the organised generosity. Again, as with the Guildford Four, the Birmingham Six used every interview as a chance to bring up Kelly's case and that of Judith Ward. Ward had almost been forgotten in the attention focused on the other cases but journalist and solicitor Michael Farrell kept her name before the public mind.

Kelly returned to Dublin on the Saturday afternoon. Granada laid on a car for him to go to the airport. The Birmingham Six went to Dublin shortly afterwards and were paraded through O'Connell Street on an open-top double-decker bus. They got a great reception. There was a *Late Late Show* appearance too, of course.

None of the Six would meet any member of the Government. They had no interest in doing so, any more than any Irish Government had any worthwhile interest in them, down all those years. Later they would participate in a commemoration of the seventy-fifth anniversary of the Easter Rising, which was organised by trade unionists, actors, musicians and other people involved with the arts. Nicky Kelly was also involved.

The Kelly case was now receiving more attention than ever before. Support for his exoneration was widespread and growing. A certain inevitability was beginning to set in. Trade unions, city and county councils, bishops and politicians were now all calling for a presidential pardon to be granted to him. MEPs Pat Cox, Niall Andrews and Neil Blaney put down a motion about the case in the European Parliament. The Labour Party put down a motion in the Dáil calling for a presidential pardon and for compensation to be paid to him.

In Britain interest was also growing. Now that the Birmingham Six were free, Kelly felt able to focus on his own case there. Fr Bobby Gilmore and Earl Smaley set up a Justice for Nicky Kelly Committee at a special and well-attended meeting in the House of Commons. Cardinal Basil Hume began to interest himself in the case; by contrast, Ireland's new Catholic Primate, Archbishop (later Cardinal) Cahal Daly did not appear to have any interest in the case, unlike his predecessor Cardinal Tomas Ó Fiaich, who had died suddenly in May 1990.

A good number of Tory MPs were also interested. In fact Kelly made it into Hansard, the House of Commons record, as "Éire's human rights problem". A joint letter from the Birmingham Six and the Guildford Four, accusing the Irish Government of hypocrisy in dealing with his case, was published. The heat was on.

Among the major Human Rights conferences Kelly attended around the world, where invariably he would be described as "the Irish torture case", there was the Helsinki Watch Conference, an Amnesty conference in New York and another in Paris. One of the most interesting of these gatherings was the Conference for Security and Co-operation in Europe (CSCE), held in Moscow in

September 1991, which he attended with Labour Senator Joe Costello (now a TD and Labour front bench spokesman on European Affairs and Defence).

"It was a remarkable time to visit that city, then still in a post-Communist flux. We flew into the airport four hours behind schedule. Not surprisingly, then, there was no one there to meet us and we were not sure where to go. We rang the conference organisers, who must have misunderstood what was meant by "a delegation from Ireland" because they sent a 40-seater bus and a huge old black limousine to pick the two of us up. We took the limousine and played VIPs, waving to people as we passed by, until we saw the hatred in their response. VIPs were not very popular in Moscow then."

They thought it a beautiful city that was falling apart. People's expectations at the time were "frightening". "Everything was very cheap; you could get a four-course meal for a dollar, $2 with wine. Everywhere we went all people wanted were dollars. The people were very generous and couldn't do enough for us.

"One day Joe and myself decided to travel somewhere on the metro – an amazing creation with its marble, its chandeliers, and its cleanliness – but on getting there we discovered that all the signs were written in Cyrillic. We had to ask people for directions. They were not satisfied simply to point, but would insist on accompanying us to within eyeshot of our destination."

They went to visit Lenin's tomb one day, but it was closed. Instead they came across a long queue of people waiting to pray at a religious shrine. Nearly as long were the queues they saw in the city outside McDonalds and Pizza Hut.

In one place they met a former head of the CIA in Moscow, who regaled them with stories about the "good old" cold war days. "The city was full of American merchant adventurers, passing themselves off as philanthropists, all looking forward to big bucks in the good days ahead."

Russian nationalism was making itself felt too, even in their hotel. As they were heading to a lift to get their luggage one day, someone in the company made a reference to Leningrad. "The lift operator, in his fifties, refused to budge until the man corrected himself and said 'St Petersburg' instead."

The CSCE conference was chaired by one of Boris Yeltsin's right-hand men, who sounded very aggressive on the subject of human rights abuse in the various former Soviet Republics. Kathleen Kennedy, daughter of the late Senator Robert Kennedy, was at the conference, representing a Robert Kennedy memorial group. She was *au fait* with Kelly's history and gave him useful advice on the case itself and provided contacts who might help.

In October 1991 Michael Heney of RTÉ presented a *Wednesday Report* programme on the Kelly case. It was the first time RTÉ's TV current affairs department had interested itself in Nicky Kelly in the 15 years since the mail train robbery. Indeed, as recently as 1989 Nicky Kelly had come up against the "ban" mentality at RTÉ. Journalist Kevin O'Kelly, then involved with the Religious Affairs department at the station, prepared a programme on the Kelly case, featuring an extensive interview with Nicky Kelly. Neither it nor the rest of the programme dealing with his case was broadcast.

The Heney *Wednesday Report* programme, however, was well worth the wait. It later won a well-deserved Jacob's Award for excellent broadcast journalism. As well as being a powerful portrayal of what had happened to Kelly, it included a test on his confession conducted by the linguistics expert, Professor Andrew Morton, who concluded that three people had written the confession, none of them Kelly, and that it "cannot be accepted as the utterance of Kelly". On the same programme another linguistics expert, Dr Malcolm Coulthard, thought "the whole statement [the confession] has features typical of police report and this seems to put the onus on the police to explain how this could have occurred in a supposed verbatim record of a dictated statement".

A presidential pardon began to seem more and more certain, but Kelly was just as anxious there should be an inquiry into how he had confessed to something he didn't do. And there was still his civil action appeal to the Supreme Court to be considered.

One man he met for the first time in this period was Brian Keenan, the freed Beirut kidnap victim. Both were waiting to use the same phone box on Dublin's Parnell Street and neither was certain the other was who he seemed to be. They kept eyeing each other. "I introduced myself. We shook hands and adjourned to the Royal Dublin Hotel, just around the corner. It was the beginning of a right royal day. Later we moved to Conway's pub nearby, called our girlfriends and continued talking into the night."

They met on a number of occasions afterwards, whether in Mayo or Dublin. Keenan then spent quite a lot of time around Westport and Kelly often visited Ballyhaunis, where his then girl-friend Helena Caulfield, later his wife, is from. Kelly also has many friends there including then local TDs Jim Higgins of Fine Gael and PJ Morley of Fianna Fáil.

"Brian Keenan has always impressed me for one quality – his compassion for people, considering the hardships and torture he was put through in captivity in the Lebanon. He is just one of a number of exceptional people I have been fortunate to meet and talk to over the years, most of whom I would probably not have met but for my own experiences."

HE WAS AT DUBLIN AIRPORT when he got the word on the after-noon of 28 April 1992. He was on his way to London for a Judith Ward appeal hearing. Nuala Kelly of the ICJP was with him.

Earlier in the afternoon he had got a sense that something was happening, but he took no heed. There had been too many before, none of which amounted to anything. Before he left the house he got a phone call from RTÉ news editor Eddie Liston wondering whether he had heard anything. Liston told him they were saying on the grapevine that a major statement would be made on the case that evening. He wanted to know where Kelly might be con-tacted later. Kelly told him and set out for the airport.

He was no sooner there than he was paged over the PA and asked to go to the Information desk. He did, to discover there were two phone calls for him. One was from East Coast Radio in Wicklow. It was they who told him about the announcement that he had been granted a presidential pardon.

Dublin radio station 98FM was on the other line. Both stations had found out he was going to London. They rang Paul Hill there, who was to meet him on arrival, and had traced him to Dublin Airport. There followed a deluge of calls. RTÉ wanted him to go to Donnybrook for the *Six-One News*. He decided to do so. Nuala Kelly went on to London.

"Then I went into a toilet cubicle at the airport and cried. I couldn't get my father out of my mind. If only he had lived a few more months." He went back to his house on his way to RTÉ. The tape on the answer machine had run out, there were so many messages congratulating him. He drove out to Donnybrook and was met there by his solicitor Greg O'Neill who had a copy of the statement.

He had barely time to look at it before he was "live", on air. But he had studied it sufficiently to be clear that there was no inbuilt qualification or hidden formula. It was unequivocal exoneration, no "ifs", "ands" or "buts". No "humanitarian grounds". In Ireland, unlike Britain or the US for instance, a presidential pardon means total exoneration. It is a declaration that the State is satisfied the relevant person is completely innocent of whatever they had been convicted of. Kelly was just the third person in the history of the Irish State to be so pardoned and the first for over 50 years.

But there was nothing about an inquiry. He was not happy with that. There must be an inquiry, he felt, if only to ensure that what had happened to him could never happen again. The British authorities had initiated inquiries into the Guildford Four and Birmingham Six cases. There was an official acknowledgement there that something out of order had happened and should be investigated. The threat of such an inquiry/investigation would act as a powerful deterrent to any Government or senior Garda figure(s) who might in the future be tempted to allow the law be broken to safeguard the law, he believes.

He agreed to stay on for RTÉ's *Today Tonight* programme that night. The then recently appointed Minister for Justice, Padraig Flynn, was a guest. He explained the details of the presidential pardon and its announcement. "I thought he was smug and self-satisfied, as though he had just bestowed a gift on me. Had he – or any of the seven Ministers for Justice preceding him in the six Governments which had held office since my arrest – had they had the courage and honesty to do their job properly, I would have had no need of a presidential pardon in the first place. And he still shilly-shallied about an inquiry.

"It was one of the lawyers in the Birmingham Six case who best summed up Irish politicians for me. He said that when a British politician said 'yes' it meant 'yes', whereas when an Irish politician said 'yes' but it could also mean 'no'."

The presidential pardon announcement set off a series of celebrations that threatened to go on forever. One of the biggest was at McGann's pub in Doolin, County Clare on the coast between the Burren and the Cliffs of Mother. Doolin had become a favourite place of Kelly's over the years. The celebration party was organised by Tony and Teresa McGann themselves and took place about two weeks after the announcement of his pardon. Over the years Tony and Teresa, Ann and Davog Rynne, Brid and Miceál Shannon, who all live in that part of the world, had become good friends of Kelly's.

Among those who travelled to the party in McCann's were members of the Justice for Nicky Kelly Committee, including Peter Graves, who came over from London for it, and also Paul Hill and Courtney Kennedy. There too were all the local patrons, as well as the customers and staff from the other two pubs in Doolin, McDermotts and O'Connors. Billy Power, Gerry Hunter, and Paddy Hill of the Birmingham Six didn't make it. They had hired a minibus in London and it broke down on the motorway in the North of England. It took 12 hours for them and their families to be towed back to base. However they held their own impromptu party at a motor-way service station.

The party in Doolin lasted two days. A couple of weeks later, Kelly hosted a special "thank you" party for all who had helped him down the years. It took place at Boss Crokers on the quays in Dublin and was attended by over 300 people. Among those there were members of the Birmingham Six, the Guildford Four, and the recently released Judy Ward. It was her first time in Ireland since her release.

There was a civic reception for Kelly at Dublin's Mansion House, organised by Lord Mayor, Sean Kenny. It was attended by various dignitaries, including local and national politicians. The Lord Mayor spoke warmly of the pardon and called for an independent inquiry into the entire scandal. He then presented Kelly with a piece of Waterford crystal on behalf of the people of Dublin.

On 17 July 1992, the eighth anniversary of his release from Portlaoise, Nicky Kelly met the President, Mrs Robinson, at Áras an Uachtaráin. His mother, his fiancée Helena Caulfield, and his solicitor Greg O'Neill, went along with him. The visit lasted about an hour and a half and was a very cordial affair. All chatted over tea and scones before going for a walk in the grounds. "My mother and the President had a frank, woman-to-woman discussion about what the family had been through."

And that was that . . . but not quite. Negotiations got underway between Kelly's lawyers and the Department of Justice on the question of compensation. It was a long, drawn-out and fraught process, with officials behaving in a way that was all-too-familiar to Kelly.

"In explaining to a supporter why he couldn't act on my case – at the time I was in Portlaoise – one Minister for Justice said there would be 'murder' in the Department if he was to 'interfere'. Again and again supporters spoke to Kelly of the impresssion they were getting that various Ministers for Justice were being 'stonewalled' by officials. Again and again those officials had argued with their Ministers against any review of the case. 'There was nothing to review,' they said, 'no grounds for release'."

Where compensation was concerned, a six-figure sum was being talked about in Departmental leaks to the media, but Kelly was offered nothing like that. This set the tone and pattern for the following months, during which Kelly believes both politicians and the media were actively misled by officials. In turn the Dáil was misled on a number of occasions. "It got so bad my lawyers threatened to go public on the entire affair unless the Department came clean. It was raised in the Dáil. We seemed to be getting nowhere."

Then the Government changed and a special Labour party backbench sub-committee was set up to progress the negotiations. Included were TDs Joe Costello, Declan Bree, Liam Kavanagh, and Derek McDowell. All Labour Ministers at Cabinet took an active interest and pushed the negotiations along, while keeping the parliamentary party informed of the progress being made. A major point of contention in the negotiations became Kelly's determination to pursue his civil action appeal in the Supreme Court. The Department argued that the State could not be left in a position where it was possible it might have to indemnify him twice in connection with the same events. In theory, winning the civil action would mean Kelly could sue the State once more.

His lawyers discussed the situation with him over and over, until eventually he agreed to drop the action. "It could take years before it would be heard and, frankly, I wanted to get on with my life." Following that and even more haggling it was agreed during the summer of 1993 that he would be paid £750,000 in compensation, plus costs. Altogether the amount came to almost £1,000,000.

In September 1993 Amnesty International distributed a booklet worldwide in which Ireland was accused of "torture and other cruel treatment of prisoners". The reason for Ireland's inclusion in that most notorious of exclusive clubs – countries which torture their people – rested solely on the fact that there had never been an investigation into the circumstances surrounding Kelly's conviction and that of the others in what became known as "the Sallins case".

In the summer of 1993 Kelly moved home to Arklow, back again among his own and where they still call him "Eamonn". He bought a house and set about sorting out his health. He also started laying the foundations for a life after "Nicky Kelly".

He was 43. If, as they say, life begins at 40, he had to wait a bit longer than most.

21

THE STORY OF THIS BOOK

M Y INTEREST IN THE NICKY KELLY case went back to the late
1970s but really took off around the time of his hunger
strike in May 1983. The calibre of the people campaigning for him,
and who insisted on his innocence, certainly influenced me but
not as much as the simple facts of the case when I informed myself of them.

There was also the disturbing background which made it be-
lievable that Kelly had signed a confession for a crime he had
nothing to do with. There were the 1977 articles in *The Irish Times*
concerning the existence of a "Heavy Gang" in the Garda, whose
function it seemed was to "help" people make such admissions.
There were also a number of other disturbing cases which indicated all was not well.

In December 1980 the Supreme Court ordered the release of
Christy Lynch, who had by then served three years for murder,
solely on the basis of a confession which followed 22 hours of interrogation by gardaí. The Supreme Court found he had been subject to "harassment and oppression" and noted that there was
even evidence the murder victim was alive at the time Lynch
claimed to have killed her.

In 1982 the DPP dropped charges against Amanda McShane
when it was discovered that investigating gardaí at Crumlin in
Dublin had prepared a written confession in advance for her to
sign. She was being held in connection with a £100,000 robbery at
Tallaght post office. Her solicitor discovered the pre-prepared
confession when visiting her at Crumlin Garda station and copied

it. The interrogation of Amanda McShane continued after her solicitor left and eventually she signed another pre-prepared statement admitting to the crime. The case went to court, but when he
heard of the existence of the other pre-prepared statement, the
DPP entered a *nolle prosequi*.

In June 1983 Michael Ward signed a statement at Naas Garda
station admitting to 26 separate counts of burglary. His solicitors
later established he was in jail over a particular three-week period
when, according to his confession, he had also burgled several
houses in Naas. It emerged too that at least one of the burglaries
to which he admitted had never happened. When these facts were
disclosed in court the DPP once again entered a *nolle prosequi* and
Michael Ward was released.

In none of the above cases was there any sort of inquiry to establish how people, clearly innocent of the crimes involved, had
admitted responsibility for them.

Then in 1984 there was the Kerry Babies case, which was to
play its own part in halting this book's publication. Two dead
newborn babies were found in Kerry in April 1984. The first was
that of a baby boy with stab wounds and was discovered on
White Strand in Caherciveen. Two weeks later, the body of another baby boy was uncovered on the farm of Joanne Hayes at
Abbeydorney, 30 miles away from the first baby.

Gardaí suspected the Caherciveen baby belonged to Ms
Hayes. She signed a confession claiming she had stabbed the Caherciveen baby. Her family signed statements supporting the confession. All followed hours of questioning by gardaí.
Subsequently charges were dropped when DNA evidence established that the blood group of the Caherciveen baby was different
to that of Ms Hayes, the man she was having an affair with, and
the baby found at Abbeydorney. A tribunal of inquiry as held. It
sat for 77 days and heard 109 witnesses. It found that the gardaí
were not responsible for Ms Hayes's false confession or the false
statements by members of her family.

Growing up in small-town Ireland I became aware personally
of instances where some local gardaí had no reservation about

abusing their powers when it came to dealing with people they had personal disagreements with, or just plain disliked. In Ballaghaderreen everyone knew gardaí who set out to "get" such people. Soon I would learn this was not peculiar to a small town like Ballaghaderreen.

In one instance there a middle-aged respected man who had a disagreement with a (now deceased) garda at the local GAA club was followed around a backway in the town one Sunday night and charged with indecent exposure when he tried to relieve himself. The same man was well-known to have serious kidney problems, which later led to his premature death.

On another occasion a local priest, also active in the GAA, was summonsed for being on a pub premises after hours, following another GAA row. The priest had been attending a meeting at what was the local hotel. It was believed he was deliberately targeted by a particular (deceased) garda.

Some pubs in the town came in for close Garda attention, while others were ignored. It was the same for some local families, where the sole basis for close attention appeared to be personal disagreements or dislike on the part of some gardaí. That said, the great majority of gardaí serving in the town then were gentlemen.

When I was a student at UCG (now NUIG) I witnessed gardaí lose control at a student protest outside the Garda station in Eglinton Street, now closed. The student protesters were picketing the station over proposed legislation which would ban such protests. All was peaceful until the local senior officer lost his temper and ordered a baton charge. Several students were badly injured, one with a deep gash to the crown of her head and another left with the skin, literally, hanging from his cheekbone. Both victims were arrested and held pending charges. Those charges were never laid as students descended on Eglinton Street and staged a sit-down, blocking all traffic. They refused to move until their colleagues were released, as they finally were. There was never an inquiry into how they secured their injuries or into reasons why a baton charge was ordered.

In 1983, when Nicky Kelly was on hunger strike, I was work-ing in news with the Dublin pirate station Sunshine Radio. As news editor there between 1983 and 1987 I availed of every oppor-tunity to highlight his case.

From 1987, while freelancing for *Magill* magazine and the *Irish Press*, I wrote many reports on it. In May 1988 I wrote a 6,500-word article on the case for *Magill*. It was too long even for *Magill*. By then I had met Nicky Kelly himself.

It was the late Derek Dunne, encouraged by then *Magill* editor John Waters, who first suggested to me I should write an up-to-date book about the case, ideally with Nicky's co-operation. Derek he passed on to me a lot of documentation he had about the case. Nicky agreed it was a good idea and in early 1993 we went to see publishers Gill and Macmillan.

They asked for two sample chapters and asked that they be written in the first person, as Kelly's account of events. The chap-ters dealt with Nicky's time on the run in the US. Gill and Mac-millan were happy with them and gave the go-ahead for a book which was to be "by Nicky Kelly in collaboration with Patsy McGarry".

Writing it took up most of 1993 and it was submitted to the publishers later that year. The title was *When Justice Sleeps*. Storm clouds began to gather. In January 1994 solicitors for Gill and Macmillan informed them of "substantial difficulties" where Kelly's account of his detention and treatment by the gardaí was concerned. That account was, deliberately, based entirely on tran-scripts of the trials.

As a letter from the publishers to us put it, the basic problem was that the only court decision ever made concerning Kelly's de-tention held that he had not been mistreated by the gardaí. This was on the legal record and would create difficulties for the pub-lishers if any of the 22 gardaí then named in the book were to take action against them.

The legal advice was that, should any of the gardaí sue, they would most likely succeed because of that Special Criminal Court finding. To this day it stands in law, despite the 1992 presidential pardon, which said Nicky Kelly was "as if he had not been charged or convicted" in connection with the mail train robbery.

So it was back to the drawing board and it took a lot of time. I made substantial changes to the book through 1994, with a new draft submitted to Gill and Macmillan in October of the year. In January of 1995 they were informed by counsel that the legal difficulties presented in the book had not been resolved. In a lengthy memo, counsel concluded, "I think that this publication is likely to present a risk for our client [Gill and Macmillan], no matter what changes are made." I have always been intrigued by that legal opinion, not least as two books published in 1984 – *Round Up the Usual Suspects* and *Blind Justice* – had named most of the same gardaí without consequence.

Gill and Macmillan, who could not have been more courteous throughout all of this, withdrew their offer of publication. Their nervousness was understandable. As recently as June 1993 gardaí involved in the mail train robbery investigation had initiated contempt proceedings in the High Court against Gay Byrne and RTÉ following a radio interview Byrne conducted with Osgur Breathnach on 31 May that year. The relevant gardaí sought the jailing of Byrne and the confiscation of RTÉ's assets as, it was argued on their behalf by senior counsel Adrian Hardiman (now a Supreme Court judge), the interview was prejudicial to them in a case being brought against them by Breathnach. That action against Gay Byrne and RTÉ was thrown out by Justice Frederick Morris, currently sole member of the Morris Tribunal, which is investigating the conduct of gardaí in Donegal.

Undaunted, we set about finding another publisher. Brandon Press in Dingle was sent copies. Senior counsel Adrian Hardiman (the same as above) was sent a copy by Brandon. In a 12-page memo, dated 4 July 1995, Hardiman noted that should there be a libel action following publication of the book, "favouring us [publishers etc.] would be the pardon granted to the author, certain observations of the Court of Criminal Appeal, and perhaps a general feeling (the vote he [Nicky Kelly] obtained in the recent [Wicklow] by-election is interesting in the context) that the author was in fact a victim of injustice. Against us would be the garda evidence and the strong general propensity of juries and still more judges to attach considerable credence to it." The reference to Kelly's vote was his performance in the 1994 local elections when, as a first-time candidate, he topped the poll and was elected to Arklow UDC.

In a letter to Nicky Kelly describing their response to Adrian Hardiman's advice Brandon they had been "pleased initially that it suggested a way forward in minimising risk". However their "gut feeling said No".

Brandon too had every reason to be wary. They were almost put out of business when successfully sued by gardaí involved with the Kerry Babies investigation, following publication of a book by Brandon on the case. They wrote that they had sent *When Justice Sleeps* for legal opinion because they were "keen to publish it" but then felt "intimidated by the defamation laws".

They continued that *When Justice Sleeps* was "very 'right' for Brandon, it fits in with our character and tradition over the past 14 years. But perhaps it is too right for us. Perhaps because we have had so much struggle over other books we know too much about the strain that can be involved."

They added, as further explanation of their decision not to go ahead with publication, that at the back of their minds was "the experience of intense isolation at the time that we were brought to our knees over the Joanne Hayes book." They could "still hear the silence" when they asked people "to help us set up a fighting fund".

In a final paragraph they said they had "absolutely no doubt but that the book deserves to be published and should be published with great success", and offered their counsel's and solicitor's help towards that end.

Six other publishers were then contacted. Most were enthusiastic until their lawyers became involved. It rested there for a while. In 1996 Blackstaff Press in Belfast were sent a copy. They were keen and asked Dublin barrister Alex White to look at it. He, two representatives from Blackstaff and I met subsequently in

Dublin. Alex White has given a lot of time to the book, then and since. His infinite patience with it over the years deserves grateful acknowledgement here. After that meeting with Blackstaff and Alex I felt that in order to make the book absolutely risk-free of legal action I would have to make it unreadable. It was my decision not to do that. It was time to move on.

Before I did so, I wrote an "Irishman's Diary" on the saga of the book for *The Irish Times*, which was published on 22 April 1996. I was interviewed that day about it on RTÉ Radio by Sean O'Rourke on the *News At One* programme.

I moved on. Nicky Kelly moved on. Life moved on.

Then in summer 2004 I was contacted by The Liffey Press asking whether I had any ideas for a book. I sent them *When Justice Sleeps*. Subsequently Nicky and myself met them. It was agreed the book should be rewritten and that it would be in the third person. Writing in the first person is a very restrictive form.

With less than enthusiasm I set about the task, helped greatly by old friend Ben Wrafter, who saved me much time and effort by scanning the hard copy onto computer disk so that I could work onscreen.

The book has had a slight change of title. *While Justice Slept* is quite different from *When Justice Sleeps*, while retaining much of the latter's content.

As well as being written in the third person it has been radically restructured with much additional and up-to-date material. A major difference between the two books is that none of the gardaí involved in the case is named. A significant addition is that it contains the first ever interview with any of the IRA gang which actually robbed the mail train on 31 March 1976, the crime for which an innocent Nicky Kelly was sentenced to 12 years' penal servitude.

But, as you read this, far and away the greatest difference between *When Justice Sleeps* and this book is that *While Justice Slept* has been published!

የ   የ   የ

AS WE COME TOWARDS THE BOOK'S CONCLUSION, it seems merely proper to thank and acknowledge the co-operation of Nicky Kelly himself, without whose suffering it could not have happened. He will bear the effects of his experiences for the rest of his days.

He still believes there must be an inquiry into what happened him and the others arrested following the 1976 mail train robbery, convinced that therein may lie a key to what has gone wrong with other Garda investigations since.

For himself he might remember the words of Cork Lord Mayor Terence MacSwiney, that it is not those who inflict the most who win out, but those who endure the most. MacSwiney died in London's Brixton prison on 25 October 1920 after spending seventy-four days on hunger strike – the longest hunger strike in Irish history.

The final words we will leave to Nicky Kelly. He said that "passing through life one encounters many invidious situations. But disloyalty or betrayal, inflicted either by an individual or the State, may be forgiven but should never, ever be forgotten."

POSTSCRIPT

NICKY KELLY IS NOW A FULL-TIME public representative and currently a Labour party councillor on Wicklow County Council and a Labour councillor on Arklow Town Council. In 1994, as a first-time candidate in the local elections that year, he topped the poll when elected to Arklow UDC.

In 1997 he stood as an Independent candidate in the general election, polling over 5,000 first preference votes. In 1999 he was re-elected to Arklow UDC, topping the poll with three quotas. That same year he was also elected as first-time candidate to Wicklow County Council. He again topped the poll and received a record-breaking vote. In the 2002 general election, following a protracted recount, he was short by six votes for the final seat in the 29th (and current) Dáil. He will be standing as a candidate in the general election next year.

He is a representative on the Health Services Executive, a director of Wicklow County Enterprise Board, a member of Wicklow Vocational Education Committee, chair of the county Special Policy Committee on Housing, and a member of the Council's Corporate Committee. He was a member of the Special Olympics Committee in the county, a director of its Community Business Centre, chair of Arklow UDC, chair of Arklow and District Health Care Improvement Committee, chair of the Building Committee Arklow Swimming Pool 1995–1999, and a member of the Arklow Community College board of management. He has also been actively involved with Wicklow GAA down the years and many other sports groups in the county.